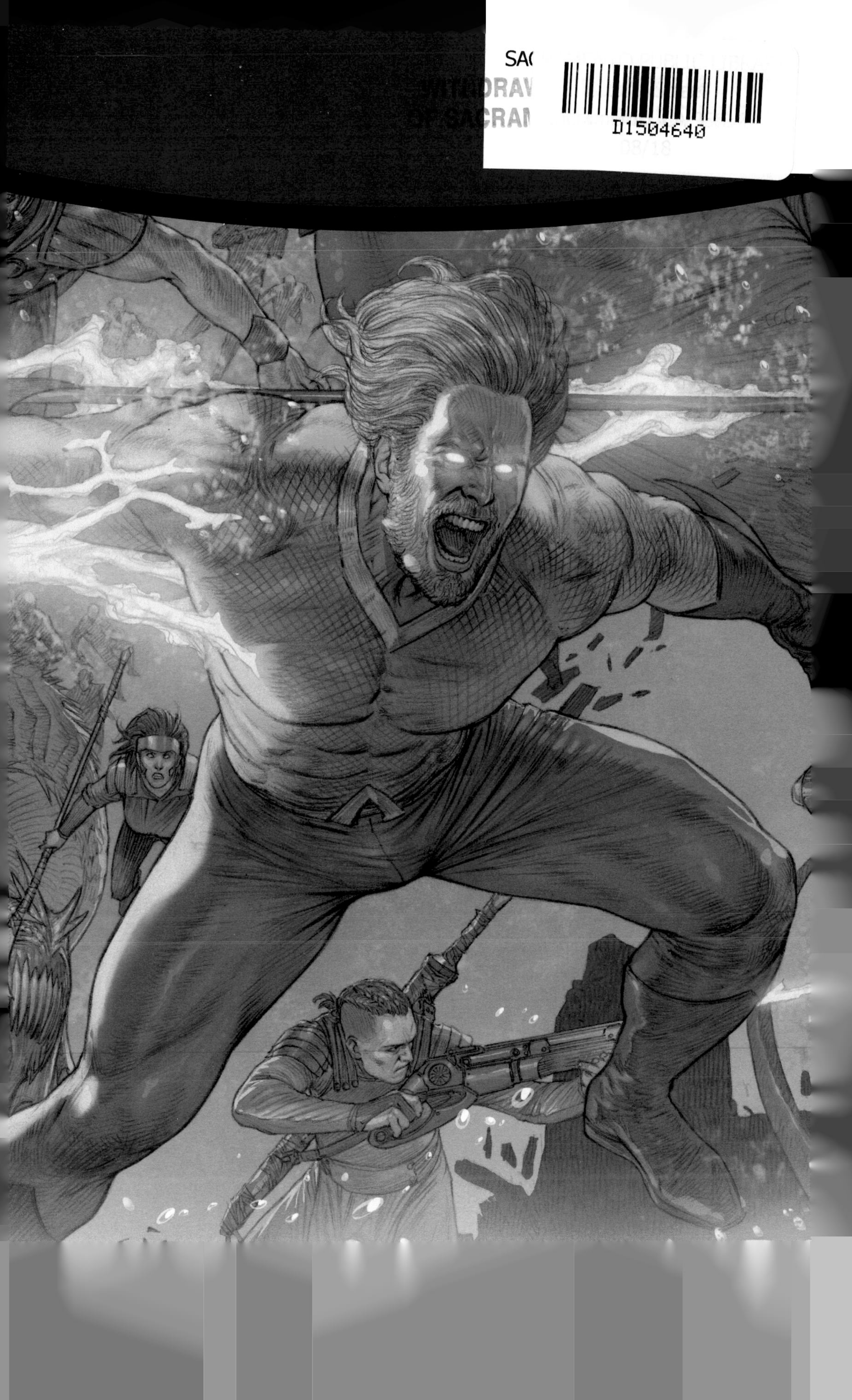

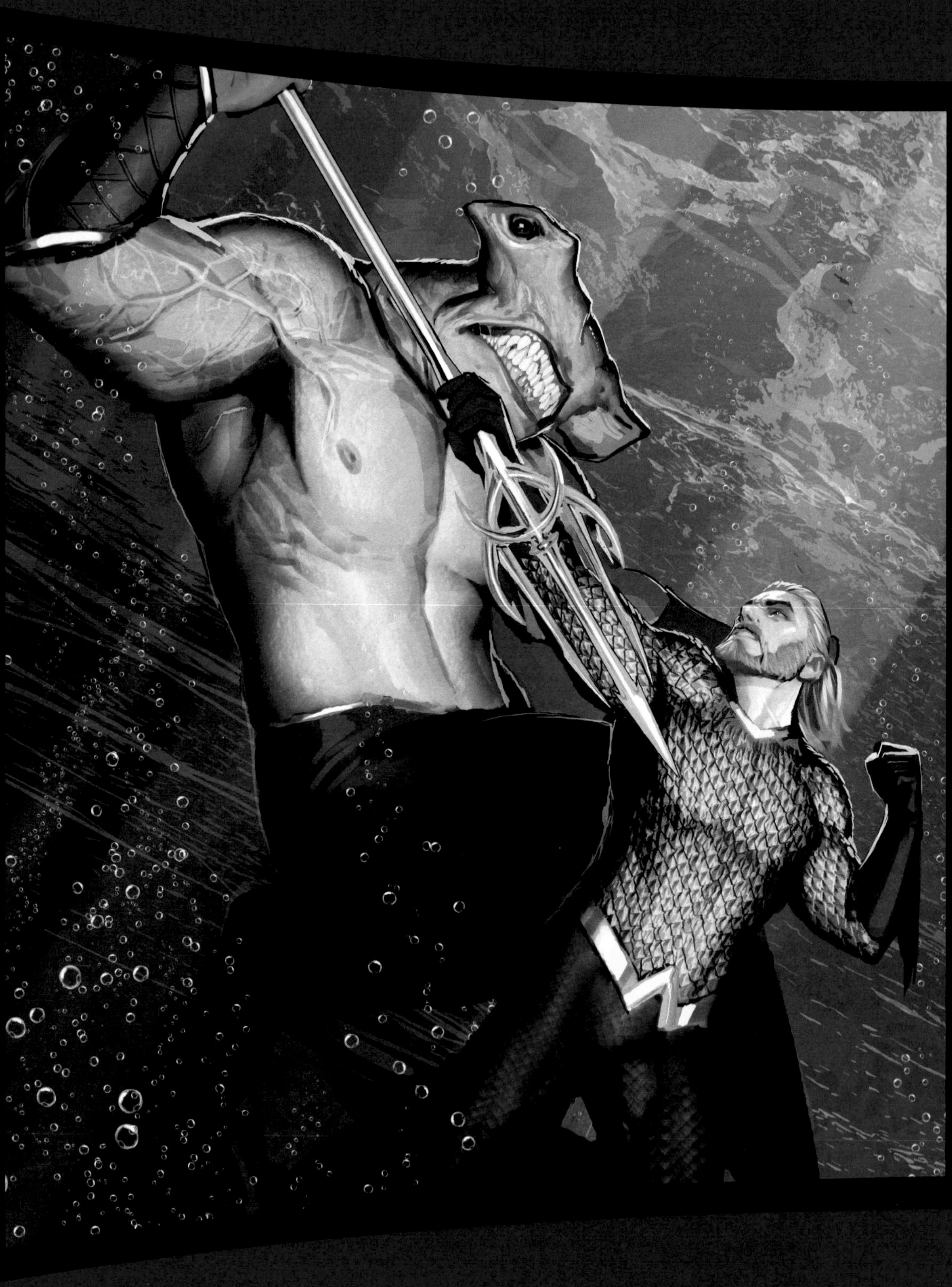

AQUAMAN
VOL.5 THE CROWN COMES DOWN

DAN ABNETT
PHILLIP KENNEDY JOHNSON
writers

RICCARDO FEDERICI
MAX FIUMARA
RICK LEONARDI
artists

SUNNY GHO
DAVE STEWART
colorists

STEVE WANDS
DERON BENNETT
letterers

STJEPAN SEJIC
collection cover artist

AQUAMAN created by PAUL NORRIS
SUPERMAN created by JERRY SIEGEL and JOE SHUSTER
By special arrangement with the Jerry Siegel family

ALEX ANTONE BRIAN CUNNINGHAM Editors - Original Series ✴ **AMEDEO TURTURRO** Associate Editor - Original Series
DAVE WIELGOSZ DIEGO LOPEZ Assistant Editors - Original Series ✴ **JEB WOODARD** Group Editor - Collected Editions
ERIKA ROTHBERG Editor - Collected Edition ✴ **STEVE COOK** Design Director - Books

BOB HARRAS Senior VP - Editor-in-Chief, DC Comics ✴ **PAT McCALLUM** Executive Editor, DC Comics

DIANE NELSON President ✴ **DAN DiDIO** Publisher ✴ **JIM LEE** Publisher ✴ **GEOFF JOHNS** President & Chief Creative Officer
AMIT DESAI Executive VP - Business & Marketing Strategy, Direct to Consumer & Global Franchise Management
SAM ADES Senior VP & General Manager, Digital Services ✴ **BOBBIE CHASE** VP & Executive Editor, Young Reader & Talent Development
MARK CHIARELLO Senior VP - Art, Design & Collected Editions ✴ **JOHN CUNNINGHAM** Senior VP - Sales & Trade Marketing
ANNE DePIES Senior VP - Business Strategy, Finance & Administration ✴ **DON FALLETTI** VP - Manufacturing Operations
LAWRENCE GANEM VP - Editorial Administration & Talent Relations ✴ **ALISON GILL** Senior VP - Manufacturing & Operations
HANK KANALZ Senior VP - Editorial Strategy & Administration ✴ **JAY KOGAN** VP - Legal Affairs ✴ **JACK MAHAN** VP - Business Affairs
NICK J. NAPOLITANO VP - Manufacturing Administration ✴ **EDDIE SCANNELL** VP - Consumer Marketing
COURTNEY SIMMONS Senior VP - Publicity & Communications ✴ **JIM (SKI) SOKOLOWSKI** VP - Comic Book Specialty Sales & Trade Marketing
NANCY SPEARS VP - Mass, Book, Digital Sales & Trade Marketing ✴ **MICHELE R. WELLS** VP - Content Strategy

AQUAMAN VOL. 5: THE CROWN COMES DOWN

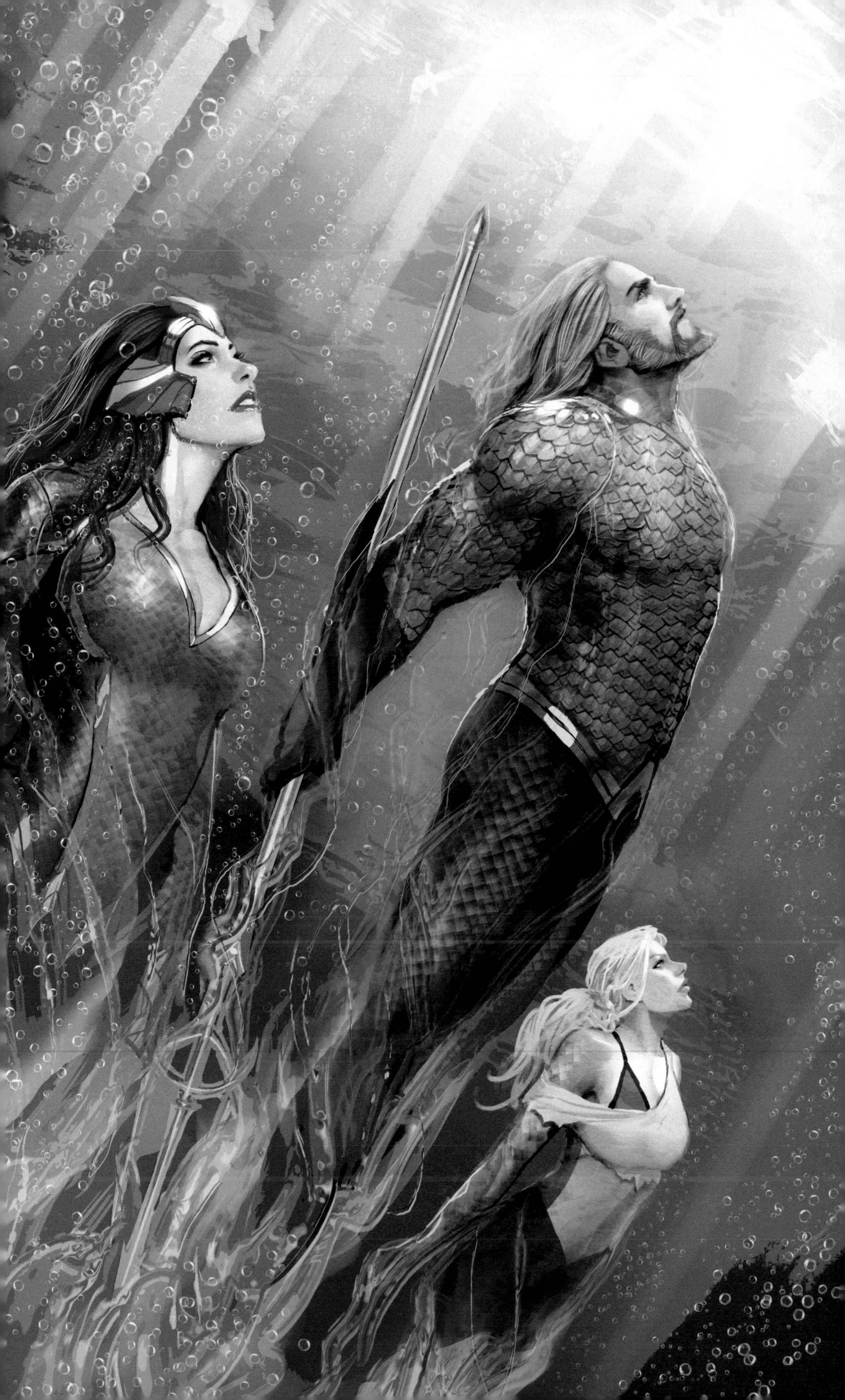

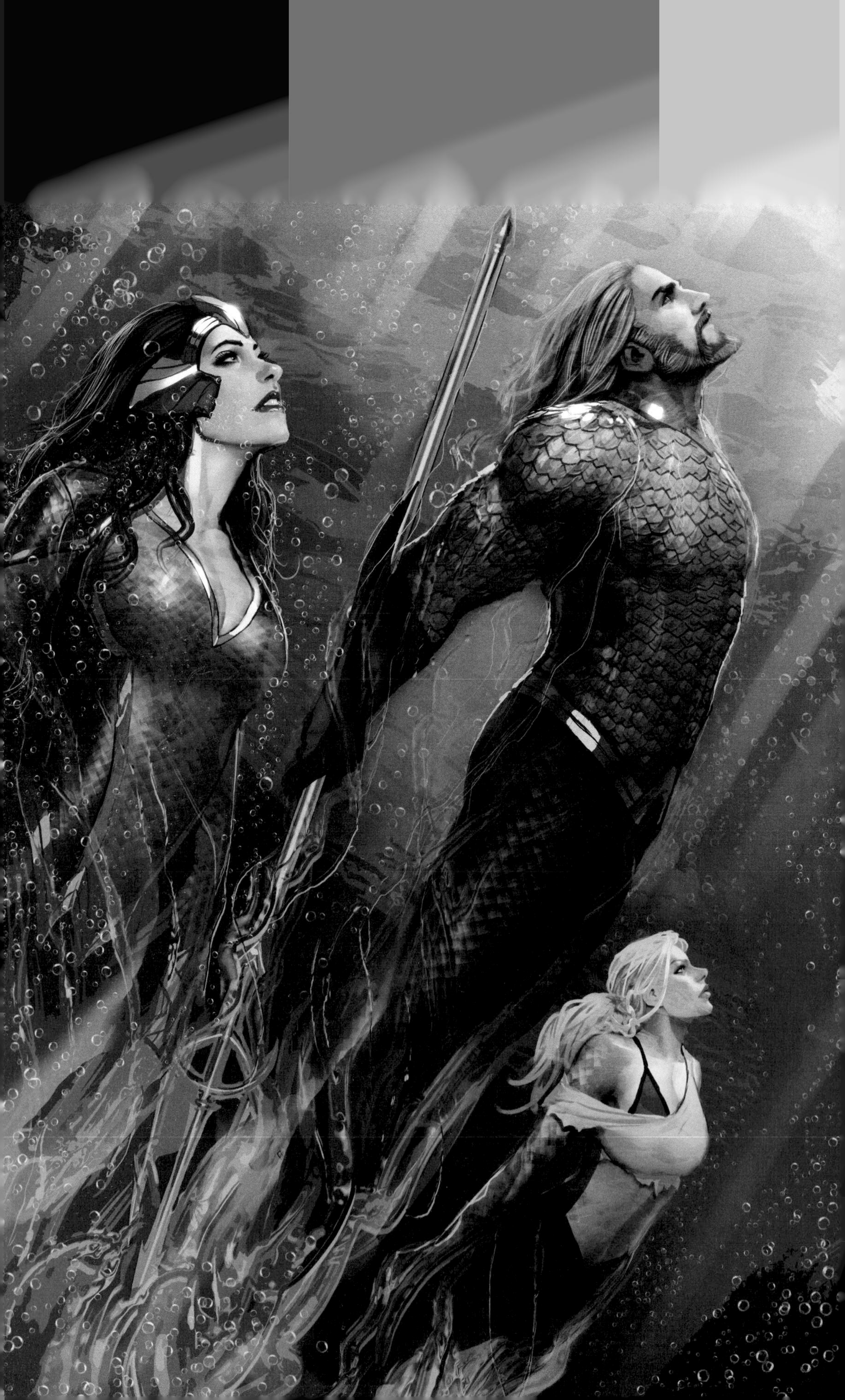

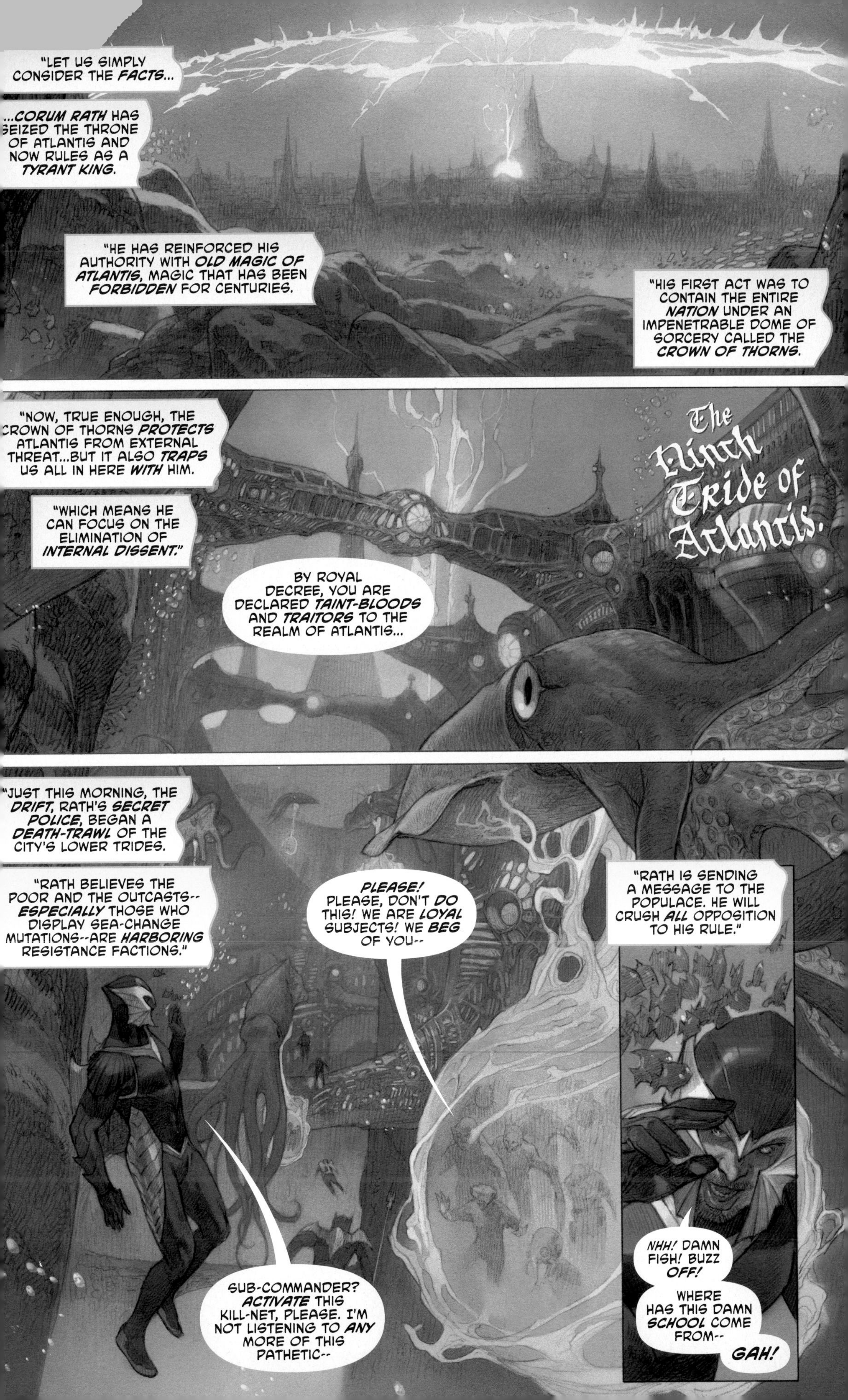
"LET US SIMPLY CONSIDER THE FACTS...
...CORUM RATH HAS SEIZED THE THRONE OF ATLANTIS AND NOW RULES AS A TYRANT KING.
"HE HAS REINFORCED HIS AUTHORITY WITH OLD MAGIC OF ATLANTIS, MAGIC THAT HAS BEEN FORBIDDEN FOR CENTURIES.
"HIS FIRST ACT WAS TO CONTAIN THE ENTIRE NATION UNDER AN IMPENETRABLE DOME OF SORCERY CALLED THE CROWN OF THORNS.
"NOW, TRUE ENOUGH, THE CROWN OF THORNS PROTECTS ATLANTIS FROM EXTERNAL THREAT...BUT IT ALSO TRAPS US ALL IN HERE WITH HIM.
"WHICH MEANS HE CAN FOCUS ON THE ELIMINATION OF INTERNAL DISSENT."
The Ninth Tride of Atlantis.
BY ROYAL DECREE, YOU ARE DECLARED TAINT-BLOODS AND TRAITORS TO THE REALM OF ATLANTIS...
"JUST THIS MORNING, THE DRIFT, RATH'S SECRET POLICE, BEGAN A DEATH-TRAWL OF THE CITY'S LOWER TRIDES.
"RATH BELIEVES THE POOR AND THE OUTCASTS--ESPECIALLY THOSE WHO DISPLAY SEA-CHANGE MUTATIONS--ARE HARBORING RESISTANCE FACTIONS."
PLEASE! PLEASE, DON'T DO THIS! WE ARE LOYAL SUBJECTS! WE BEG OF YOU--
SUB-COMMANDER? ACTIVATE THIS KILL-NET, PLEASE. I'M NOT LISTENING TO ANY MORE OF THIS PATHETIC--
"RATH IS SENDING A MESSAGE TO THE POPULACE. HE WILL CRUSH ALL OPPOSITION TO HIS RULE."
NHH! DAMN FISH! BUZZ OFF!
WHERE HAS THIS DAMN SCHOOL COME FROM--
GAH!

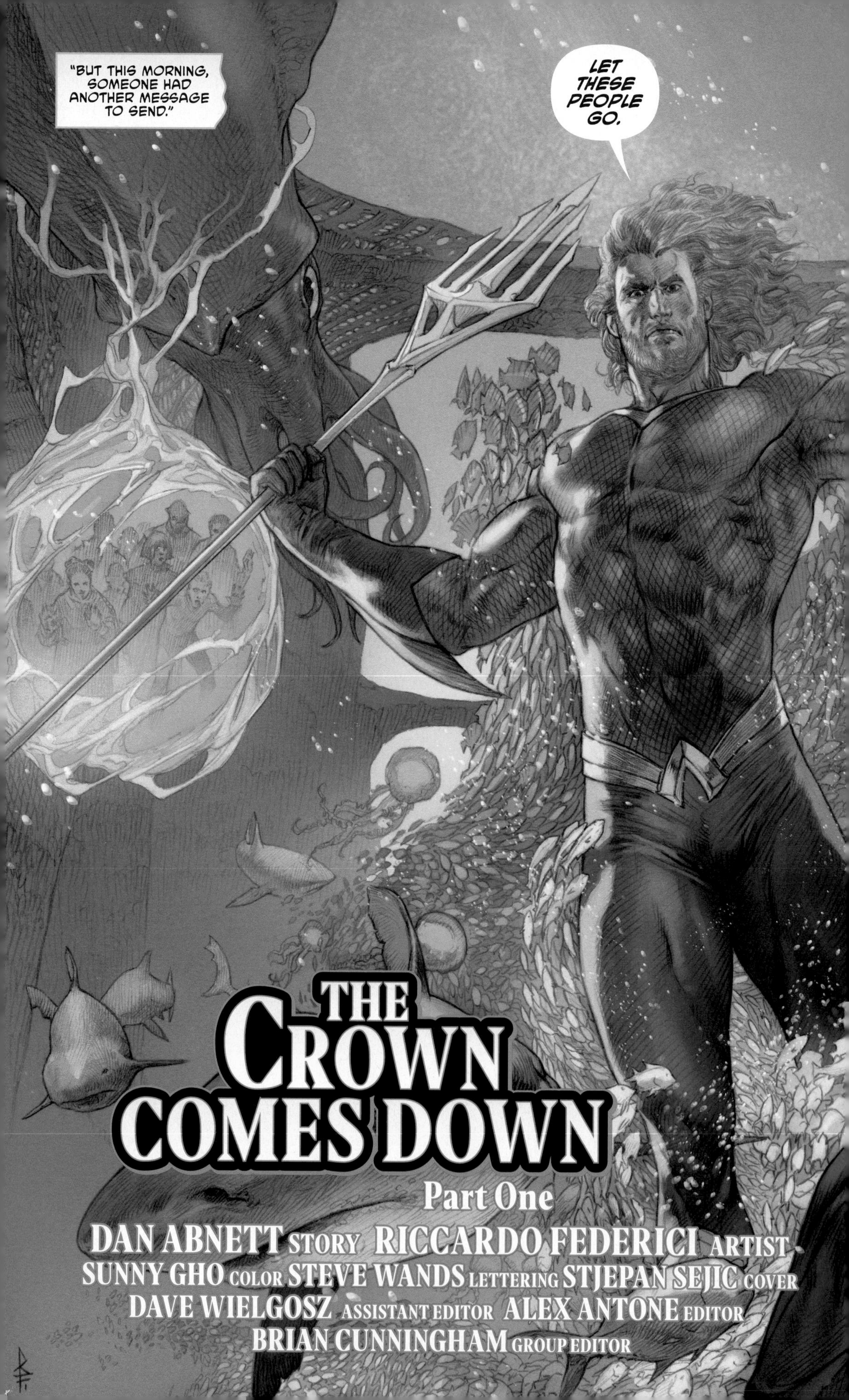
"BUT THIS MORNING, SOMEONE HAD ANOTHER MESSAGE TO SEND."
LET THESE PEOPLE GO.
THE CROWN COMES DOWN
Part One
DAN ABNETT STORY RICCARDO FEDERICI ARTIST
SUNNY GHO COLOR STEVE WANDS LETTERING STJEPAN SEJIC COVER
DAVE WIELGOSZ ASSISTANT EDITOR ALEX ANTONE EDITOR
BRIAN CUNNINGHAM GROUP EDITOR

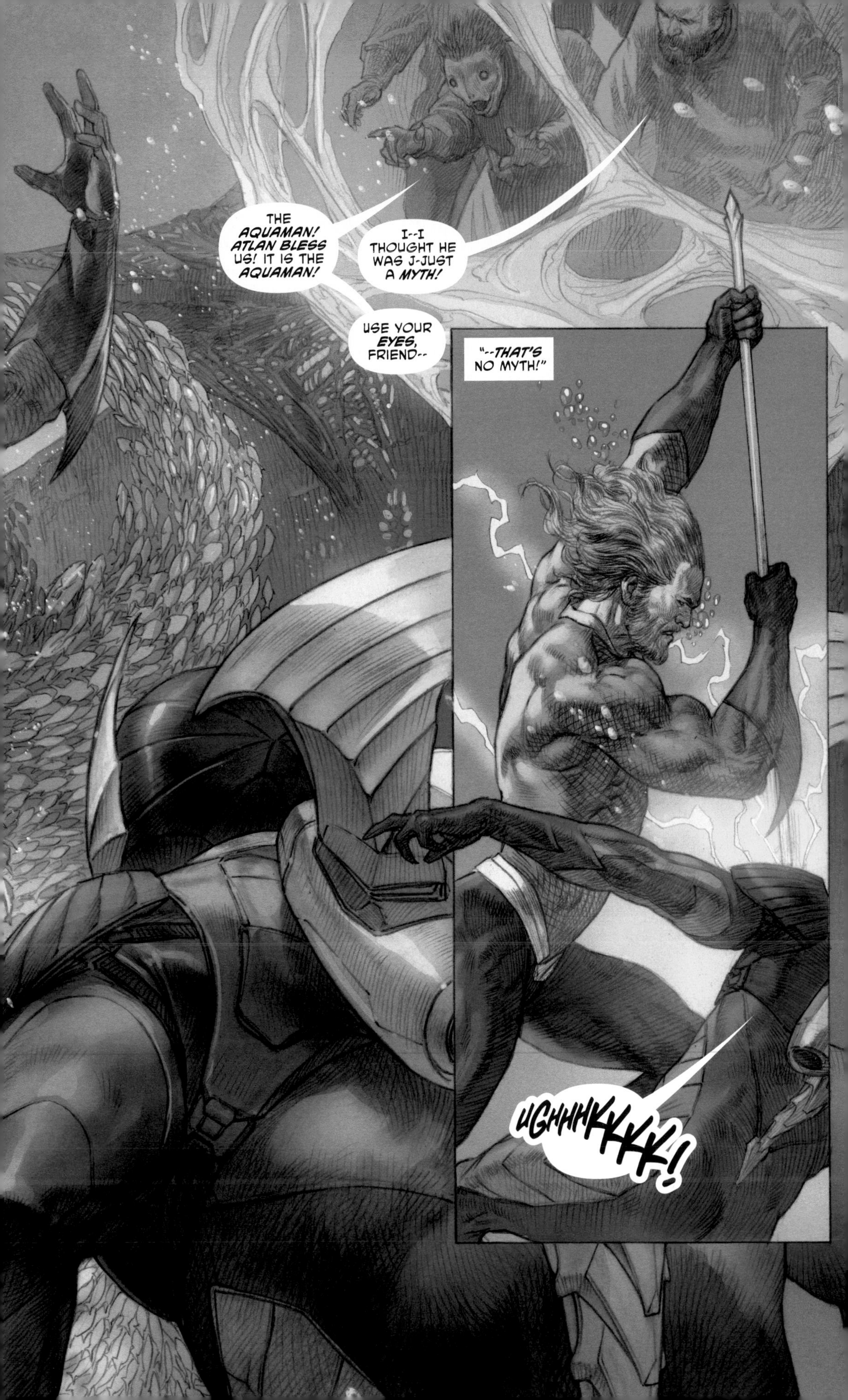
THE AQUAMAN! ATLAN BLESS US! IT IS THE AQUAMAN!
I--I THOUGHT HE WAS J-JUST A MYTH!
USE YOUR EYES, FRIEND--
"--THAT'S NO MYTH!"
UGHHHKKKK!

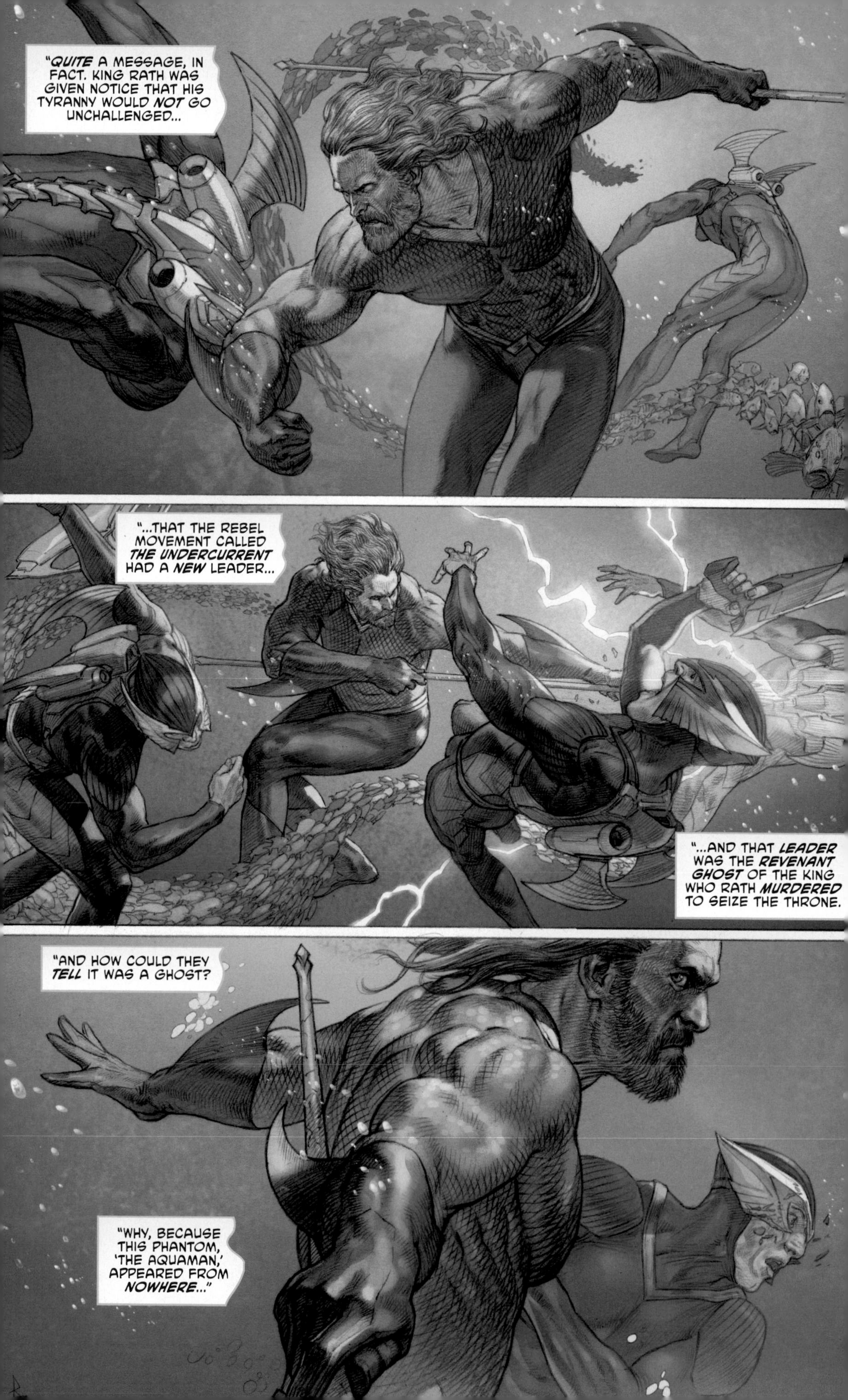
"QUITE A MESSAGE, IN FACT. KING RATH WAS GIVEN NOTICE THAT HIS TYRANNY WOULD NOT GO UNCHALLENGED...
"...THAT THE REBEL MOVEMENT CALLED THE UNDERCURRENT HAD A NEW LEADER...
"...AND THAT LEADER WAS THE REVENANT GHOST OF THE KING WHO RATH MURDERED TO SEIZE THE THRONE.
"AND HOW COULD THEY TELL IT WAS A GHOST?
"WHY, BECAUSE THIS PHANTOM, 'THE AQUAMAN,' APPEARED FROM NOWHERE..."

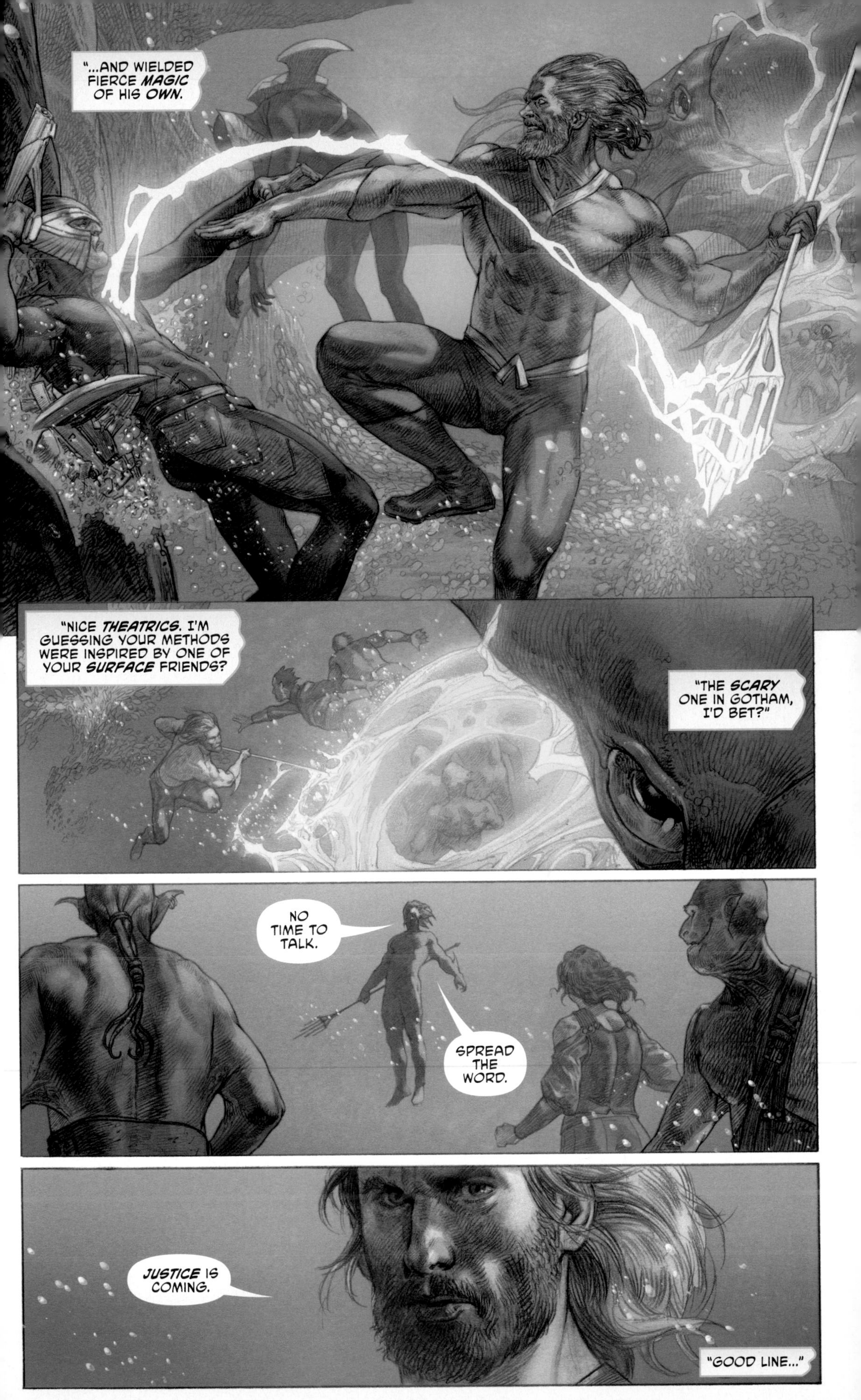
"...AND WIELDED FIERCE MAGIC OF HIS OWN.
"NICE THEATRICS. I'M GUESSING YOUR METHODS WERE INSPIRED BY ONE OF YOUR SURFACE FRIENDS?
"THE SCARY ONE IN GOTHAM, I'D BET?"
NO TIME TO TALK.
SPREAD THE WORD.
JUSTICE IS COMING.
"GOOD LINE..."

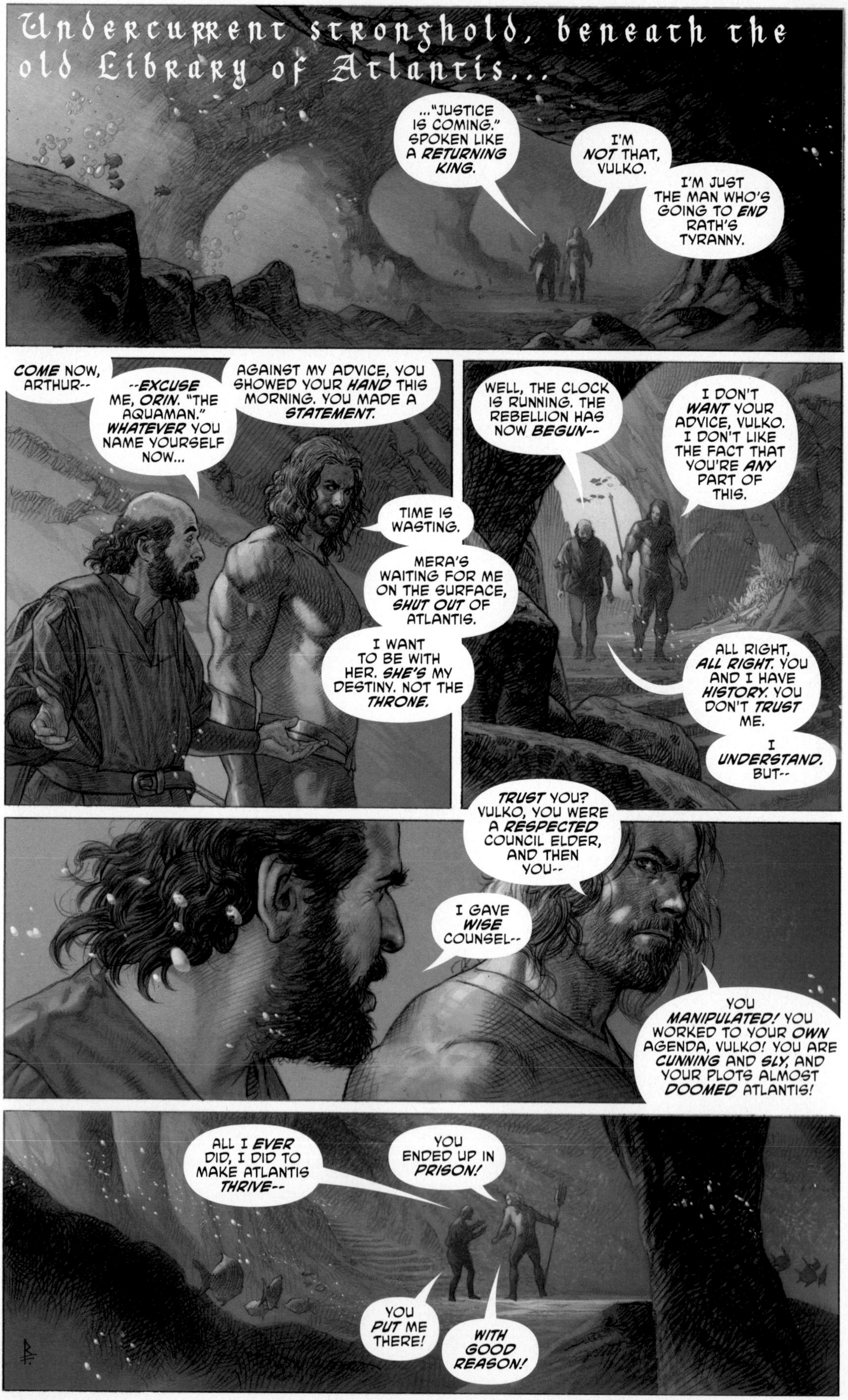
Undercurrent stronghold, beneath the old Library of Atlantis...
..."JUSTICE IS COMING." SPOKEN LIKE A RETURNING KING.
I'M NOT THAT, VULKO.
I'M JUST THE MAN WHO'S GOING TO END RATH'S TYRANNY.
COME NOW, ARTHUR--
--EXCUSE ME, ORIN. "THE AQUAMAN." WHATEVER YOU NAME YOURSELF NOW...
AGAINST MY ADVICE, YOU SHOWED YOUR HAND THIS MORNING. YOU MADE A STATEMENT.
TIME IS WASTING.
MERA'S WAITING FOR ME ON THE SURFACE, SHUT OUT OF ATLANTIS.
I WANT TO BE WITH HER. SHE'S MY DESTINY. NOT THE THRONE.
WELL, THE CLOCK IS RUNNING. THE REBELLION HAS NOW BEGUN--
I DON'T WANT YOUR ADVICE, VULKO. I DON'T LIKE THE FACT THAT YOU'RE ANY PART OF THIS.
ALL RIGHT, ALL RIGHT. YOU AND I HAVE HISTORY. YOU DON'T TRUST ME.
I UNDERSTAND. BUT--
TRUST YOU? VULKO, YOU WERE A RESPECTED COUNCIL ELDER, AND THEN YOU--
I GAVE WISE COUNSEL--
YOU MANIPULATED! YOU WORKED TO YOUR OWN AGENDA, VULKO! YOU ARE CUNNING AND SLY, AND YOUR PLOTS ALMOST DOOMED ATLANTIS!
ALL I EVER DID, I DID TO MAKE ATLANTIS THRIVE--
YOU ENDED UP IN PRISON!
YOU PUT ME THERE!
WITH GOOD REASON!

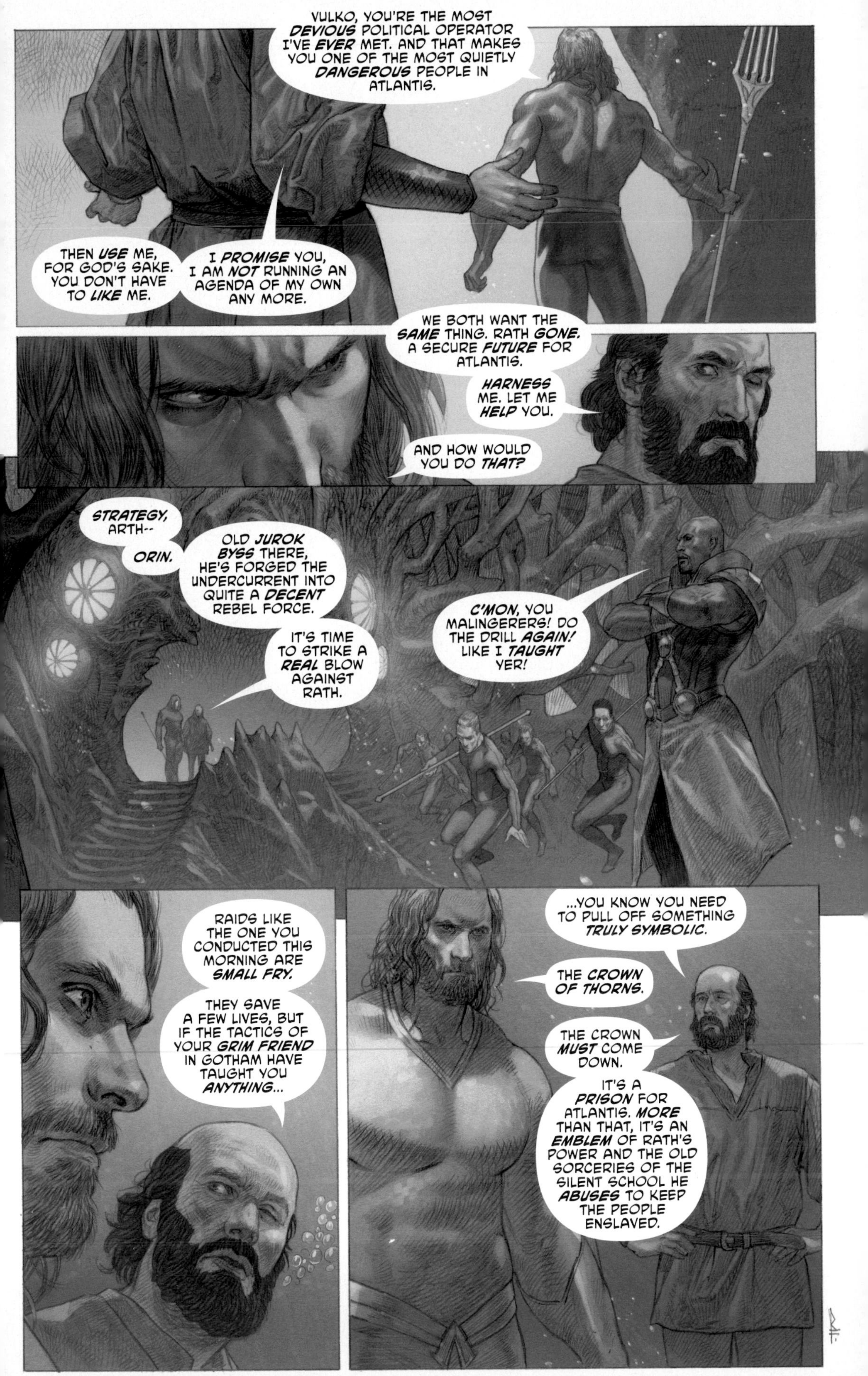
VULKO, YOU'RE THE MOST DEVIOUS POLITICAL OPERATOR I'VE EVER MET. AND THAT MAKES YOU ONE OF THE MOST QUIETLY DANGEROUS PEOPLE IN ATLANTIS.
THEN USE ME, FOR GOD'S SAKE. YOU DON'T HAVE TO LIKE ME.
I PROMISE YOU, I AM NOT RUNNING AN AGENDA OF MY OWN ANY MORE.
WE BOTH WANT THE SAME THING. RATH GONE. A SECURE FUTURE FOR ATLANTIS.
HARNESS ME. LET ME HELP YOU.
AND HOW WOULD YOU DO THAT?
STRATEGY, ARTH--
ORIN.
OLD JUROK BYSS THERE, HE'S FORGED THE UNDERCURRENT INTO QUITE A DECENT REBEL FORCE.
IT'S TIME TO STRIKE A REAL BLOW AGAINST RATH.
C'MON, YOU MALINGERERS! DO THE DRILL AGAIN! LIKE I TAUGHT YER!
RAIDS LIKE THE ONE YOU CONDUCTED THIS MORNING ARE SMALL FRY.
THEY SAVE A FEW LIVES, BUT IF THE TACTICS OF YOUR GRIM FRIEND IN GOTHAM HAVE TAUGHT YOU ANYTHING...
...YOU KNOW YOU NEED TO PULL OFF SOMETHING TRULY SYMBOLIC.
THE CROWN OF THORNS.
THE CROWN MUST COME DOWN.
IT'S A PRISON FOR ATLANTIS. MORE THAN THAT, IT'S AN EMBLEM OF RATH'S POWER AND THE OLD SORCERIES OF THE SILENT SCHOOL HE ABUSES TO KEEP THE PEOPLE ENSLAVED.

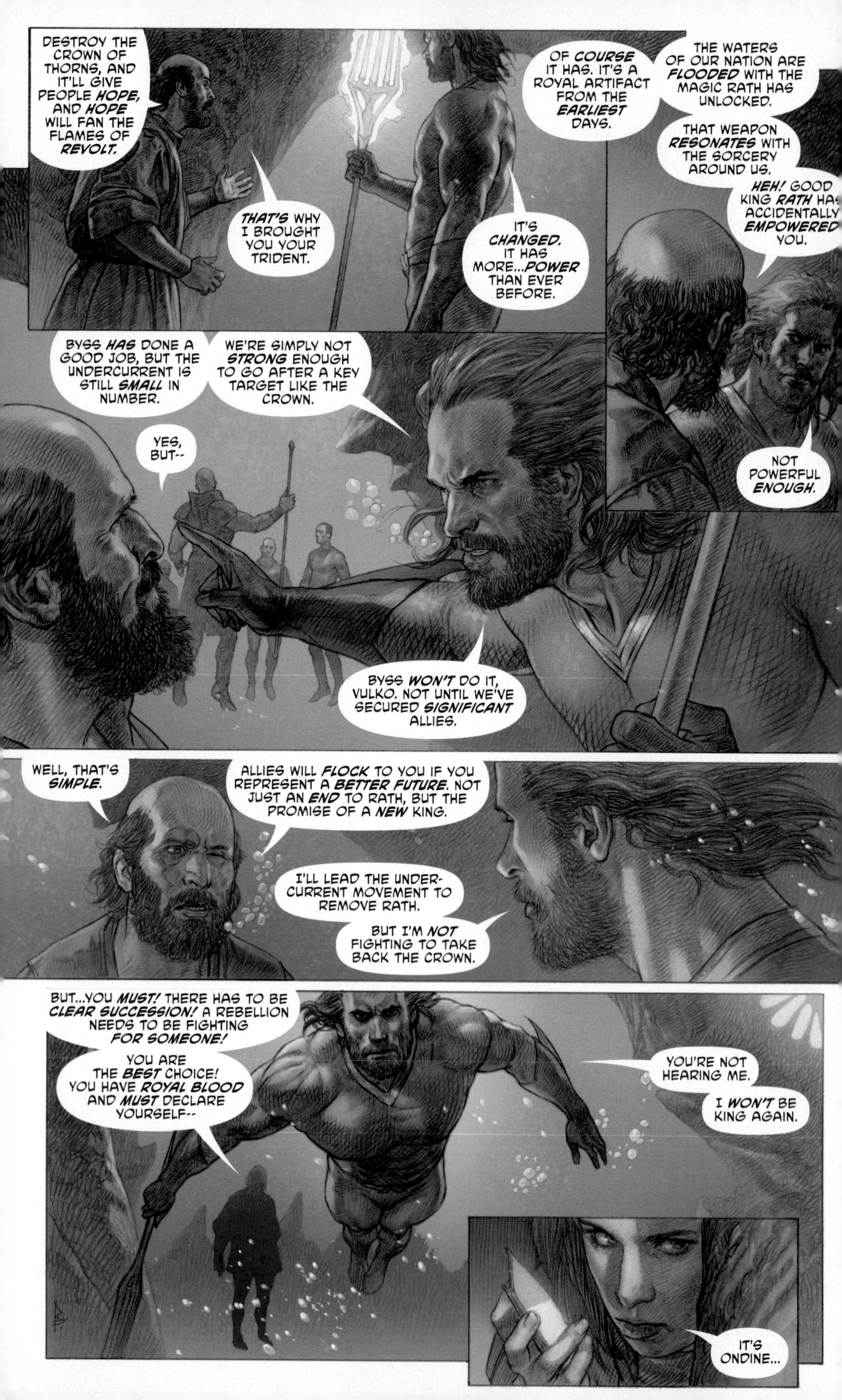

DESTROY THE CROWN OF THORNS, AND IT'LL GIVE PEOPLE HOPE, AND HOPE WILL FAN THE FLAMES OF REVOLT.
THAT'S WHY I BROUGHT YOU YOUR TRIDENT.
IT'S CHANGED. IT HAS MORE...POWER THAN EVER BEFORE.
OF COURSE IT HAS. IT'S A ROYAL ARTIFACT FROM THE EARLIEST DAYS.
THE WATERS OF OUR NATION ARE FLOODED WITH THE MAGIC RATH HAS UNLOCKED.
THAT WEAPON RESONATES WITH THE SORCERY AROUND US.
HEH! GOOD KING RATH HAS ACCIDENTALLY EMPOWERED YOU.
NOT POWERFUL ENOUGH.
BYSS HAS DONE A GOOD JOB, BUT THE UNDERCURRENT IS STILL SMALL IN NUMBER.
WE'RE SIMPLY NOT STRONG ENOUGH TO GO AFTER A KEY TARGET LIKE THE CROWN.
YES, BUT--
BYSS WON'T DO IT, VULKO. NOT UNTIL WE'VE SECURED SIGNIFICANT ALLIES.
WELL, THAT'S SIMPLE.
ALLIES WILL FLOCK TO YOU IF YOU REPRESENT A BETTER FUTURE. NOT JUST AN END TO RATH, BUT THE PROMISE OF A NEW KING.
I'LL LEAD THE UNDER-CURRENT MOVEMENT TO REMOVE RATH.
BUT I'M NOT FIGHTING TO TAKE BACK THE CROWN.
BUT...YOU MUST! THERE HAS TO BE CLEAR SUCCESSION! A REBELLION NEEDS TO BE FIGHTING FOR SOMEONE!
YOU ARE THE BEST CHOICE! YOU HAVE ROYAL BLOOD AND MUST DECLARE YOURSELF--
YOU'RE NOT HEARING ME.
I WON'T BE KING AGAIN.
IT'S ONDINE...

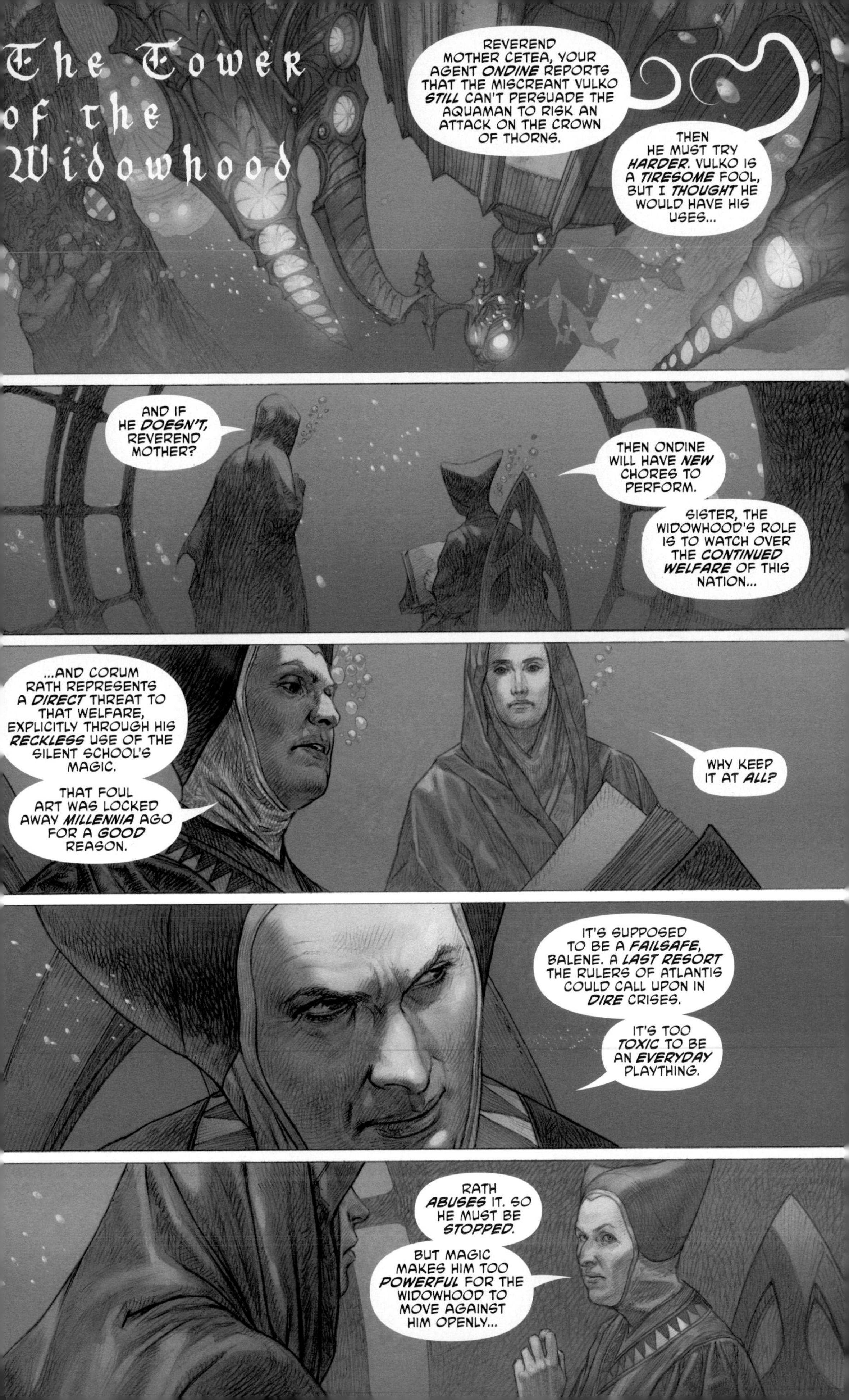
The Tower of the Widowhood
REVEREND MOTHER CETEA, YOUR AGENT ONDINE REPORTS THAT THE MISCREANT VULKO STILL CAN'T PERSUADE THE AQUAMAN TO RISK AN ATTACK ON THE CROWN OF THORNS.
THEN HE MUST TRY HARDER. VULKO IS A TIRESOME FOOL, BUT I THOUGHT HE WOULD HAVE HIS USES...
AND IF HE DOESN'T, REVEREND MOTHER?
THEN ONDINE WILL HAVE NEW CHORES TO PERFORM.
SISTER, THE WIDOWHOOD'S ROLE IS TO WATCH OVER THE CONTINUED WELFARE OF THIS NATION...
...AND CORUM RATH REPRESENTS A DIRECT THREAT TO THAT WELFARE, EXPLICITLY THROUGH HIS RECKLESS USE OF THE SILENT SCHOOL'S MAGIC.
THAT FOUL ART WAS LOCKED AWAY MILLENNIA AGO FOR A GOOD REASON.
WHY KEEP IT AT ALL?
IT'S SUPPOSED TO BE A FAILSAFE, BALENE. A LAST RESORT THE RULERS OF ATLANTIS COULD CALL UPON IN DIRE CRISES.
IT'S TOO TOXIC TO BE AN EVERYDAY PLAYTHING.
RATH ABUSES IT. SO HE MUST BE STOPPED.
BUT MAGIC MAKES HIM TOO POWERFUL FOR THE WIDOWHOOD TO MOVE AGAINST HIM OPENLY...

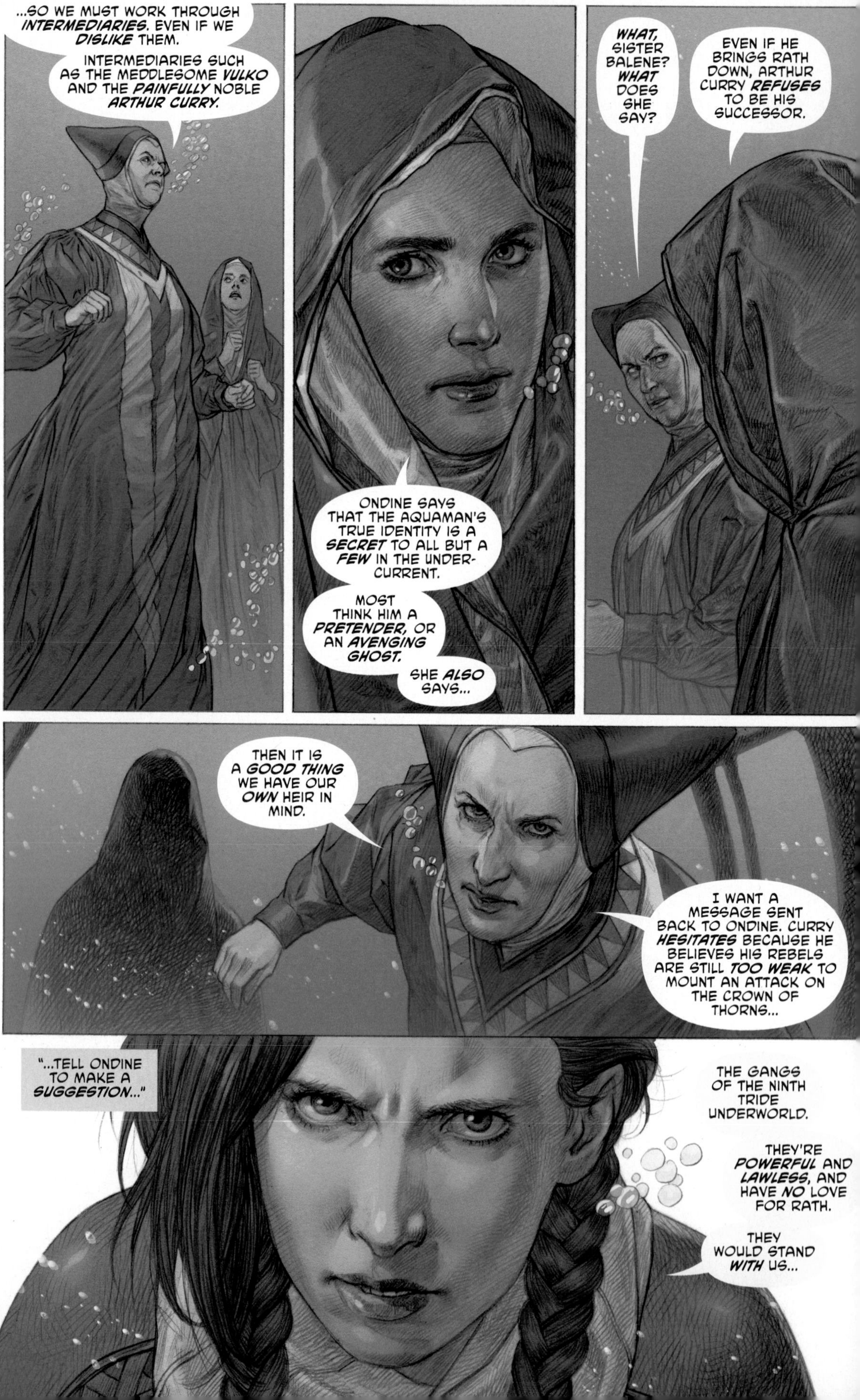
...SO WE MUST WORK THROUGH *INTERMEDIARIES*. EVEN IF WE *DISLIKE* THEM.
INTERMEDIARIES SUCH AS THE MEDDLESOME *VULKO* AND THE *PAINFULLY* NOBLE *ARTHUR CURRY*.
ONDINE SAYS THAT THE AQUAMAN'S TRUE IDENTITY IS A *SECRET* TO ALL BUT A *FEW* IN THE UNDER-CURRENT.
MOST THINK HIM A *PRETENDER*, OR AN *AVENGING GHOST*.
SHE *ALSO* SAYS...
WHAT, SISTER BALENE? *WHAT* DOES SHE SAY?
EVEN IF HE BRINGS RATH DOWN, ARTHUR CURRY *REFUSES* TO BE HIS SUCCESSOR.
THEN IT IS A *GOOD THING* WE HAVE OUR *OWN* HEIR IN MIND.
I WANT A MESSAGE SENT BACK TO ONDINE. CURRY *HESITATES* BECAUSE HE BELIEVES HIS REBELS ARE STILL *TOO WEAK* TO MOUNT AN ATTACK ON THE CROWN OF THORNS...
"...TELL ONDINE TO MAKE A *SUGGESTION*..."
THE GANGS OF THE NINTH TRIDE UNDERWORLD.
THEY'RE *POWERFUL* AND *LAWLESS*, AND HAVE *NO* LOVE FOR RATH.
THEY WOULD STAND *WITH* US...

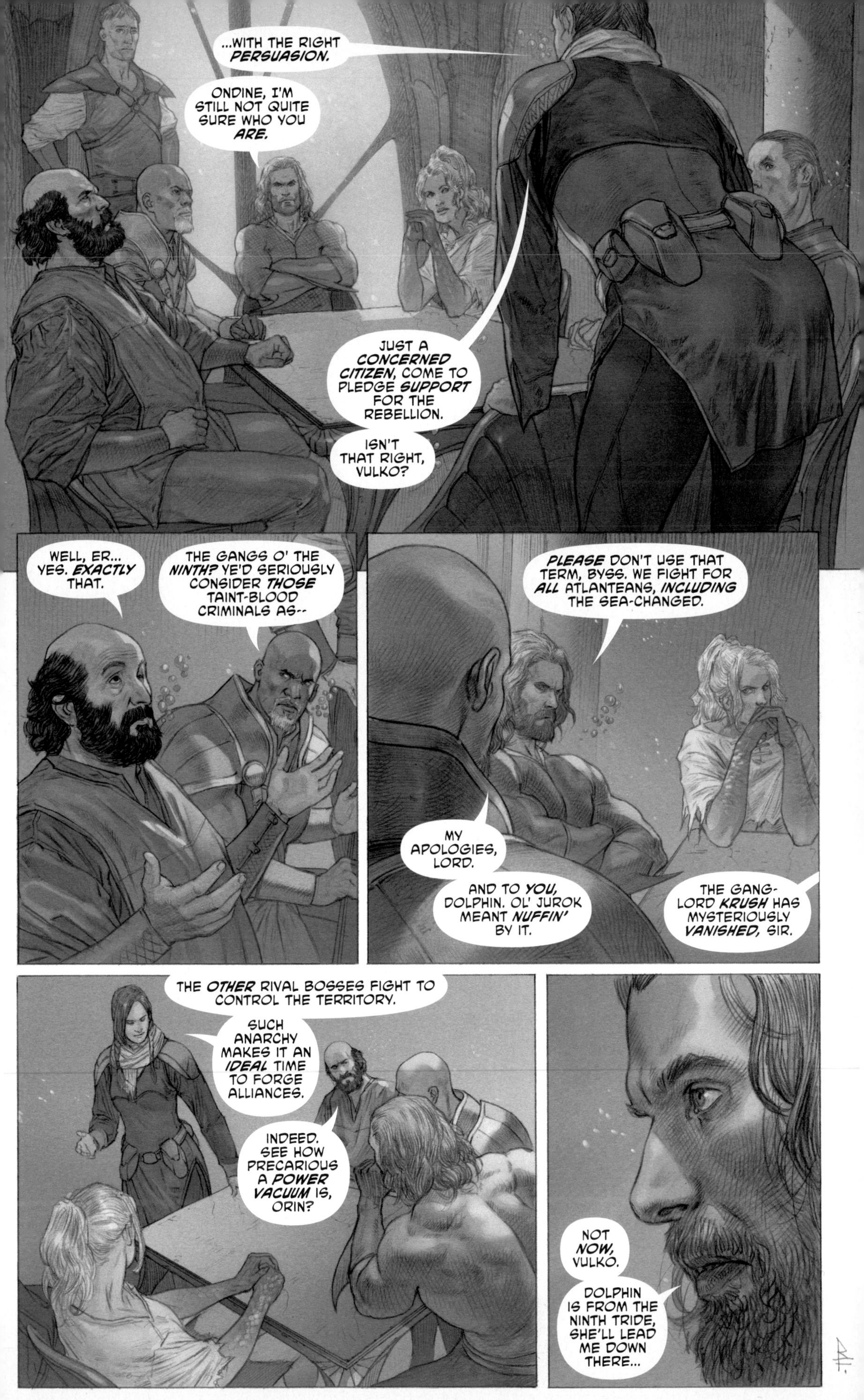
...WITH THE RIGHT PERSUASION.
ONDINE, I'M STILL NOT QUITE SURE WHO YOU ARE.
JUST A CONCERNED CITIZEN, COME TO PLEDGE SUPPORT FOR THE REBELLION.
ISN'T THAT RIGHT, VULKO?
WELL, ER... YES. EXACTLY THAT.
THE GANGS O' THE NINTH? YE'D SERIOUSLY CONSIDER THOSE TAINT-BLOOD CRIMINALS AS--
PLEASE DON'T USE THAT TERM, BYSS. WE FIGHT FOR ALL ATLANTEANS, INCLUDING THE SEA-CHANGED.
MY APOLOGIES, LORD.
AND TO YOU, DOLPHIN. OL' JUROK MEANT NUFFIN' BY IT.
THE GANG-LORD KRUSH HAS MYSTERIOUSLY VANISHED, SIR.
THE OTHER RIVAL BOSSES FIGHT TO CONTROL THE TERRITORY.
SUCH ANARCHY MAKES IT AN IDEAL TIME TO FORGE ALLIANCES.
INDEED. SEE HOW PRECARIOUS A POWER VACUUM IS, ORIN?
NOT NOW, VULKO.
DOLPHIN IS FROM THE NINTH TRIDE, SHE'LL LEAD ME DOWN THERE...

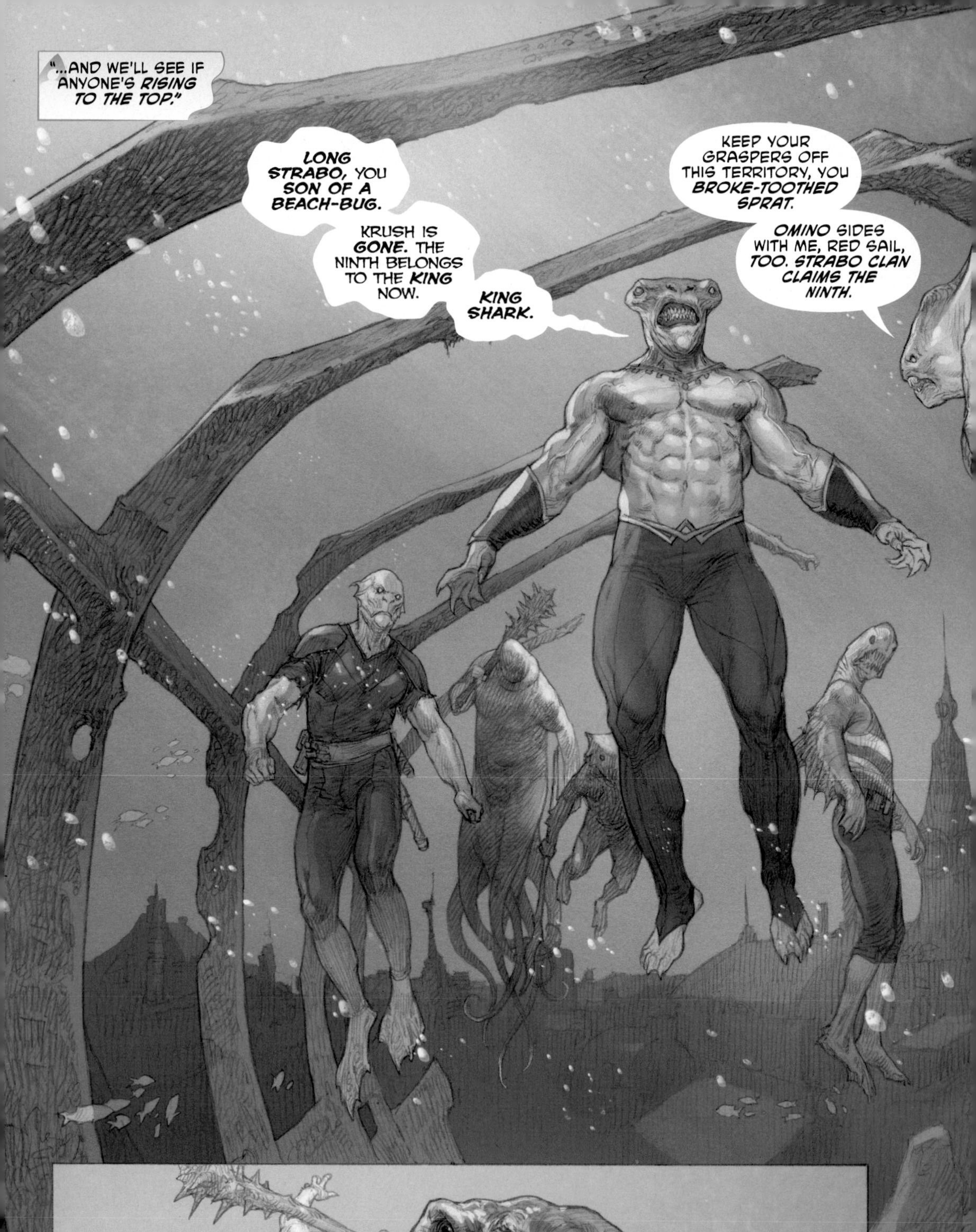
"...AND WE'LL SEE IF ANYONE'S *RISING TO THE TOP.*"
LONG STRABO, YOU **SON OF A BEACH-BUG.**
KRUSH IS **GONE.** THE NINTH BELONGS TO THE ***KING*** NOW.
KING SHARK.
KEEP YOUR GRASPERS OFF THIS TERRITORY, YOU *BROKE-TOOTHED SPRAT.*
OMINO SIDES WITH ME, RED SAIL, *TOO. STRABO CLAN CLAIMS THE NINTH.*

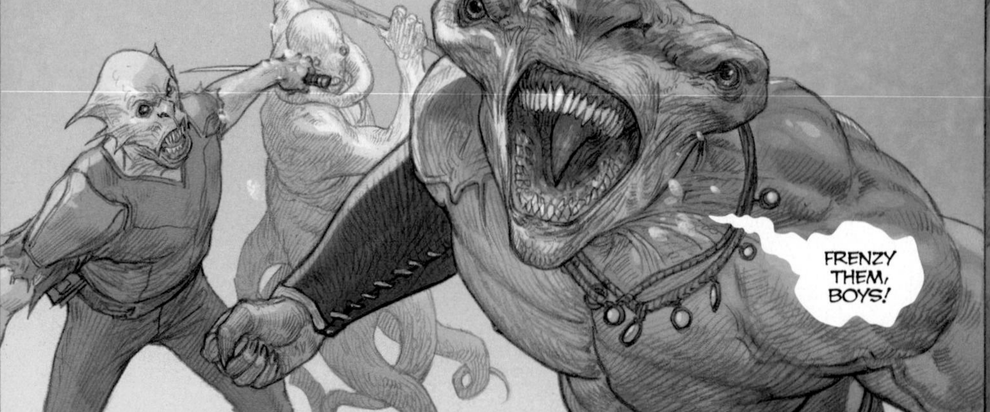
FRENZY THEM, BOYS!

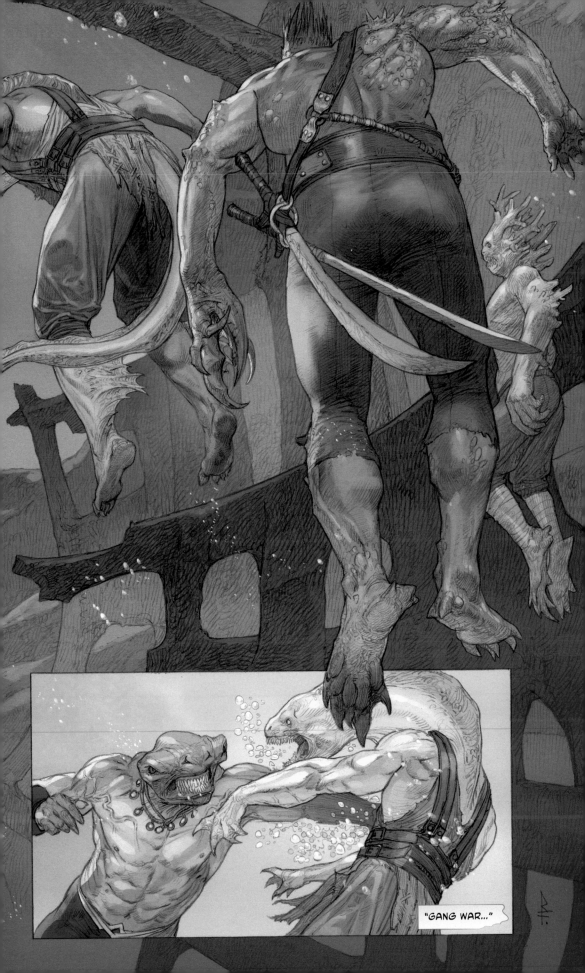

"GANG WAR..."

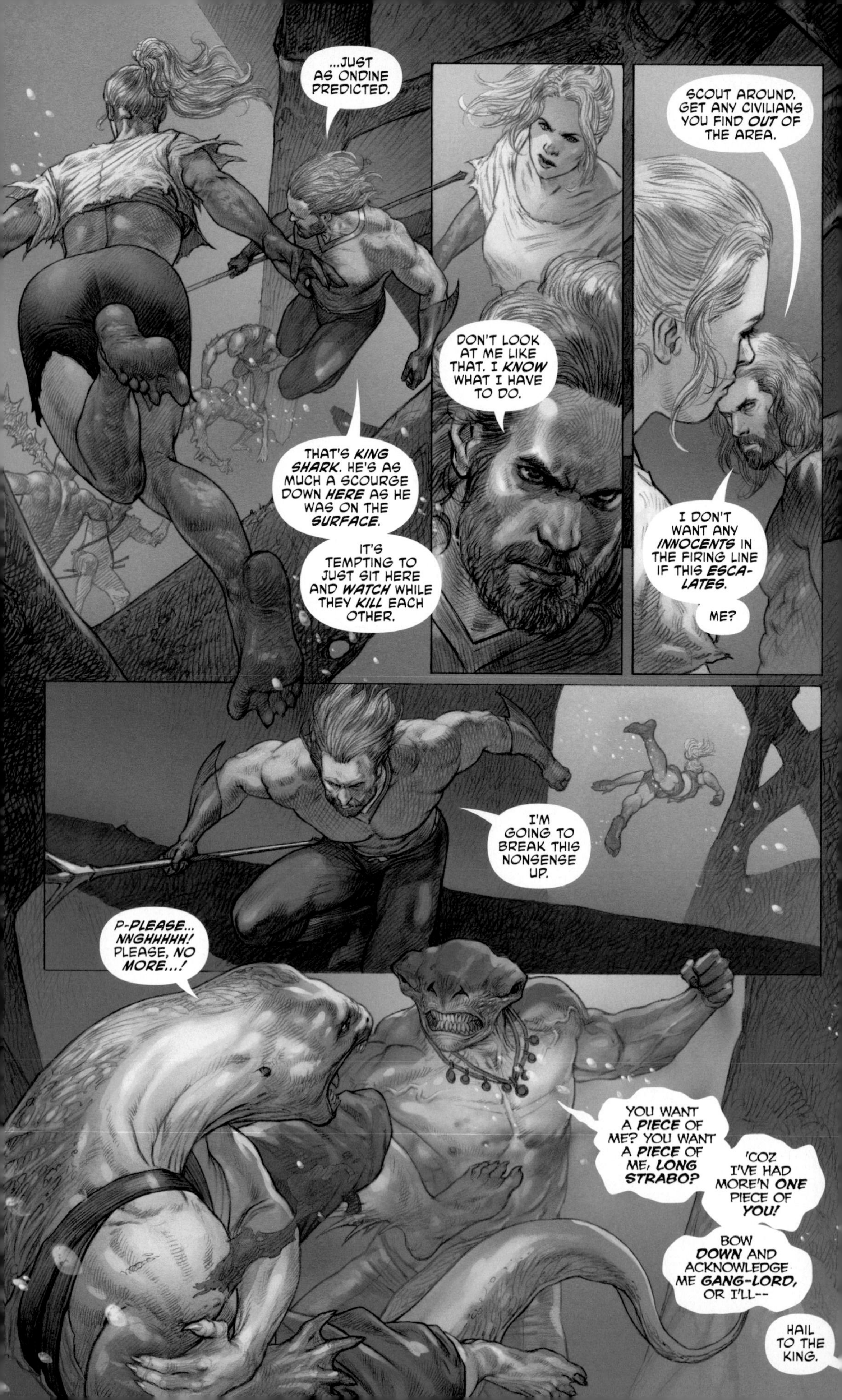
...JUST AS ONDINE PREDICTED.
THAT'S KING SHARK. HE'S AS MUCH A SCOURGE DOWN HERE AS HE WAS ON THE SURFACE.
IT'S TEMPTING TO JUST SIT HERE AND WATCH WHILE THEY KILL EACH OTHER.
DON'T LOOK AT ME LIKE THAT. I KNOW WHAT I HAVE TO DO.
SCOUT AROUND. GET ANY CIVILIANS YOU FIND OUT OF THE AREA.
I DON'T WANT ANY INNOCENTS IN THE FIRING LINE IF THIS ESCA- LATES.
ME?
I'M GOING TO BREAK THIS NONSENSE UP.
P-PLEASE... NNGHHHHH! PLEASE, NO MORE...!
YOU WANT A PIECE OF ME? YOU WANT A PIECE OF ME, LONG STRABO?
'COZ I'VE HAD MORE'N ONE PIECE OF YOU!
BOW DOWN AND ACKNOWLEDGE ME GANG-LORD, OR I'LL--
HAIL TO THE KING.

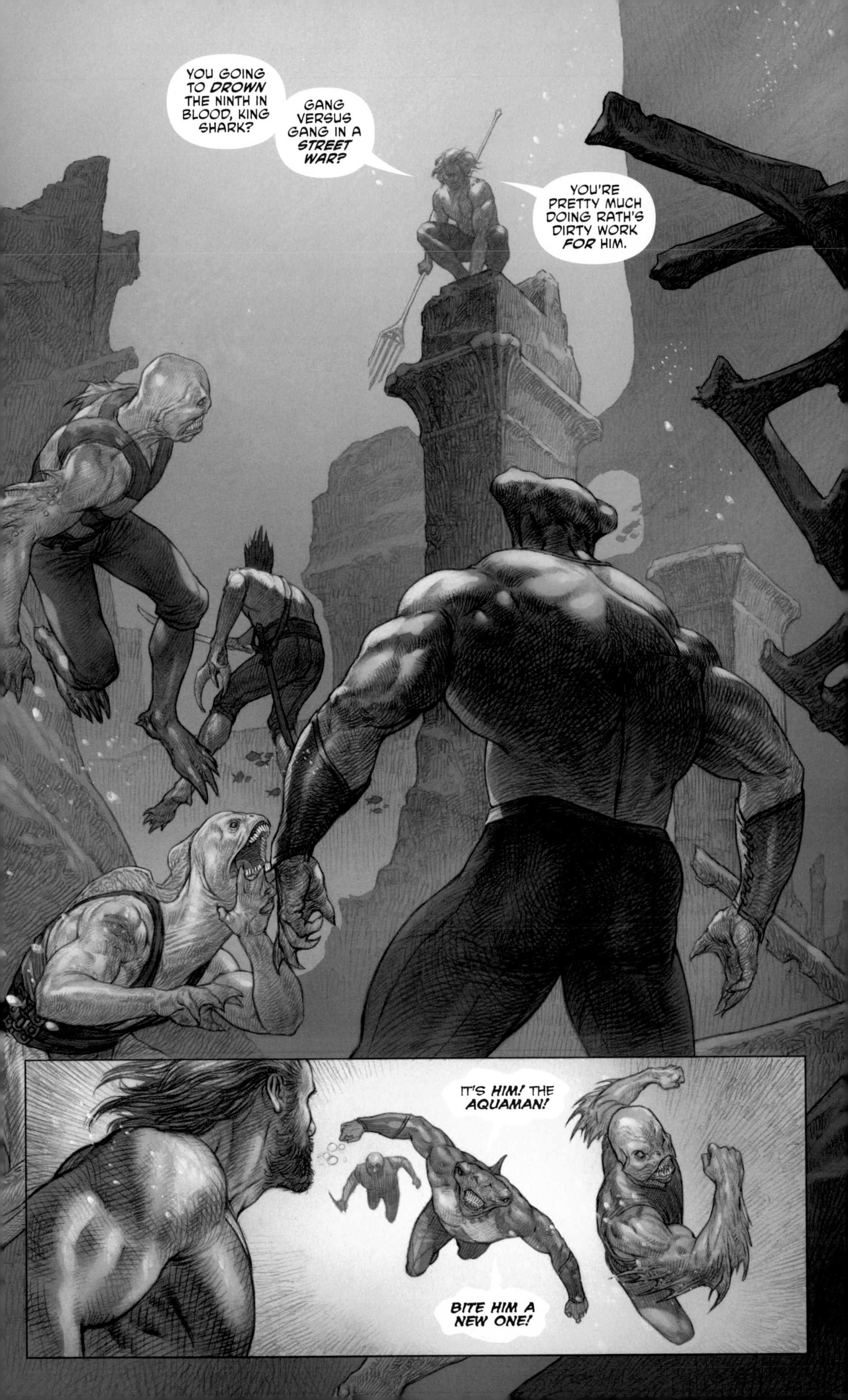
YOU GOING TO DROWN THE NINTH IN BLOOD, KING SHARK?
GANG VERSUS GANG IN A STREET WAR?
YOU'RE PRETTY MUCH DOING RATH'S DIRTY WORK FOR HIM.
IT'S HIM! THE AQUAMAN!
BITE HIM A NEW ONE!

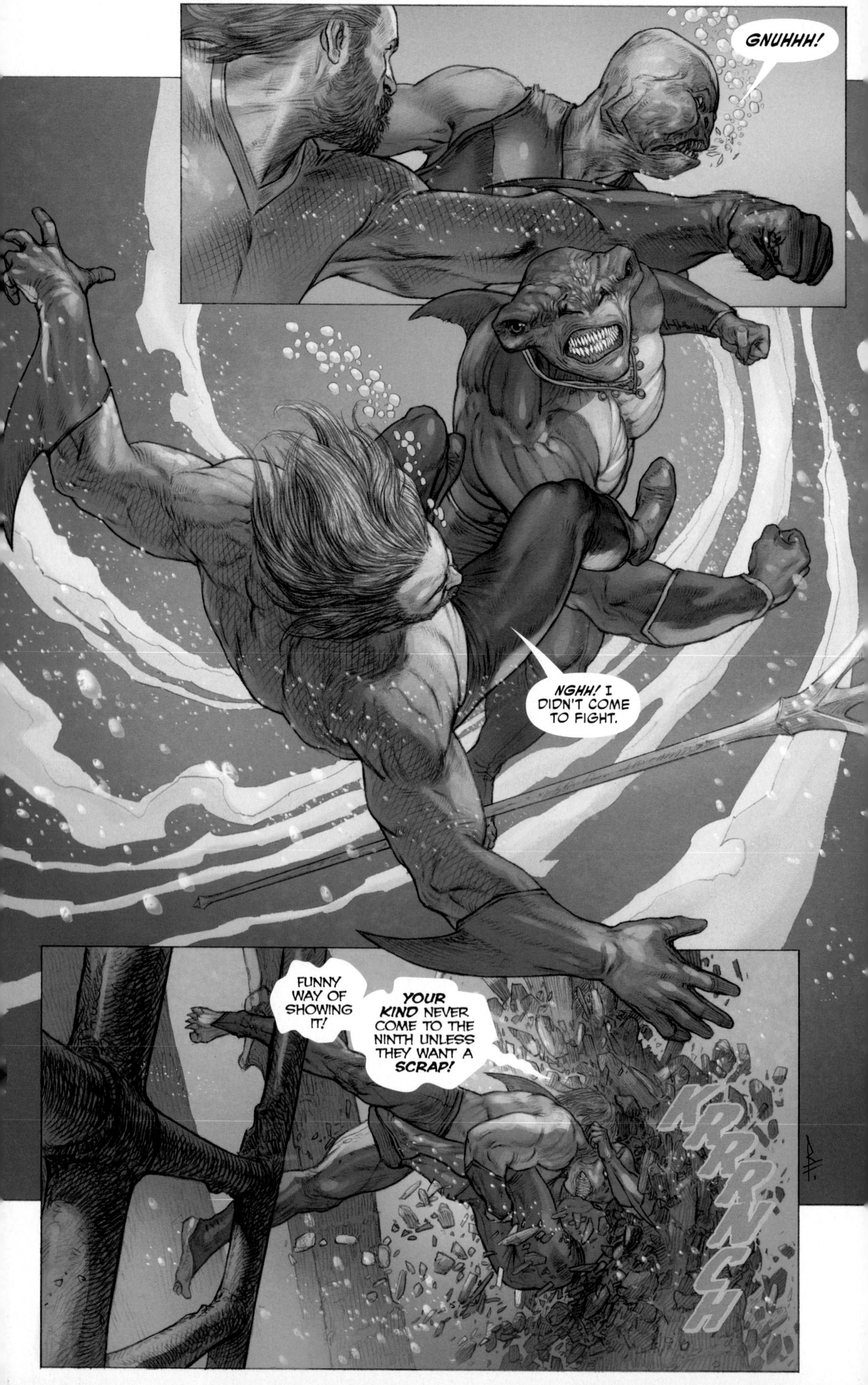
GNUHHH!
NGHH! I DIDN'T COME TO FIGHT.
FUNNY WAY OF SHOWING IT!
YOUR KIND NEVER COME TO THE NINTH UNLESS THEY WANT A SCRAP!
KRRRNCH

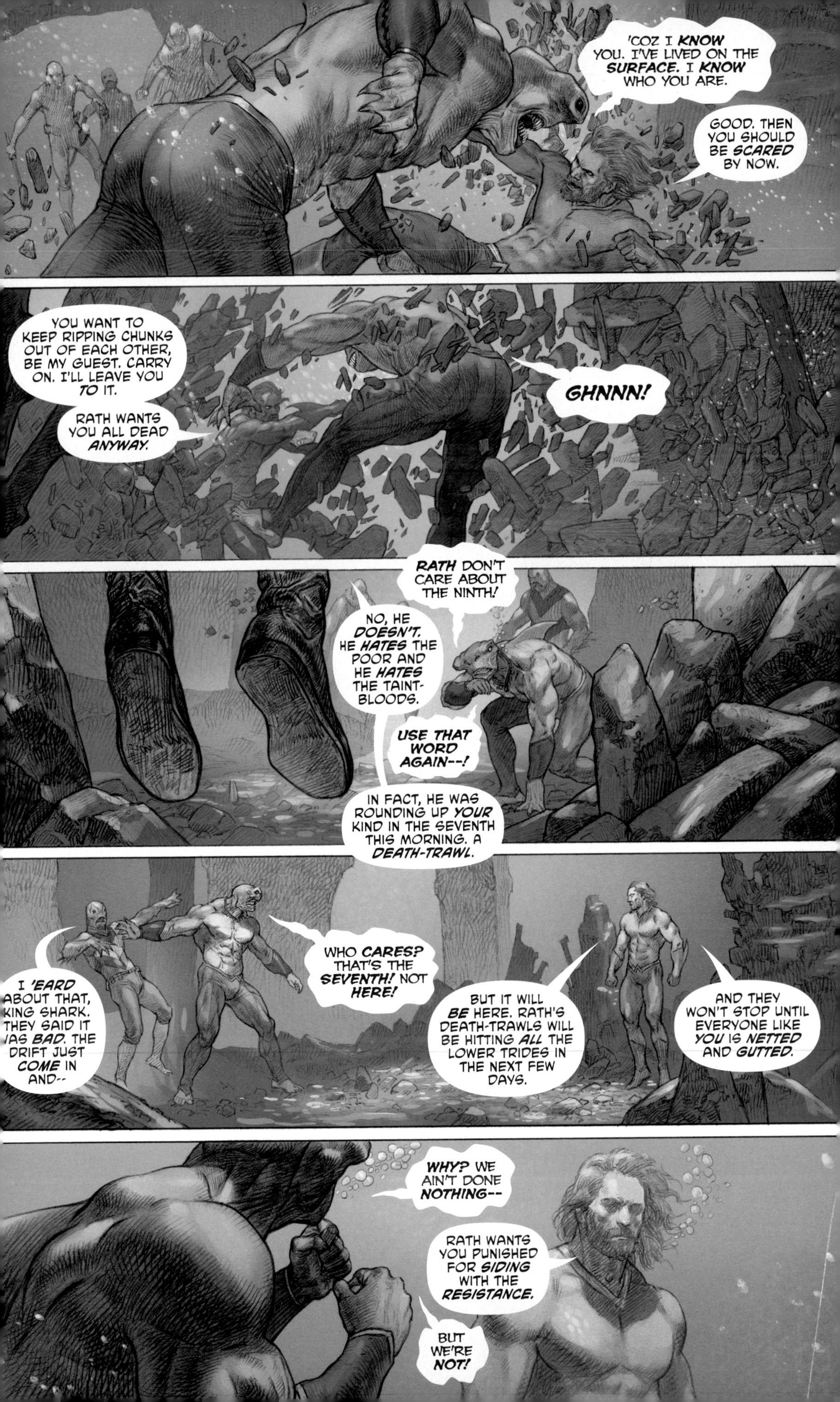
'COZ I KNOW YOU. I'VE LIVED ON THE SURFACE. I KNOW WHO YOU ARE.
GOOD. THEN YOU SHOULD BE SCARED BY NOW.
YOU WANT TO KEEP RIPPING CHUNKS OUT OF EACH OTHER, BE MY GUEST. CARRY ON. I'LL LEAVE YOU TO IT.
RATH WANTS YOU ALL DEAD ANYWAY.
GHNNN!
RATH DON'T CARE ABOUT THE NINTH!
NO, HE DOESN'T. HE HATES THE POOR AND HE HATES THE TAINT-BLOODS.
USE THAT WORD AGAIN--!
IN FACT, HE WAS ROUNDING UP YOUR KIND IN THE SEVENTH THIS MORNING. A DEATH-TRAWL.
I 'EARD ABOUT THAT, KING SHARK. THEY SAID IT WAS BAD. THE DRIFT JUST COME IN AND--
WHO CARES? THAT'S THE SEVENTH! NOT HERE!
BUT IT WILL BE HERE. RATH'S DEATH-TRAWLS WILL BE HITTING ALL THE LOWER TRIDES IN THE NEXT FEW DAYS.
AND THEY WON'T STOP UNTIL EVERYONE LIKE YOU IS NETTED AND GUTTED.
WHY? WE AIN'T DONE NOTHING--
RATH WANTS YOU PUNISHED FOR SIDING WITH THE RESISTANCE.
BUT WE'RE NOT!

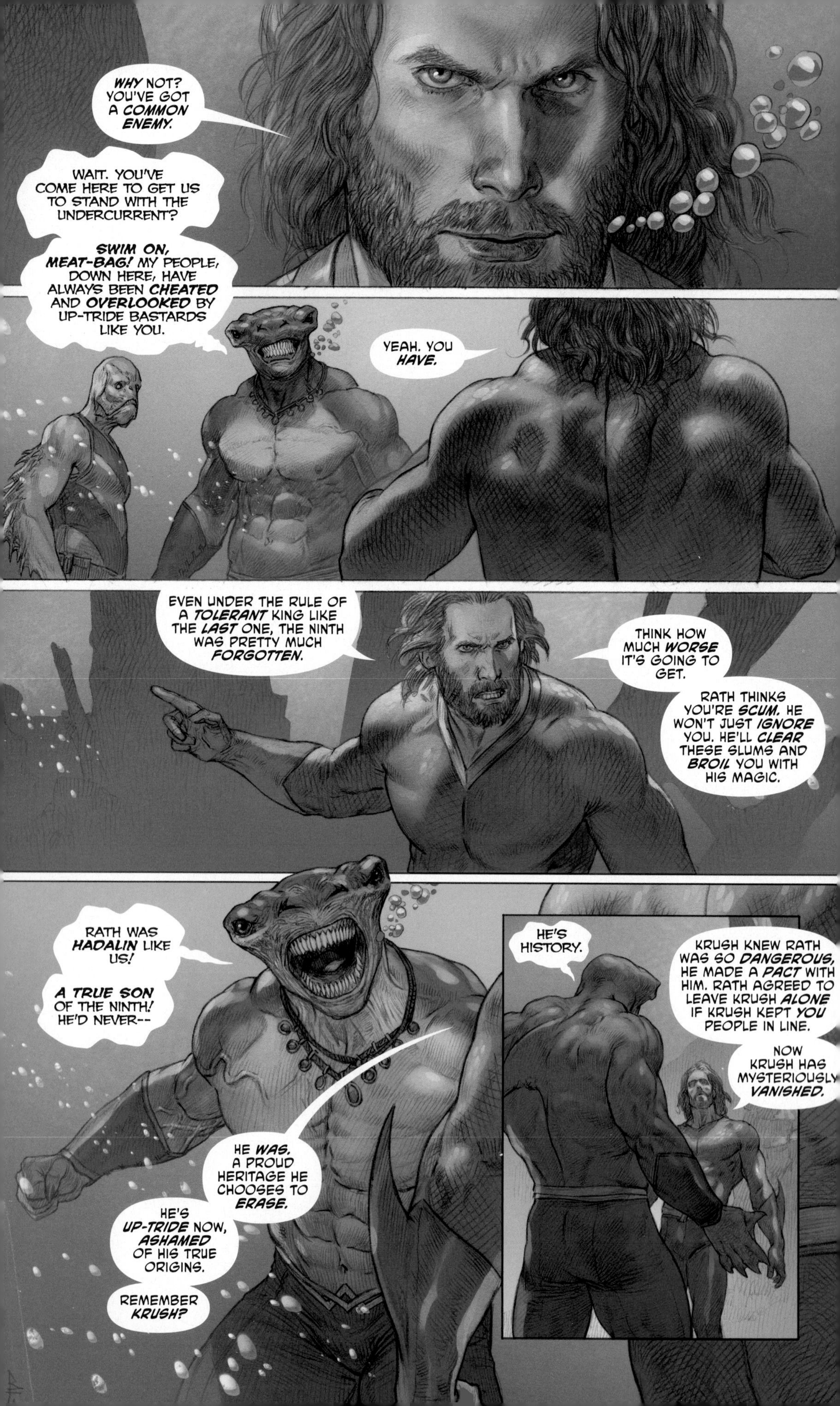
WHY NOT? YOU'VE GOT A COMMON ENEMY.
WAIT. YOU'VE COME HERE TO GET US TO STAND WITH THE UNDERCURRENT?
SWIM ON, MEAT-BAG! MY PEOPLE, DOWN HERE, HAVE ALWAYS BEEN CHEATED AND OVERLOOKED BY UP-TRIDE BASTARDS LIKE YOU.
YEAH. YOU HAVE.
EVEN UNDER THE RULE OF A TOLERANT KING LIKE THE LAST ONE, THE NINTH WAS PRETTY MUCH FORGOTTEN.
THINK HOW MUCH WORSE IT'S GOING TO GET.
RATH THINKS YOU'RE SCUM. HE WON'T JUST IGNORE YOU. HE'LL CLEAR THESE SLUMS AND BROIL YOU WITH HIS MAGIC.
RATH WAS HADALIN LIKE US!
A TRUE SON OF THE NINTH! HE'D NEVER--
HE WAS. A PROUD HERITAGE HE CHOOSES TO ERASE.
HE'S UP-TRIDE NOW, ASHAMED OF HIS TRUE ORIGINS.
REMEMBER KRUSH?
HE'S HISTORY.
KRUSH KNEW RATH WAS SO DANGEROUS, HE MADE A PACT WITH HIM. RATH AGREED TO LEAVE KRUSH ALONE IF KRUSH KEPT YOU PEOPLE IN LINE.
NOW KRUSH HAS MYSTERIOUSLY VANISHED.

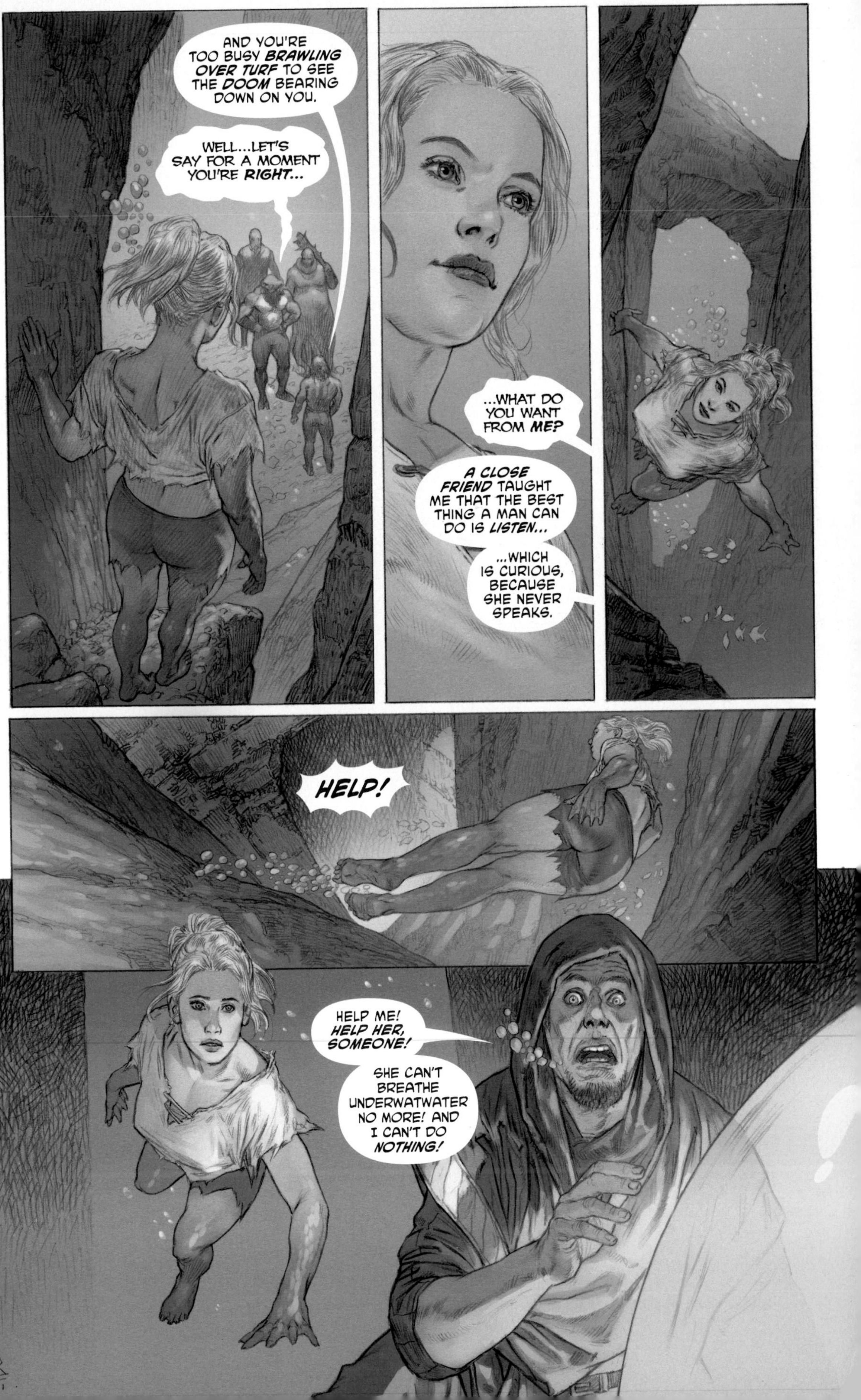
AND YOU'RE TOO BUSY BRAWLING OVER TURF TO SEE THE DOOM BEARING DOWN ON YOU.
WELL...LET'S SAY FOR A MOMENT YOU'RE RIGHT...
...WHAT DO YOU WANT FROM ME?
A CLOSE FRIEND TAUGHT ME THAT THE BEST THING A MAN CAN DO IS LISTEN...
...WHICH IS CURIOUS, BECAUSE SHE NEVER SPEAKS.
HELP!
HELP ME! HELP HER, SOMEONE!
SHE CAN'T BREATHE UNDERWATWATER NO MORE! AND I CAN'T DO NOTHING!

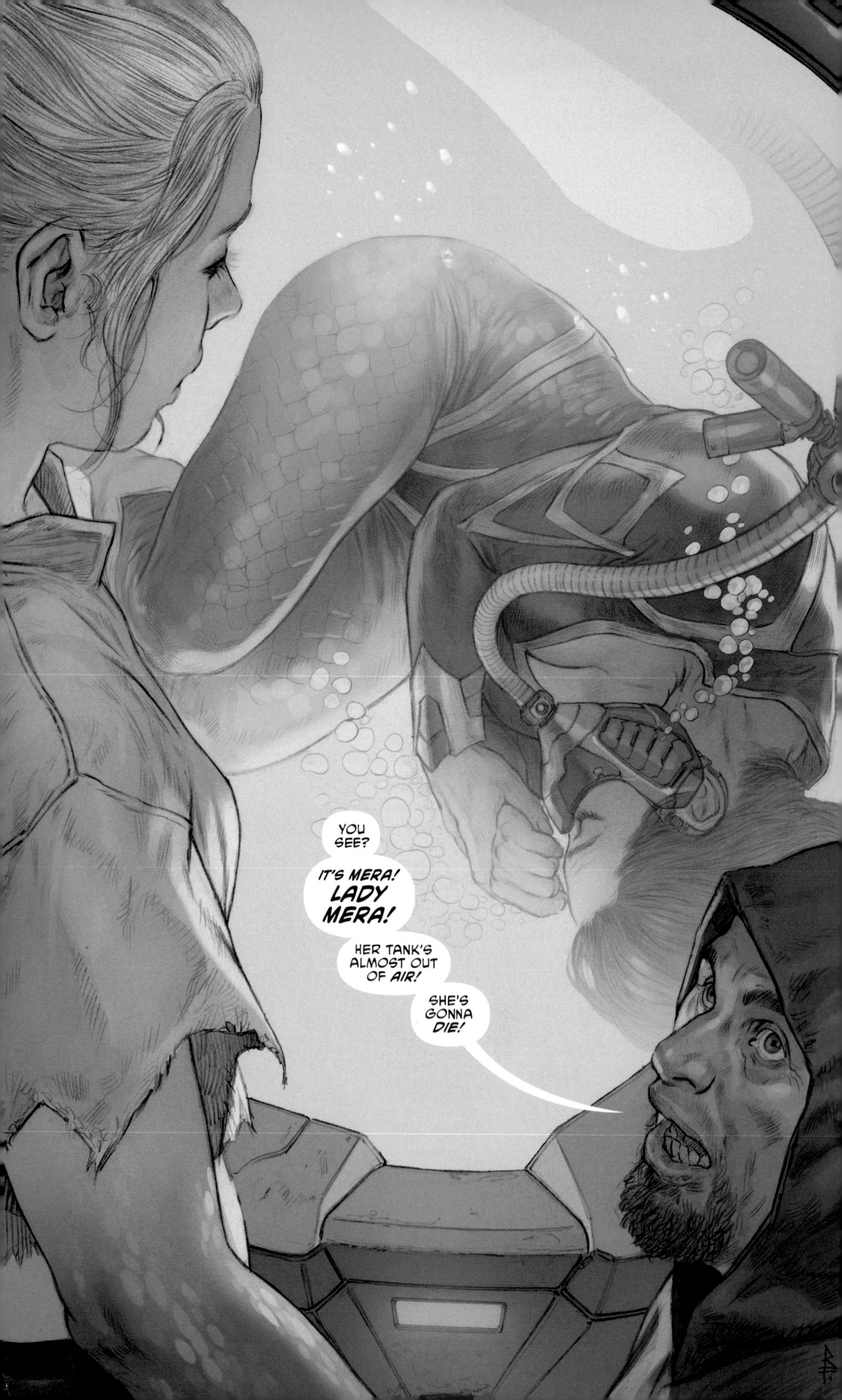
YOU SEE?
IT'S MERA! LADY MERA!
HER TANK'S ALMOST OUT OF AIR!
SHE'S GONNA DIE!

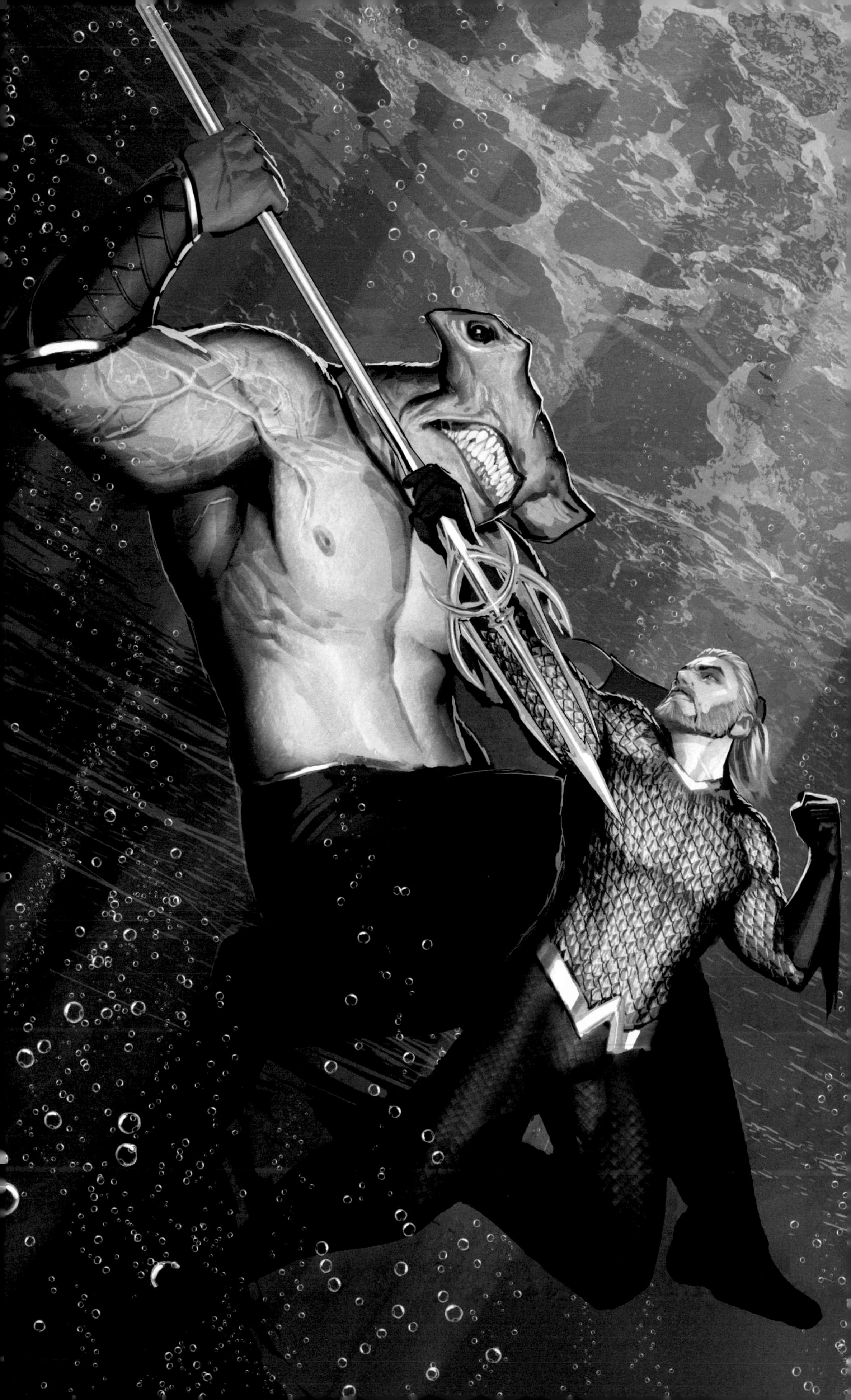

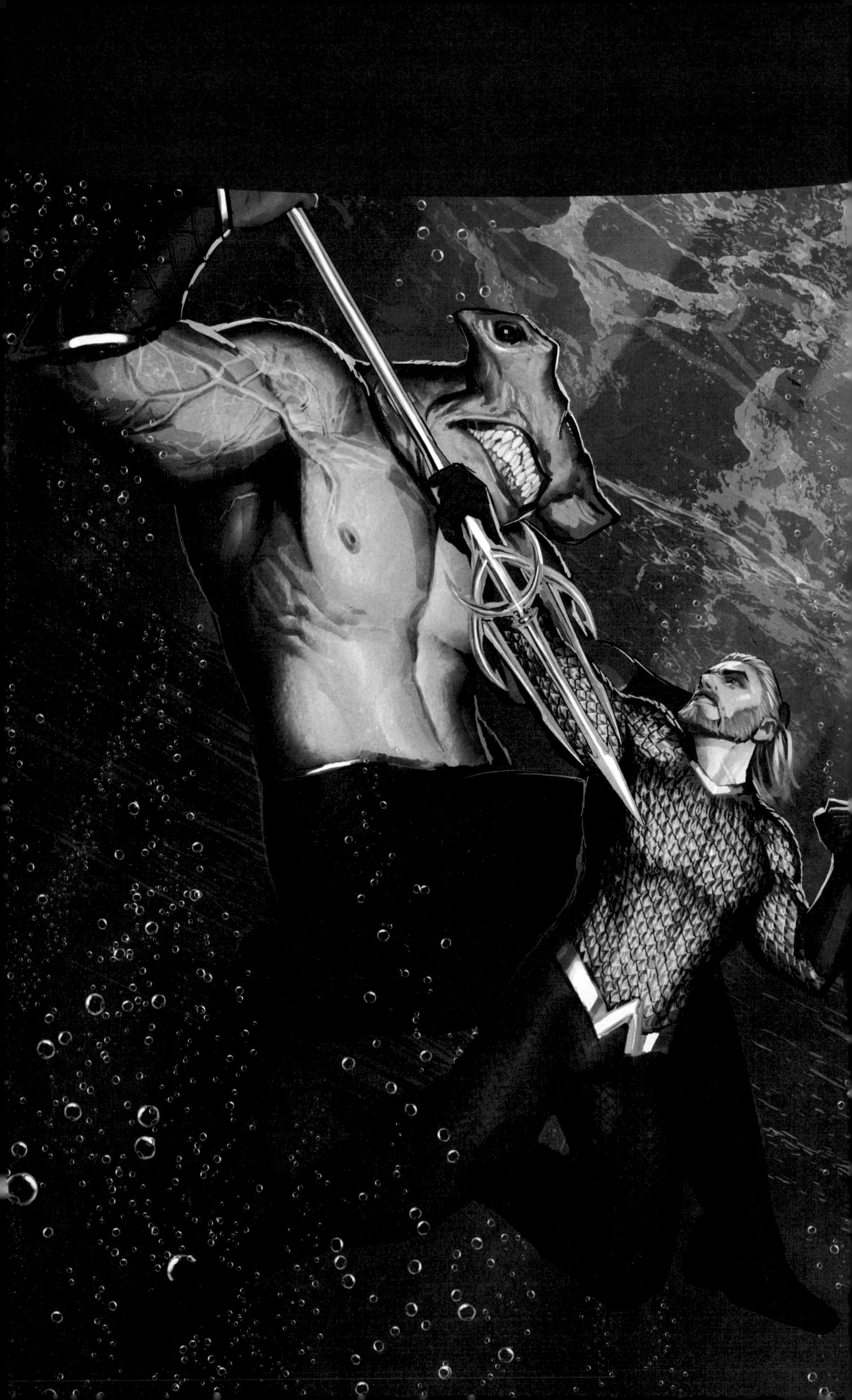

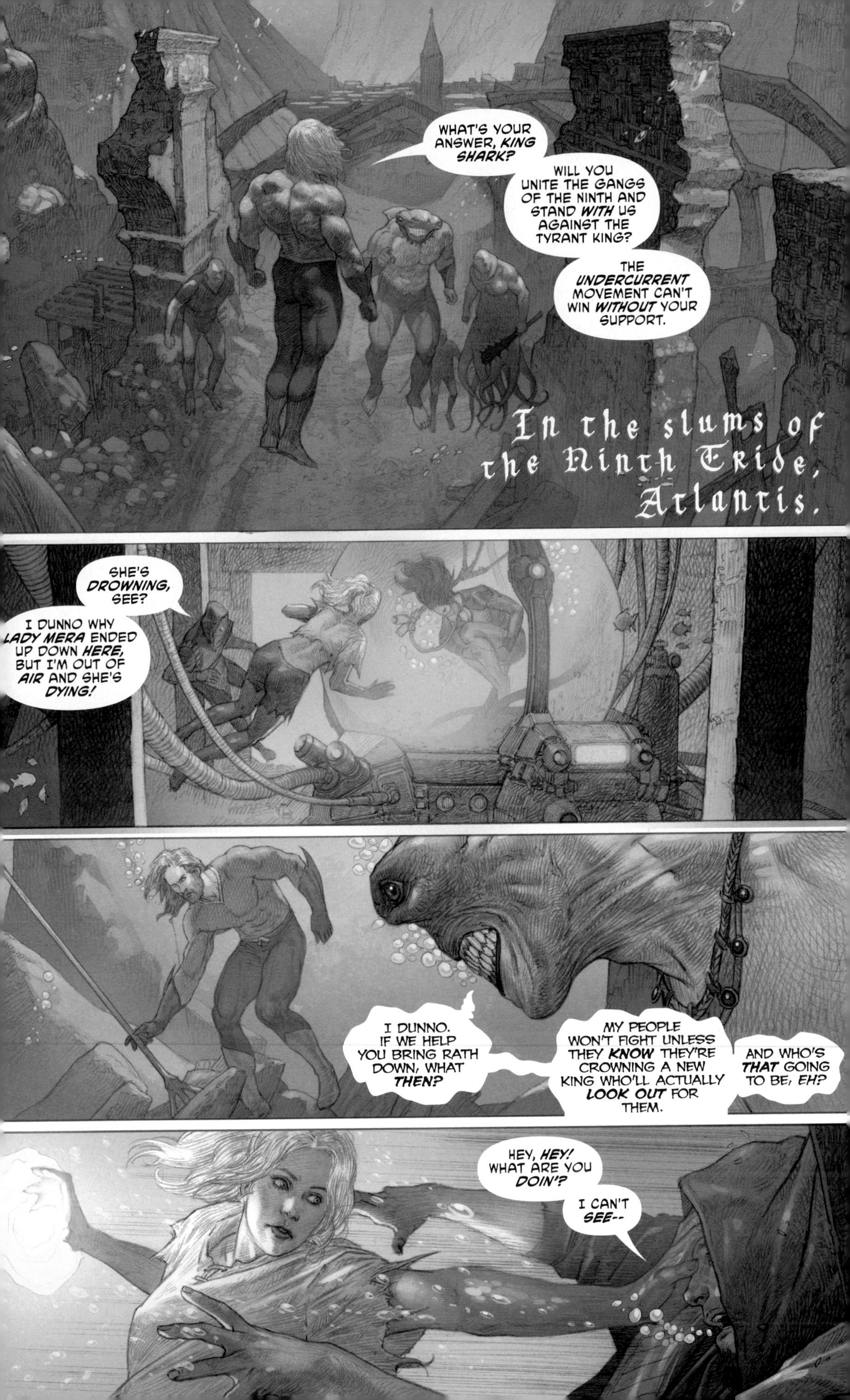

WHAT'S YOUR ANSWER, KING SHARK?
WILL YOU UNITE THE GANGS OF THE NINTH AND STAND WITH US AGAINST THE TYRANT KING?
THE UNDERCURRENT MOVEMENT CAN'T WIN WITHOUT YOUR SUPPORT.
In the slums of the Ninth Tride, Atlantis.
SHE'S DROWNING, SEE?
I DUNNO WHY LADY MERA ENDED UP DOWN HERE, BUT I'M OUT OF AIR AND SHE'S DYING!
I DUNNO. IF WE HELP YOU BRING RATH DOWN, WHAT THEN?
MY PEOPLE WON'T FIGHT UNLESS THEY KNOW THEY'RE CROWNING A NEW KING WHO'LL ACTUALLY LOOK OUT FOR THEM.
AND WHO'S THAT GOING TO BE, EH?
HEY, HEY! WHAT ARE YOU DOIN'?
I CAN'T SEE--

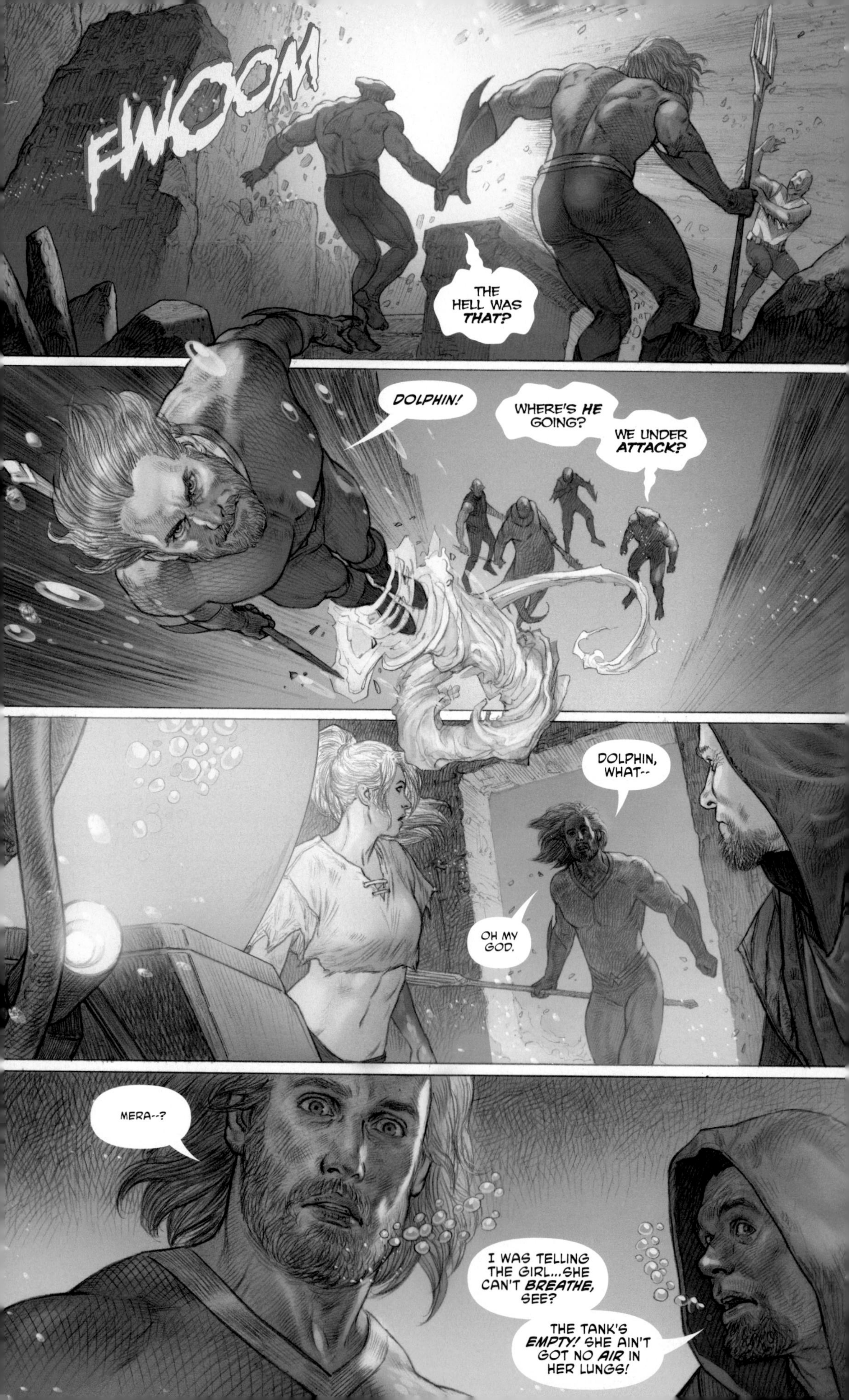
FWOOM
THE HELL WAS THAT?
DOLPHIN!
WHERE'S HE GOING?
WE UNDER ATTACK?
DOLPHIN, WHAT--
OH MY GOD.
MERA--?
I WAS TELLING THE GIRL...SHE CAN'T BREATHE, SEE?
THE TANK'S EMPTY! SHE AIN'T GOT NO AIR IN HER LUNGS!

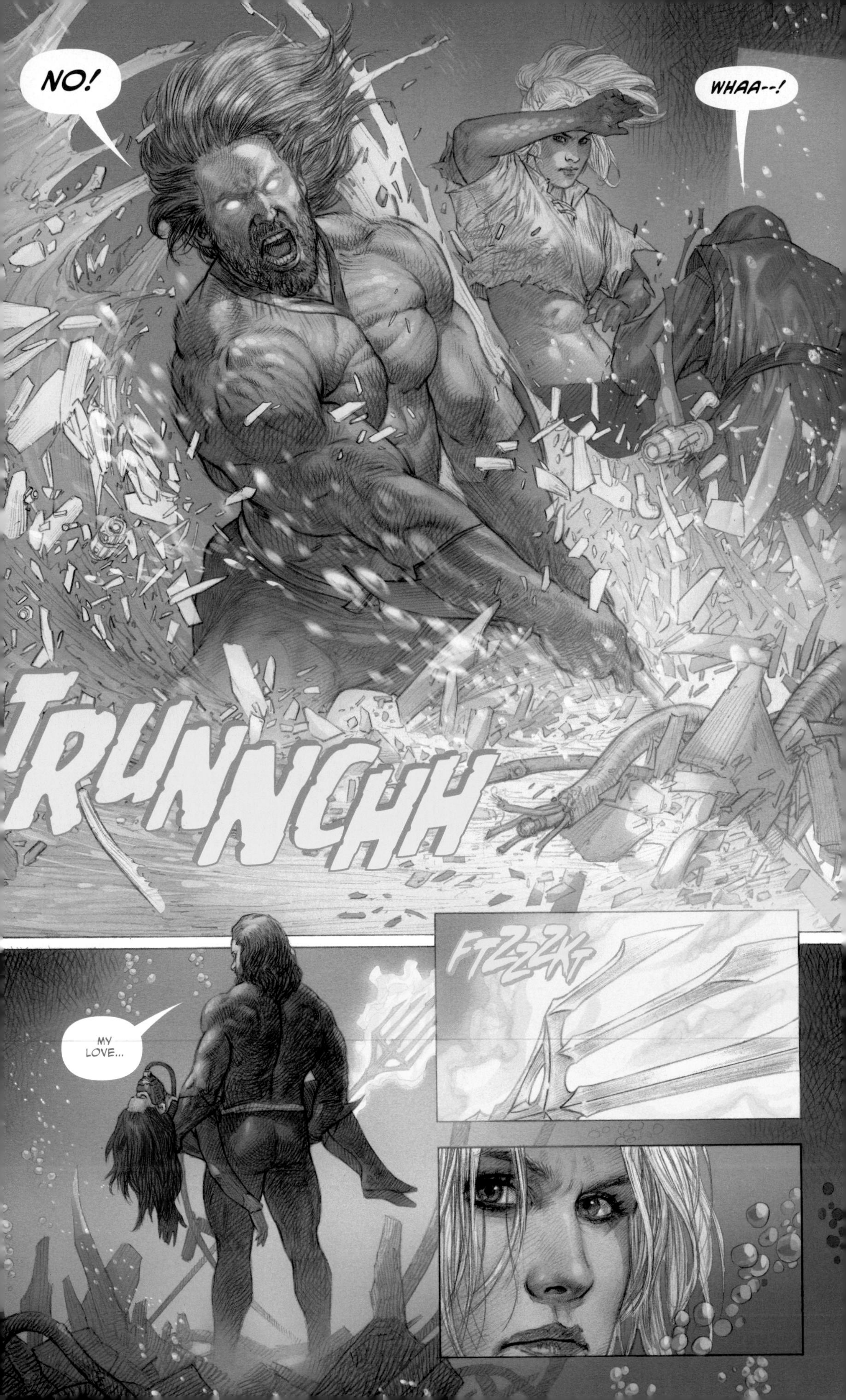
NO!
WHAA--!
TRUNNCHH
MY LOVE...
FTZZZKT

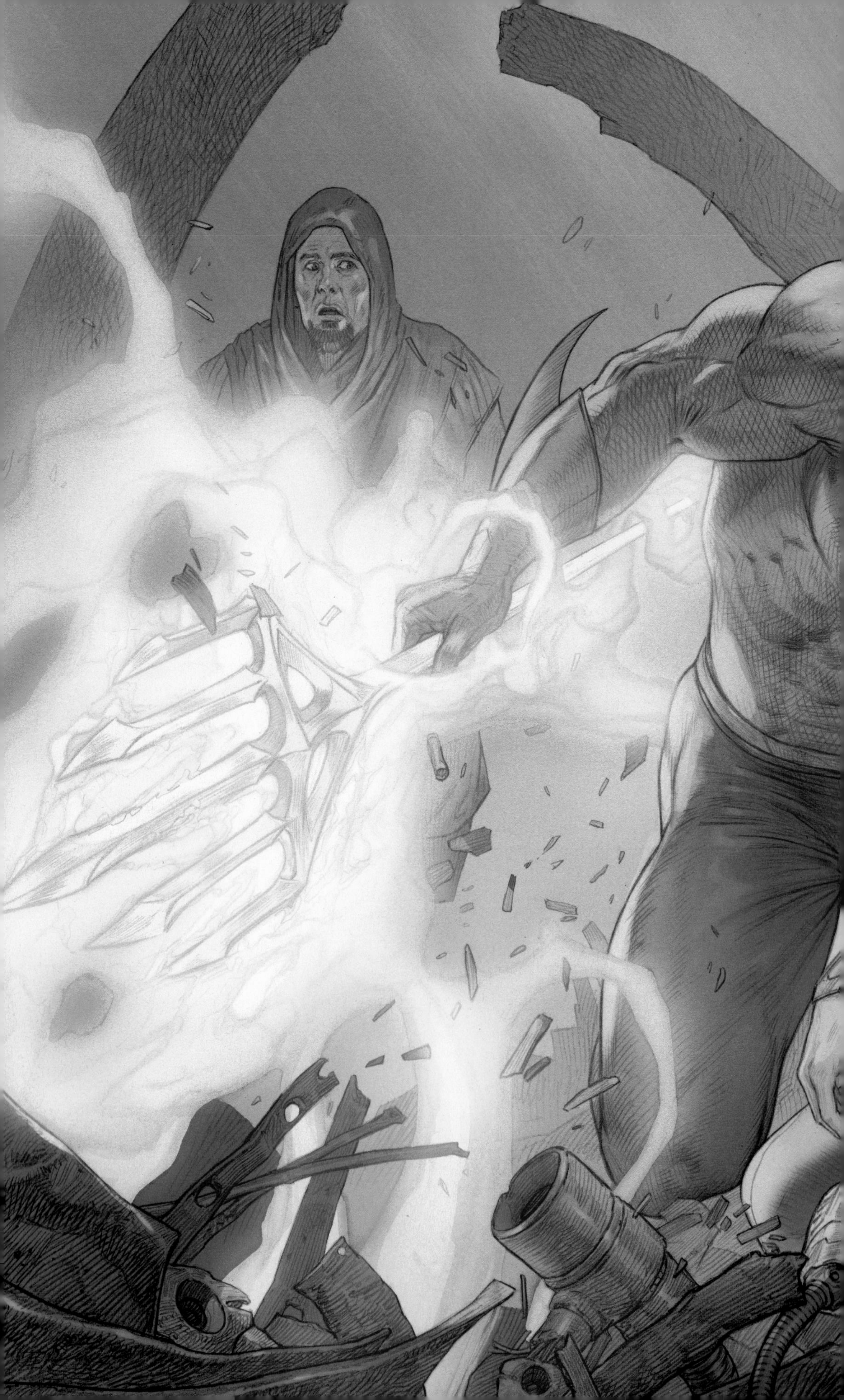

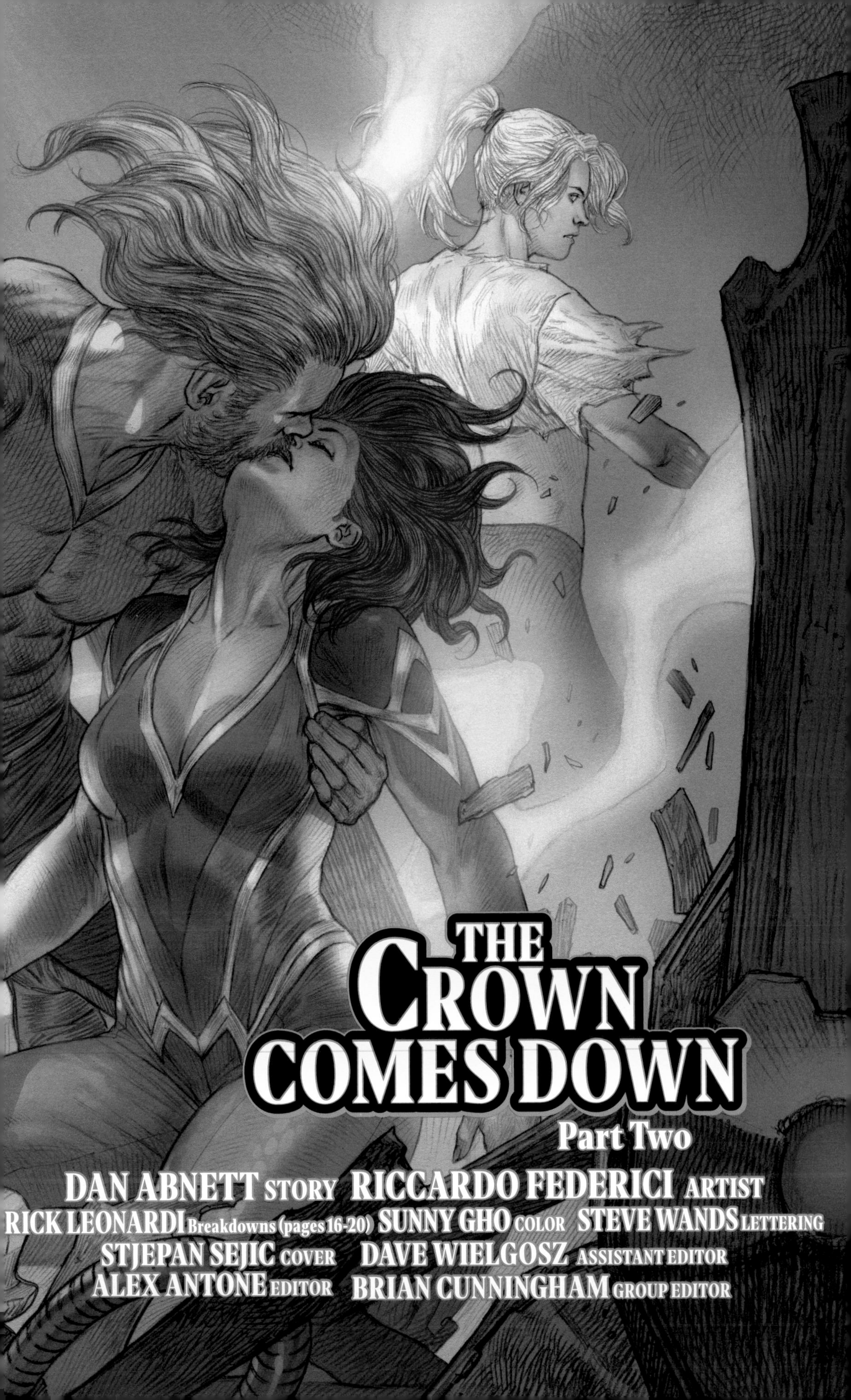
THE CROWN COMES DOWN
Part Two
DAN ABNETT STORY RICCARDO FEDERICI ARTIST
RICK LEONARDI Breakdowns (pages 16-20) SUNNY GHO COLOR STEVE WANDS LETTERING
STJEPAN SEJIC COVER DAVE WIELGOSZ ASSISTANT EDITOR
ALEX ANTONE EDITOR BRIAN CUNNINGHAM GROUP EDITOR

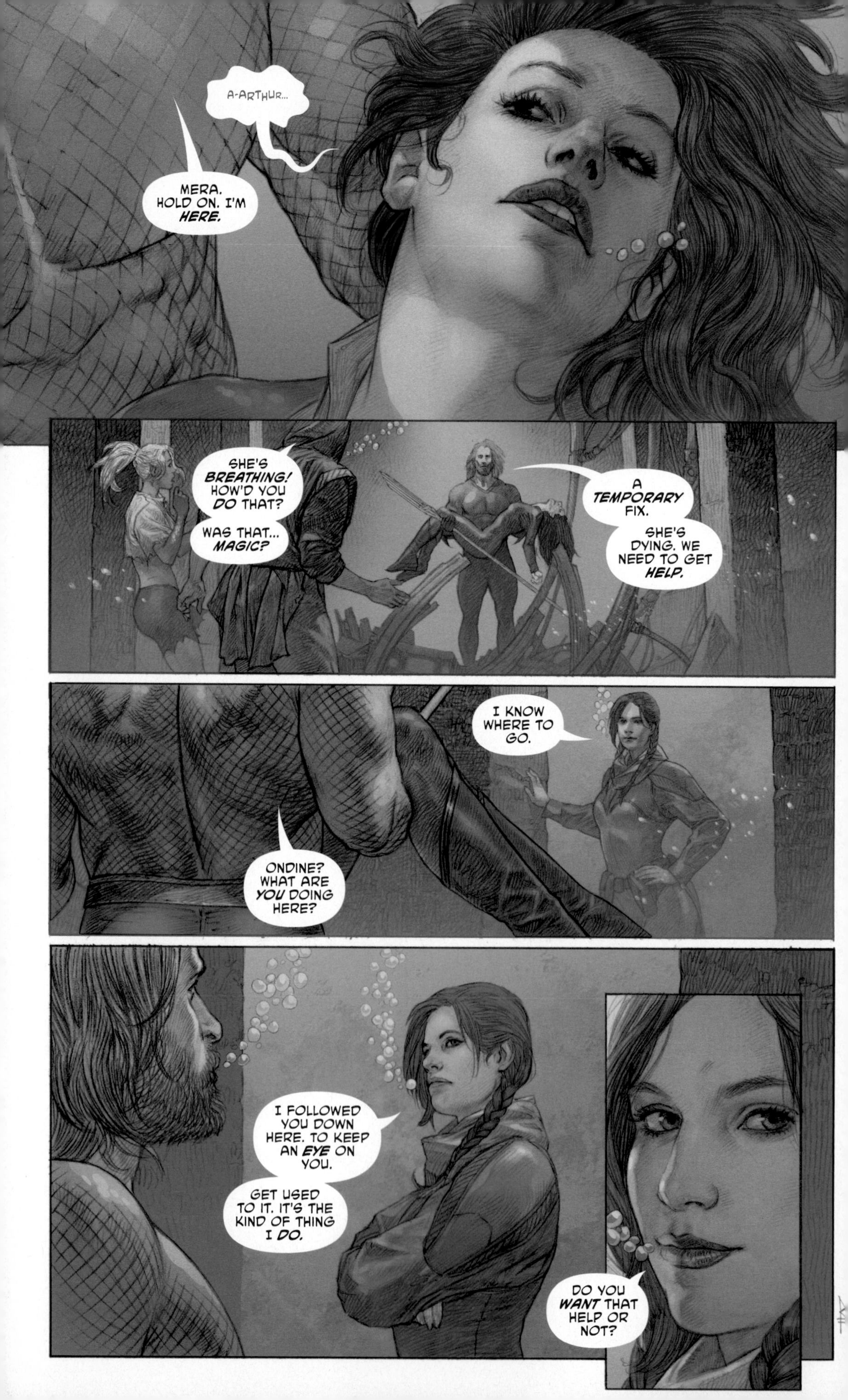
A-ARTHUR...
MERA. HOLD ON. I'M *HERE.*
SHE'S *BREATHING!* HOW'D YOU *DO* THAT?
WAS THAT... *MAGIC?*
A *TEMPORARY* FIX.
SHE'S DYING. WE NEED TO GET *HELP.*
ONDINE? WHAT ARE *YOU* DOING HERE?
I KNOW WHERE TO GO.
I FOLLOWED YOU DOWN HERE. TO KEEP AN *EYE* ON YOU.
GET USED TO IT. IT'S THE KIND OF THING I *DO.*
DO YOU *WANT* THAT HELP OR NOT?

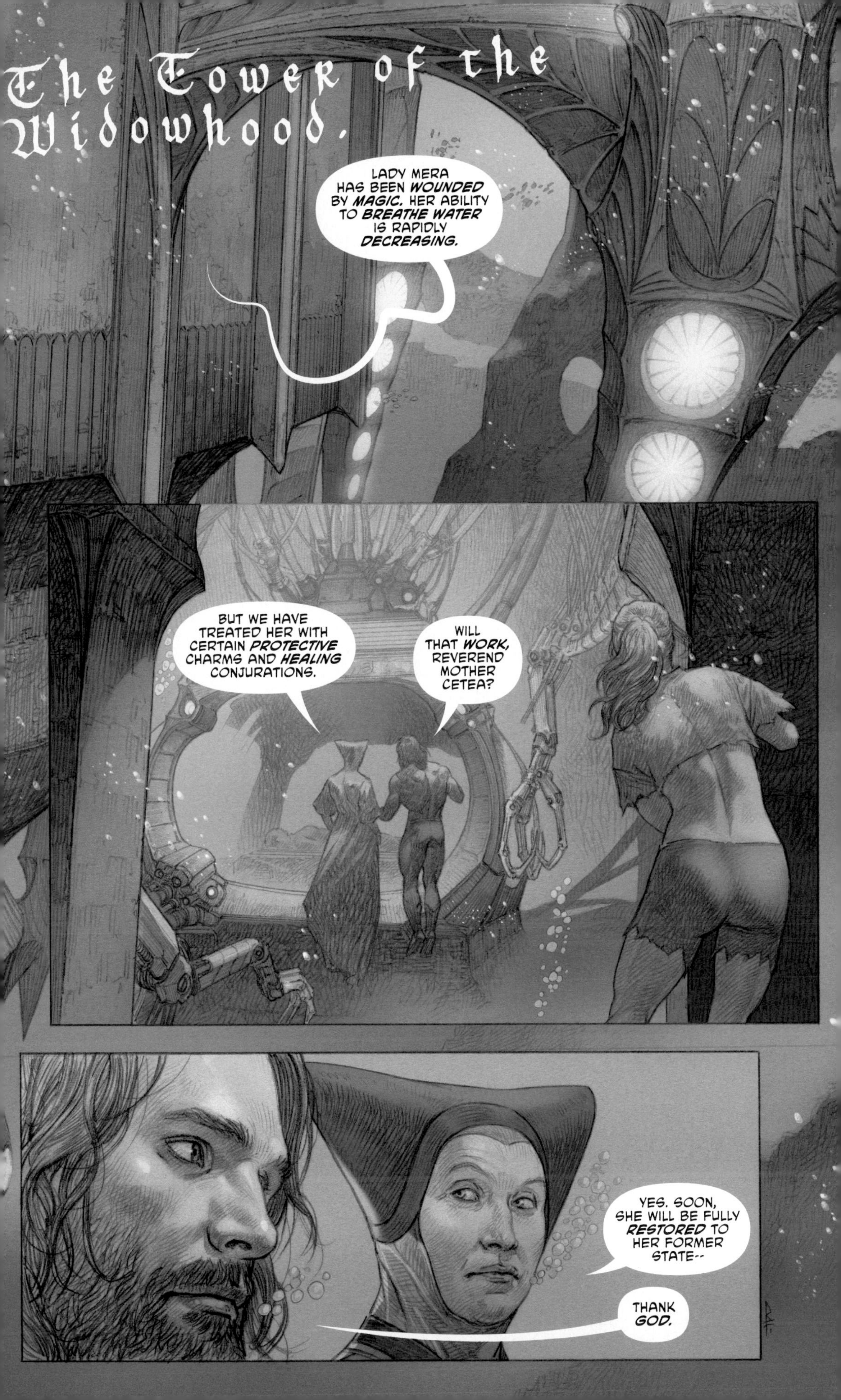
The Tower of the Widowhood.
LADY MERA HAS BEEN WOUNDED BY MAGIC. HER ABILITY TO BREATHE WATER IS RAPIDLY DECREASING.
BUT WE HAVE TREATED HER WITH CERTAIN PROTECTIVE CHARMS AND HEALING CONJURATIONS.
WILL THAT WORK, REVEREND MOTHER CETEA?
YES. SOON, SHE WILL BE FULLY RESTORED TO HER FORMER STATE--
THANK GOD.

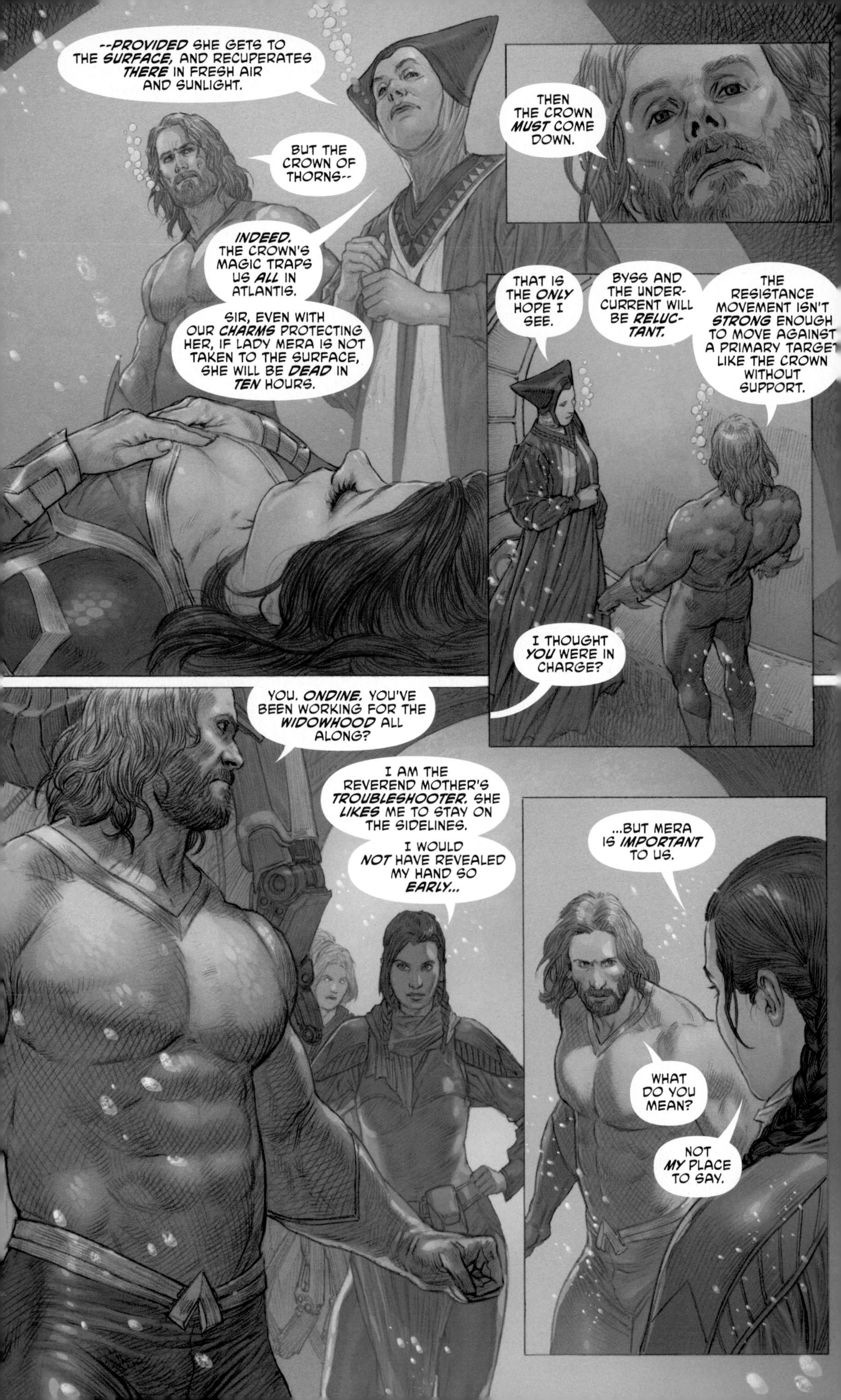
--PROVIDED SHE GETS TO THE SURFACE, AND RECUPERATES THERE IN FRESH AIR AND SUNLIGHT.
BUT THE CROWN OF THORNS--
INDEED. THE CROWN'S MAGIC TRAPS US ALL IN ATLANTIS.
SIR, EVEN WITH OUR CHARMS PROTECTING HER, IF LADY MERA IS NOT TAKEN TO THE SURFACE, SHE WILL BE DEAD IN TEN HOURS.
THEN THE CROWN MUST COME DOWN.
THE RESISTANCE MOVEMENT ISN'T STRONG ENOUGH TO MOVE AGAINST A PRIMARY TARGET LIKE THE CROWN WITHOUT SUPPORT.
BYSS AND THE UNDER-CURRENT WILL BE RELUC-TANT.
THAT IS THE ONLY HOPE I SEE.
I THOUGHT YOU WERE IN CHARGE?
YOU. ONDINE. YOU'VE BEEN WORKING FOR THE WIDOWHOOD ALL ALONG?
I AM THE REVEREND MOTHER'S TROUBLESHOOTER. SHE LIKES ME TO STAY ON THE SIDELINES.
I WOULD NOT HAVE REVEALED MY HAND SO EARLY...
...BUT MERA IS IMPORTANT TO US.
WHAT DO YOU MEAN?
NOT MY PLACE TO SAY.

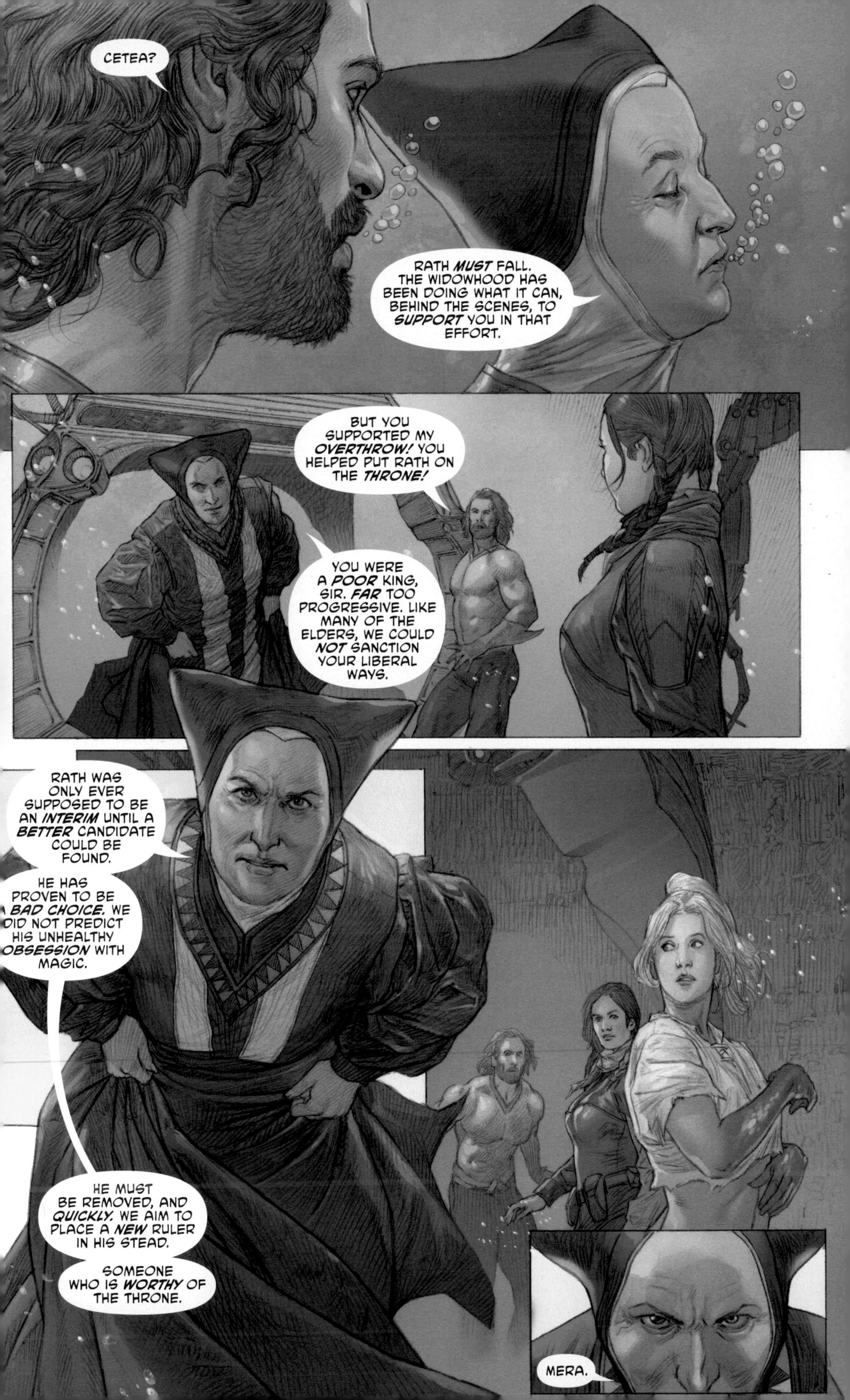
CETEA?
RATH *MUST* FALL. THE WIDOWHOOD HAS BEEN DOING WHAT IT CAN, BEHIND THE SCENES, TO *SUPPORT* YOU IN THAT EFFORT.
BUT YOU SUPPORTED MY *OVERTHROW!* YOU HELPED PUT RATH ON THE *THRONE!*
YOU WERE A *POOR* KING, SIR. *FAR* TOO PROGRESSIVE. LIKE MANY OF THE ELDERS, WE COULD *NOT* SANCTION YOUR LIBERAL WAYS.
RATH WAS ONLY EVER SUPPOSED TO BE AN *INTERIM* UNTIL A *BETTER* CANDIDATE COULD BE FOUND.
HE HAS PROVEN TO BE A *BAD CHOICE.* WE DID NOT PREDICT HIS UNHEALTHY *OBSESSION* WITH MAGIC.
HE MUST BE REMOVED, AND *QUICKLY.* WE AIM TO PLACE A *NEW* RULER IN HIS STEAD.
SOMEONE WHO IS *WORTHY* OF THE THRONE.
MERA.

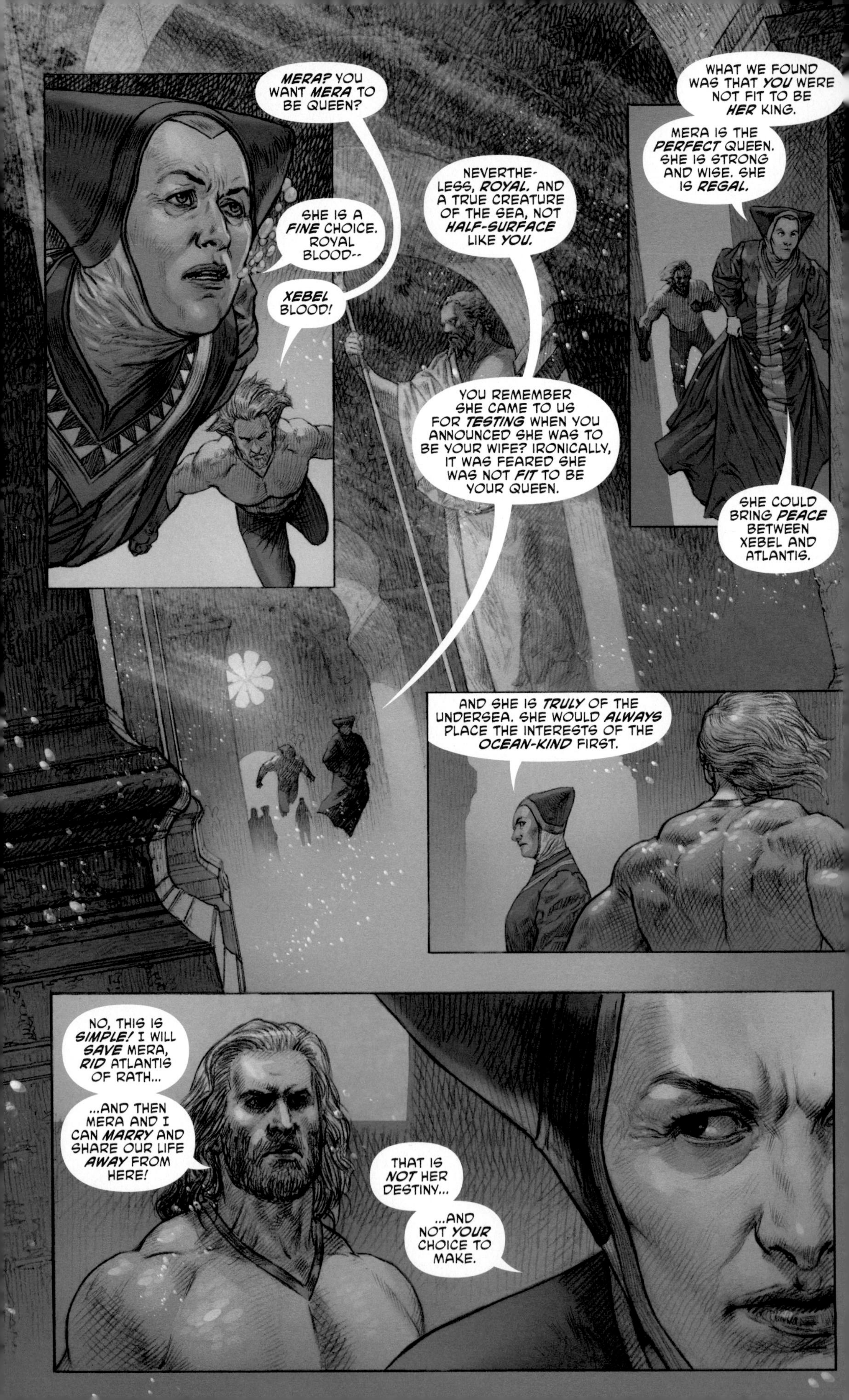
MERA? YOU WANT MERA TO BE QUEEN?
SHE IS A FINE CHOICE. ROYAL BLOOD--
XEBEL BLOOD!
NEVERTHELESS, ROYAL. AND A TRUE CREATURE OF THE SEA, NOT HALF-SURFACE LIKE YOU.
YOU REMEMBER SHE CAME TO US FOR TESTING WHEN YOU ANNOUNCED SHE WAS TO BE YOUR WIFE? IRONICALLY, IT WAS FEARED SHE WAS NOT FIT TO BE YOUR QUEEN.
WHAT WE FOUND WAS THAT YOU WERE NOT FIT TO BE HER KING.
MERA IS THE PERFECT QUEEN. SHE IS STRONG AND WISE. SHE IS REGAL.
SHE COULD BRING PEACE BETWEEN XEBEL AND ATLANTIS.
AND SHE IS TRULY OF THE UNDERSEA. SHE WOULD ALWAYS PLACE THE INTERESTS OF THE OCEAN-KIND FIRST.
NO, THIS IS SIMPLE! I WILL SAVE MERA, RID ATLANTIS OF RATH...
...AND THEN MERA AND I CAN MARRY AND SHARE OUR LIFE AWAY FROM HERE!
THAT IS NOT HER DESTINY...
...AND NOT YOUR CHOICE TO MAKE.

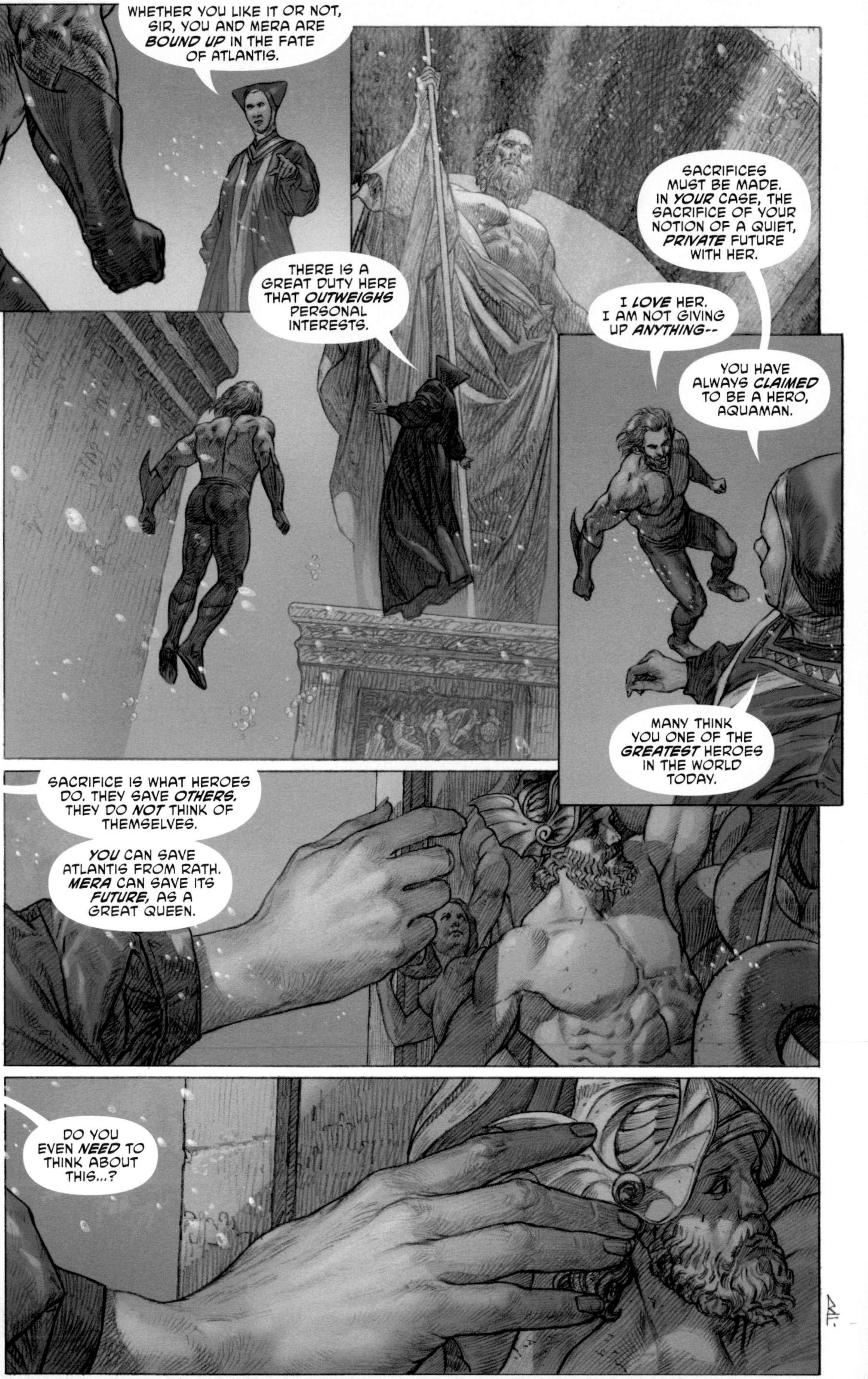
WHETHER YOU LIKE IT OR NOT, SIR, YOU AND MERA ARE *BOUND UP* IN THE FATE OF ATLANTIS.
THERE IS A GREAT DUTY HERE THAT *OUTWEIGHS* PERSONAL INTERESTS.
SACRIFICES MUST BE MADE. IN *YOUR* CASE, THE SACRIFICE OF YOUR NOTION OF A QUIET, *PRIVATE* FUTURE WITH HER.
I *LOVE* HER. I AM NOT GIVING UP *ANYTHING*--
YOU HAVE ALWAYS *CLAIMED* TO BE A HERO, AQUAMAN.
MANY THINK YOU ONE OF THE *GREATEST* HEROES IN THE WORLD TODAY.
SACRIFICE IS WHAT HEROES DO. THEY SAVE *OTHERS.* THEY DO *NOT* THINK OF THEMSELVES.
YOU CAN SAVE ATLANTIS FROM RATH. *MERA* CAN SAVE ITS *FUTURE,* AS A GREAT QUEEN.
DO YOU EVEN *NEED* TO THINK ABOUT THIS...?

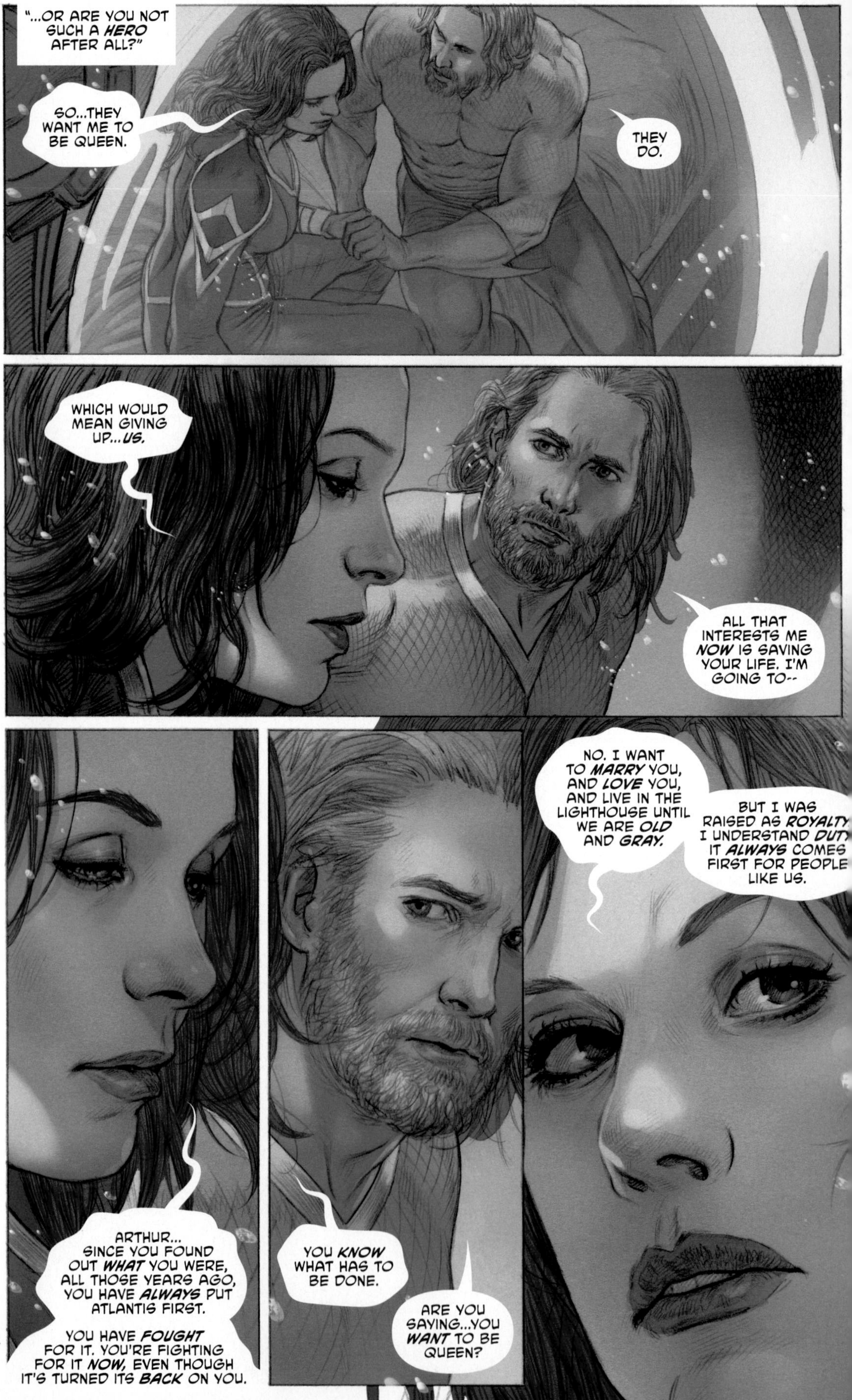
"...OR ARE YOU NOT SUCH A *HERO* AFTER ALL?"
SO...THEY WANT ME TO BE QUEEN.
THEY DO.
WHICH WOULD MEAN GIVING UP...*US.*
ALL THAT INTERESTS ME *NOW* IS SAVING YOUR LIFE. I'M GOING TO--
ARTHUR... SINCE YOU FOUND OUT *WHAT* YOU WERE, ALL THOSE YEARS AGO, YOU HAVE *ALWAYS* PUT ATLANTIS FIRST.
YOU HAVE *FOUGHT* FOR IT. YOU'RE FIGHTING FOR IT *NOW,* EVEN THOUGH IT'S TURNED ITS *BACK* ON YOU.
YOU *KNOW* WHAT HAS TO BE DONE.
ARE YOU SAYING...YOU *WANT* TO BE QUEEN?
NO. I WANT TO *MARRY* YOU, AND *LOVE* YOU, AND LIVE IN THE LIGHTHOUSE UNTIL WE ARE *OLD* AND *GRAY.*
BUT I WAS RAISED AS *ROYALTY* I UNDERSTAND *DUT* IT *ALWAYS* COMES FIRST FOR PEOPLE LIKE US.

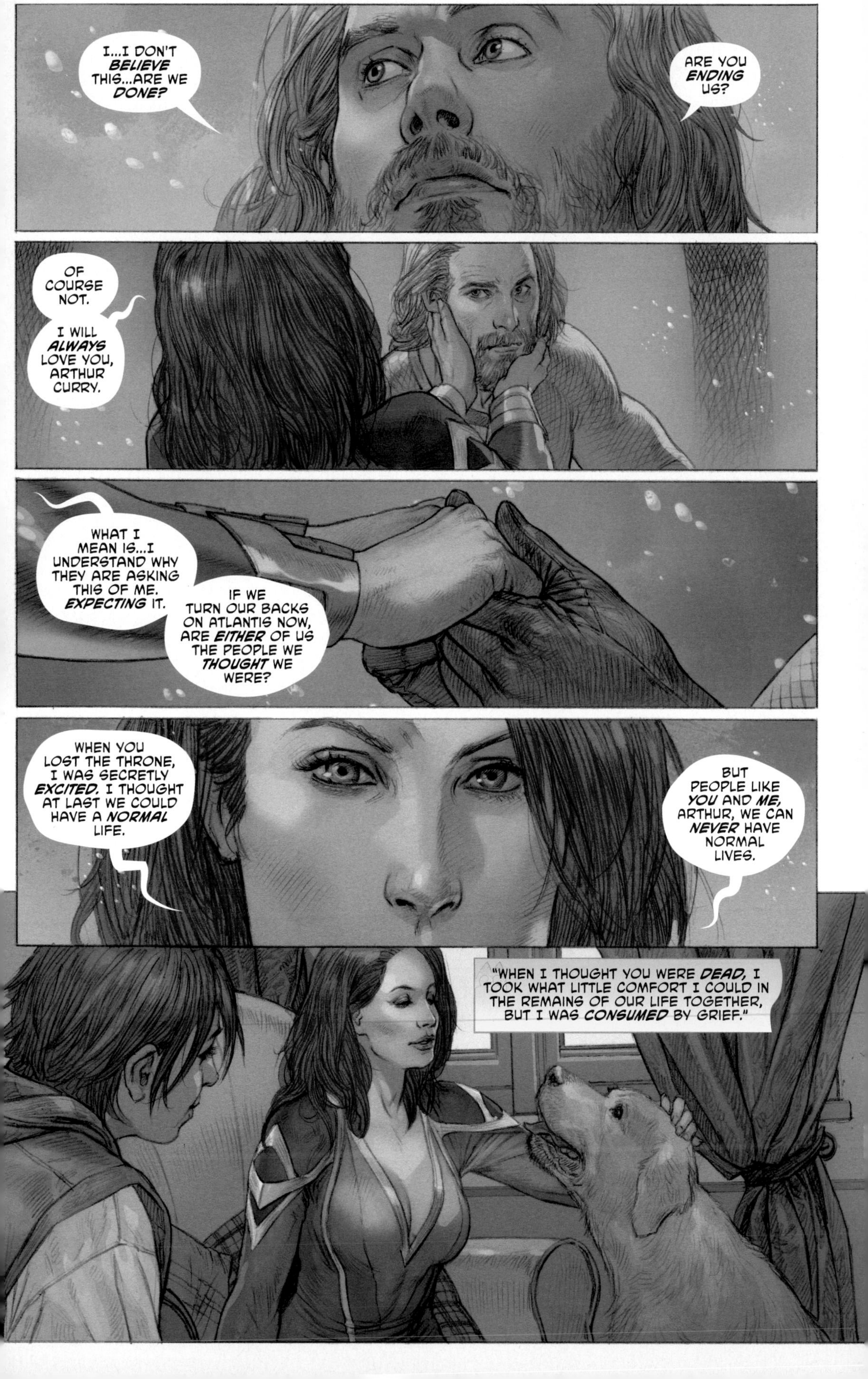
I...I DON'T BELIEVE THIS...ARE WE DONE?
ARE YOU ENDING US?
OF COURSE NOT.
I WILL ALWAYS LOVE YOU, ARTHUR CURRY.
WHAT I MEAN IS...I UNDERSTAND WHY THEY ARE ASKING THIS OF ME. EXPECTING IT.
IF WE TURN OUR BACKS ON ATLANTIS NOW, ARE EITHER OF US THE PEOPLE WE THOUGHT WE WERE?
WHEN YOU LOST THE THRONE, I WAS SECRETLY EXCITED. I THOUGHT AT LAST WE COULD HAVE A NORMAL LIFE.
BUT PEOPLE LIKE YOU AND ME, ARTHUR, WE CAN NEVER HAVE NORMAL LIVES.
"WHEN I THOUGHT YOU WERE DEAD, I TOOK WHAT LITTLE COMFORT I COULD IN THE REMAINS OF OUR LIFE TOGETHER, BUT I WAS CONSUMED BY GRIEF."

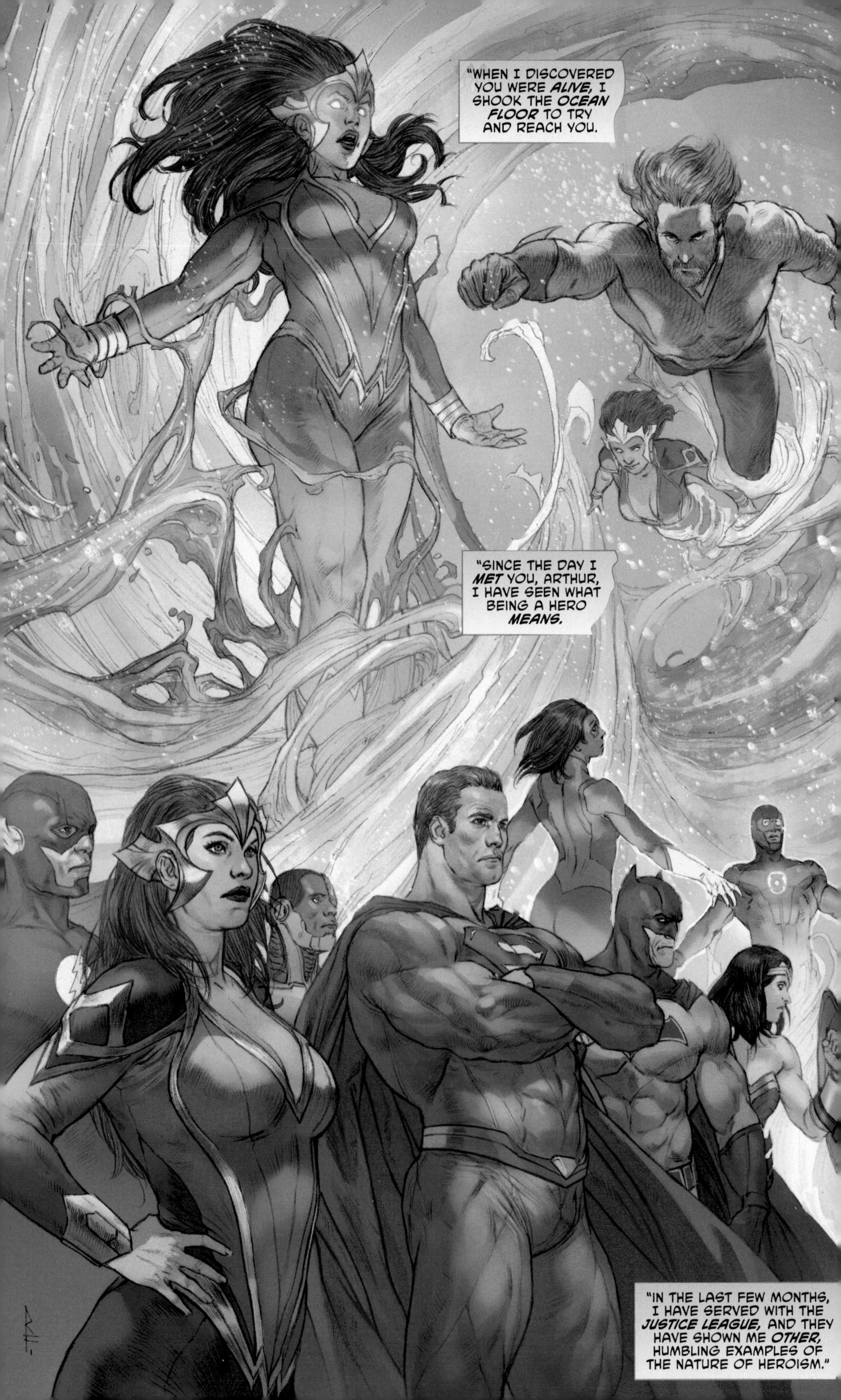
"WHEN I DISCOVERED YOU WERE *ALIVE*, I SHOOK THE *OCEAN FLOOR* TO TRY AND REACH YOU.
"SINCE THE DAY I *MET* YOU, ARTHUR, I HAVE SEEN WHAT BEING A HERO *MEANS*.
"IN THE LAST FEW MONTHS, I HAVE SERVED WITH THE *JUSTICE LEAGUE*, AND THEY HAVE SHOWN ME *OTHER*, HUMBLING EXAMPLES OF THE NATURE OF HEROISM."

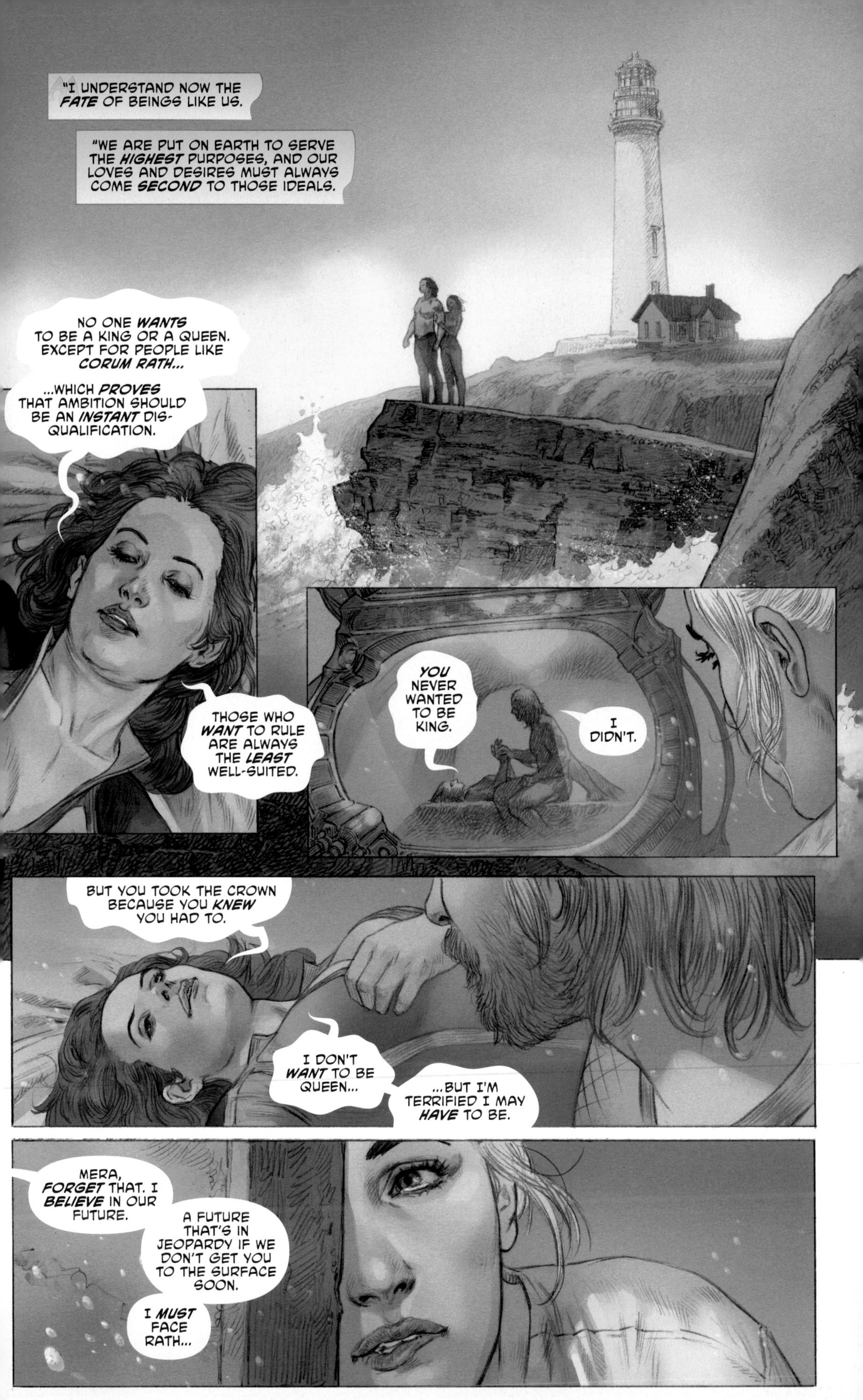

"I UNDERSTAND NOW THE FATE OF BEINGS LIKE US.
"WE ARE PUT ON EARTH TO SERVE THE HIGHEST PURPOSES, AND OUR LOVES AND DESIRES MUST ALWAYS COME SECOND TO THOSE IDEALS.
NO ONE WANTS TO BE A KING OR A QUEEN. EXCEPT FOR PEOPLE LIKE CORUM RATH...
...WHICH PROVES THAT AMBITION SHOULD BE AN INSTANT DISQUALIFICATION.
THOSE WHO WANT TO RULE ARE ALWAYS THE LEAST WELL-SUITED.
YOU NEVER WANTED TO BE KING.
I DIDN'T.
BUT YOU TOOK THE CROWN BECAUSE YOU KNEW YOU HAD TO.
I DON'T WANT TO BE QUEEN...
...BUT I'M TERRIFIED I MAY HAVE TO BE.
MERA, FORGET THAT. I BELIEVE IN OUR FUTURE.
A FUTURE THAT'S IN JEOPARDY IF WE DON'T GET YOU TO THE SURFACE SOON.
I MUST FACE RATH...

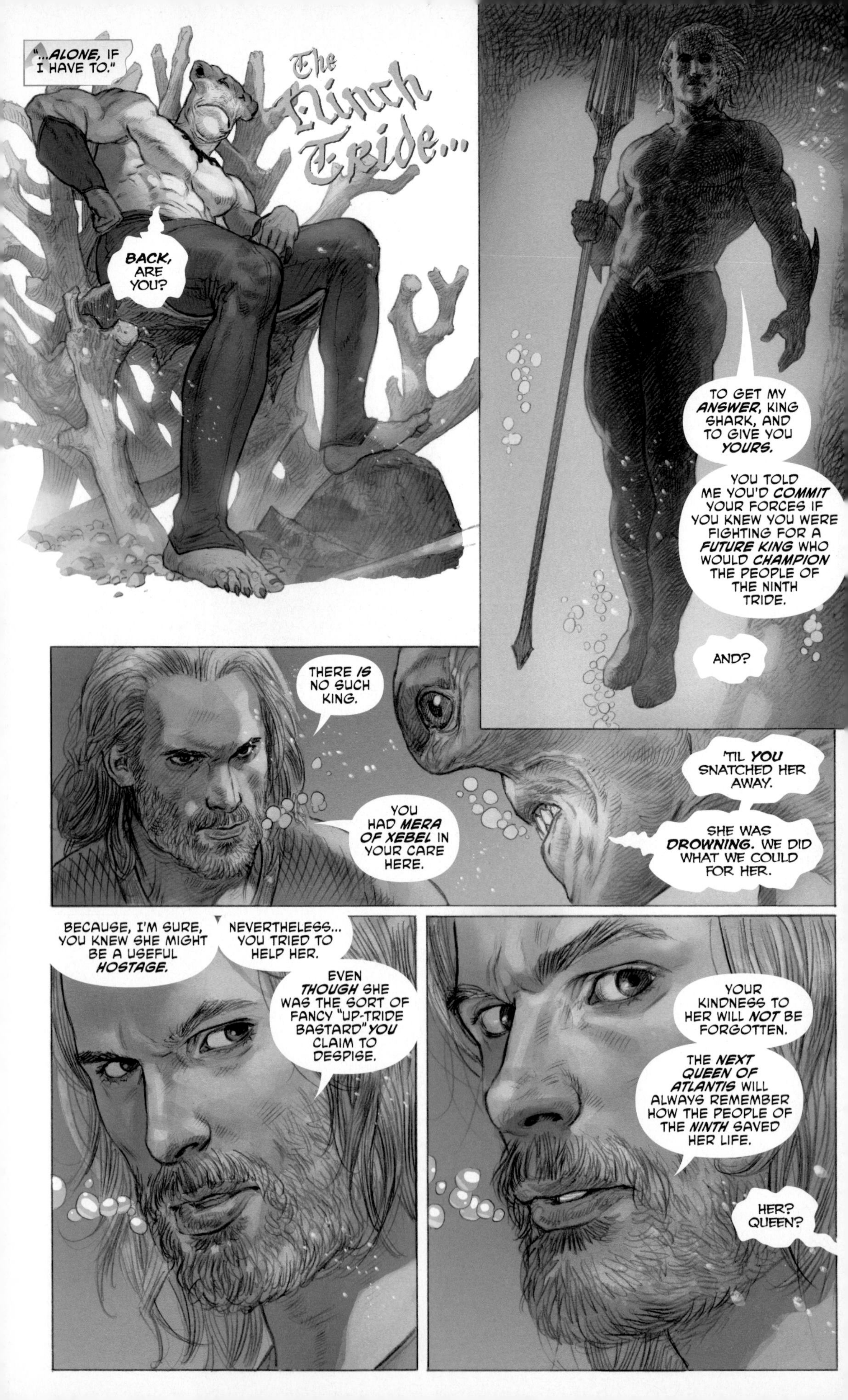
"...ALONE, IF I HAVE TO."
The Ninth Tride...
BACK, ARE YOU?
TO GET MY ANSWER, KING SHARK, AND TO GIVE YOU YOURS.
YOU TOLD ME YOU'D COMMIT YOUR FORCES IF YOU KNEW YOU WERE FIGHTING FOR A FUTURE KING WHO WOULD CHAMPION THE PEOPLE OF THE NINTH TRIDE.
AND?
THERE IS NO SUCH KING.
YOU HAD MERA OF XEBEL IN YOUR CARE HERE.
'TIL YOU SNATCHED HER AWAY.
SHE WAS DROWNING. WE DID WHAT WE COULD FOR HER.
BECAUSE, I'M SURE, YOU KNEW SHE MIGHT BE A USEFUL HOSTAGE.
NEVERTHELESS... YOU TRIED TO HELP HER.
EVEN THOUGH SHE WAS THE SORT OF FANCY "UP-TRIDE BASTARD" YOU CLAIM TO DESPISE.
YOUR KINDNESS TO HER WILL NOT BE FORGOTTEN.
THE NEXT QUEEN OF ATLANTIS WILL ALWAYS REMEMBER HOW THE PEOPLE OF THE NINTH SAVED HER LIFE.
HER? QUEEN?

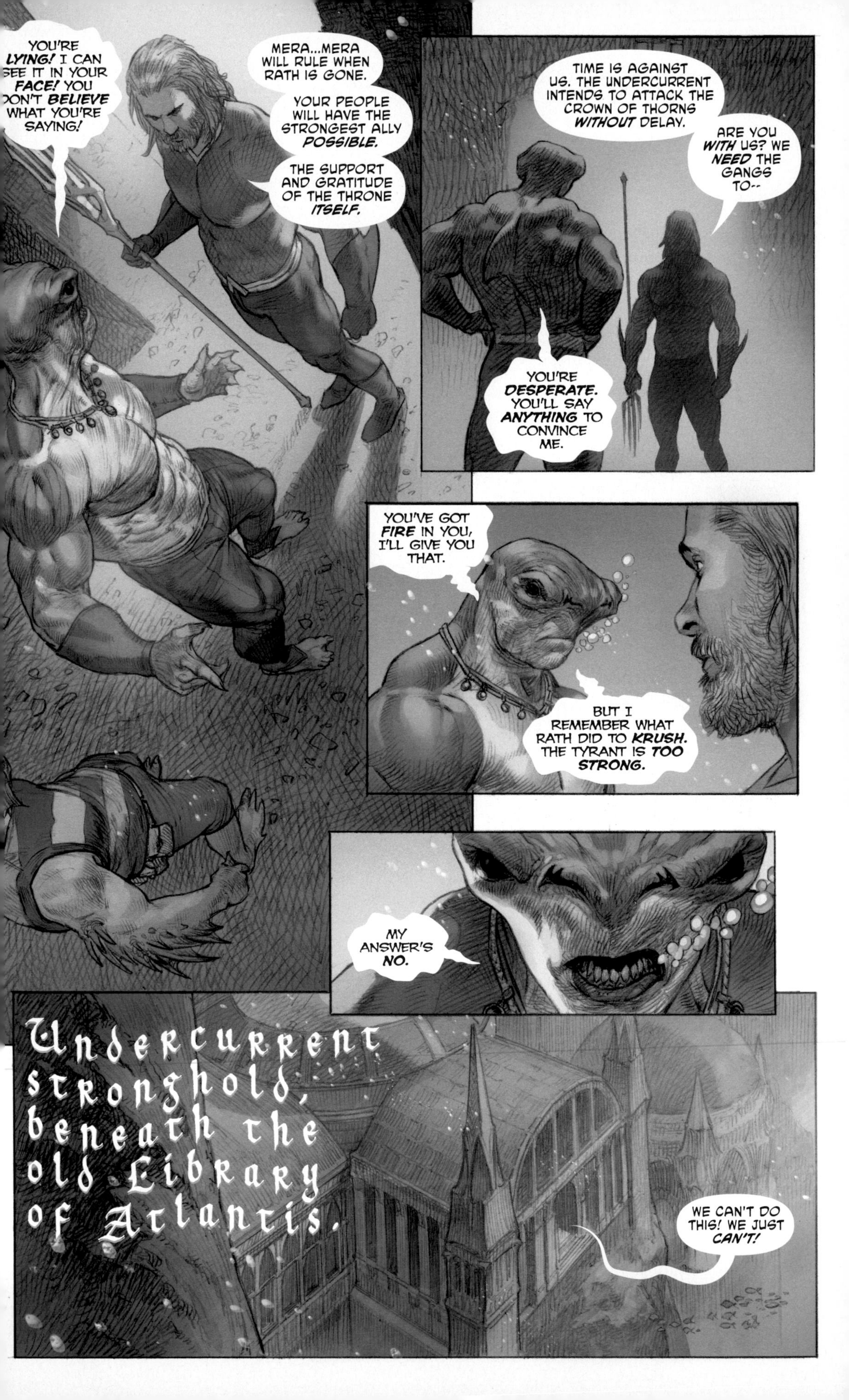

YOU'RE LYING! I CAN SEE IT IN YOUR FACE! YOU DON'T BELIEVE WHAT YOU'RE SAYING!
MERA...MERA WILL RULE WHEN RATH IS GONE.
YOUR PEOPLE WILL HAVE THE STRONGEST ALLY POSSIBLE.
THE SUPPORT AND GRATITUDE OF THE THRONE ITSELF.
TIME IS AGAINST US. THE UNDERCURRENT INTENDS TO ATTACK THE CROWN OF THORNS WITHOUT DELAY.
ARE YOU WITH US? WE NEED THE GANGS TO--
YOU'RE DESPERATE. YOU'LL SAY ANYTHING TO CONVINCE ME.
YOU'VE GOT FIRE IN YOU, I'LL GIVE YOU THAT.
BUT I REMEMBER WHAT RATH DID TO KRUSH. THE TYRANT IS TOO STRONG.
MY ANSWER'S NO.
Undercurrent stronghold, beneath the old Library of Atlantis.
WE CAN'T DO THIS! WE JUST CAN'T!

WE *HAVE* TO, JUROK.

IF THE WRETCHED *GANGS O' THE NINTH* WON'T STAND WIV US, THEN BELIEVE *ME*... MOST O' THE *UNDERCURRENT* WON'T FOLLOW YOU INTA HELL *NEITHER!*

WE JUST AIN'T *STRONG* ENOUGH! RATH WILL *BURN* US IN OUR *BOOTS*...

...AND WIV *RESPECT*, YOUR DECISION TO MOVE *NOW* HAS NUFFIN TO DO WIV THE STRUGGLE AGAINST RATH!

THIS IS *PERSONAL!* YOU WANT TO RISK THE *ENTIRE RESISTANCE* TO SAVE YOUR LADY'S *LIFE!*

NO...

...THIS IS *ABSOLUTELY* ABOUT ATLANTIS, JUROK BYSS.

QUEEN MERA IS THE *FUTURE*. SHE'S THE *SYMBOL* WE'VE BEEN WAITING FOR.

SHE IS, AT *LAST*, A RAY OF *HOPE* IN THE DARKNESS OF RATH'S REIGN.

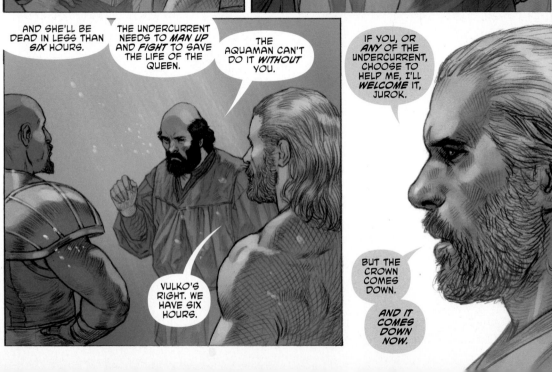

AND SHE'LL BE DEAD IN LESS THAN *SIX* HOURS.

THE UNDERCURRENT NEEDS TO *MAN UP* AND *FIGHT* TO SAVE THE LIFE OF THE QUEEN.

THE AQUAMAN CAN'T DO IT *WITHOUT* YOU.

IF YOU, OR *ANY* OF THE UNDERCURRENT, CHOOSE TO HELP ME, I'LL *WELCOME* IT, JUROK.

VULKO'S *RIGHT*. WE HAVE SIX HOURS.

BUT THE CROWN COMES DOWN.

AND IT COMES DOWN NOW.

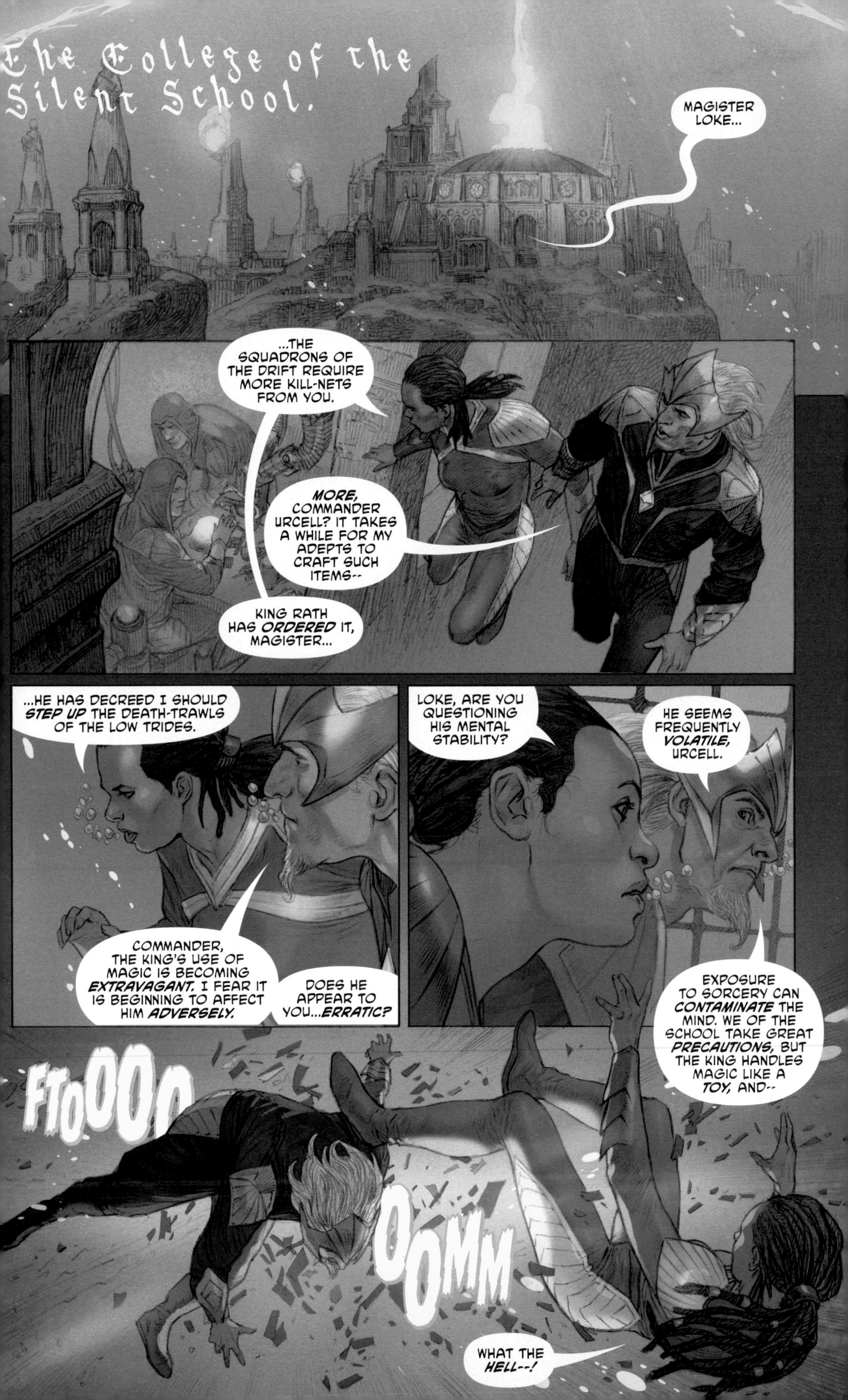

The College of the Silent School.
MAGISTER LOKE...
...THE SQUADRONS OF THE DRIFT REQUIRE MORE KILL-NETS FROM YOU.
MORE, COMMANDER URCELL? IT TAKES A WHILE FOR MY ADEPTS TO CRAFT SUCH ITEMS--
KING RATH HAS ORDERED IT, MAGISTER...
...HE HAS DECREED I SHOULD STEP UP THE DEATH-TRAWLS OF THE LOW TRIDES.
COMMANDER, THE KING'S USE OF MAGIC IS BECOMING EXTRAVAGANT. I FEAR IT IS BEGINNING TO AFFECT HIM ADVERSELY.
DOES HE APPEAR TO YOU...ERRATIC?
LOKE, ARE YOU QUESTIONING HIS MENTAL STABILITY?
HE SEEMS FREQUENTLY VOLATILE, URCELL.
EXPOSURE TO SORCERY CAN CONTAMINATE THE MIND. WE OF THE SCHOOL TAKE GREAT PRECAUTIONS, BUT THE KING HANDLES MAGIC LIKE A TOY, AND--
FTOOOOOOOMM
WHAT THE HELL--!

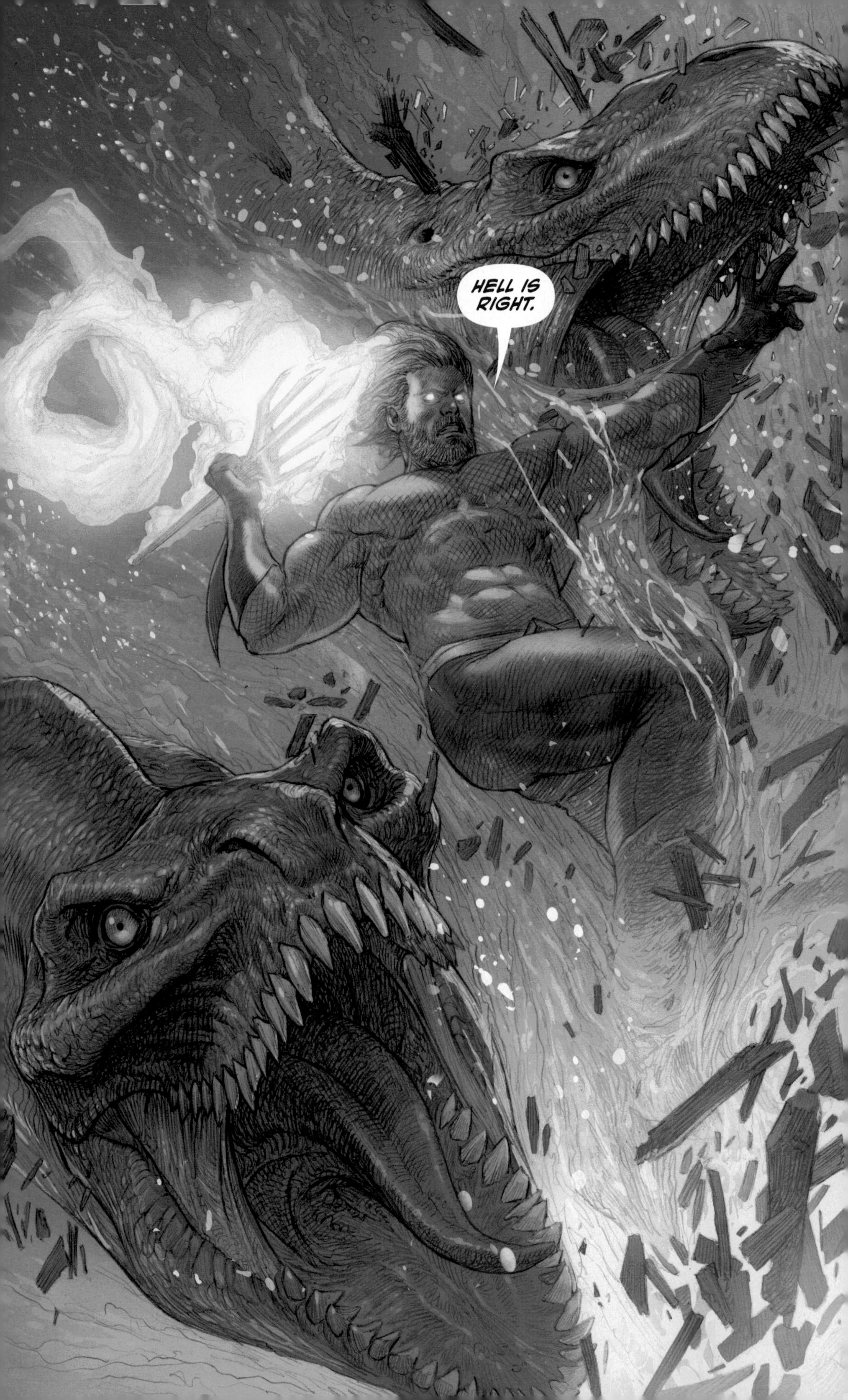
HELL IS RIGHT.

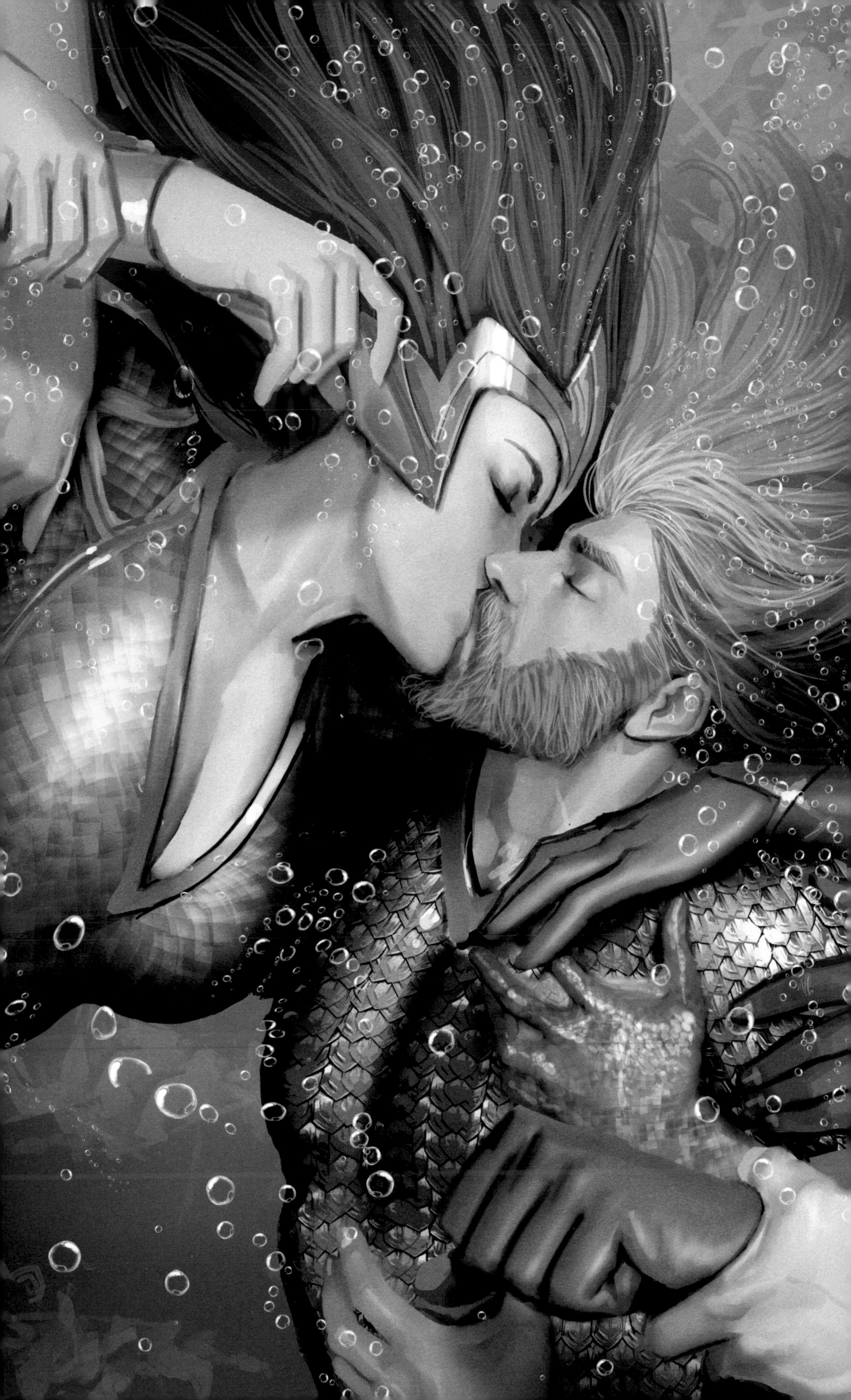

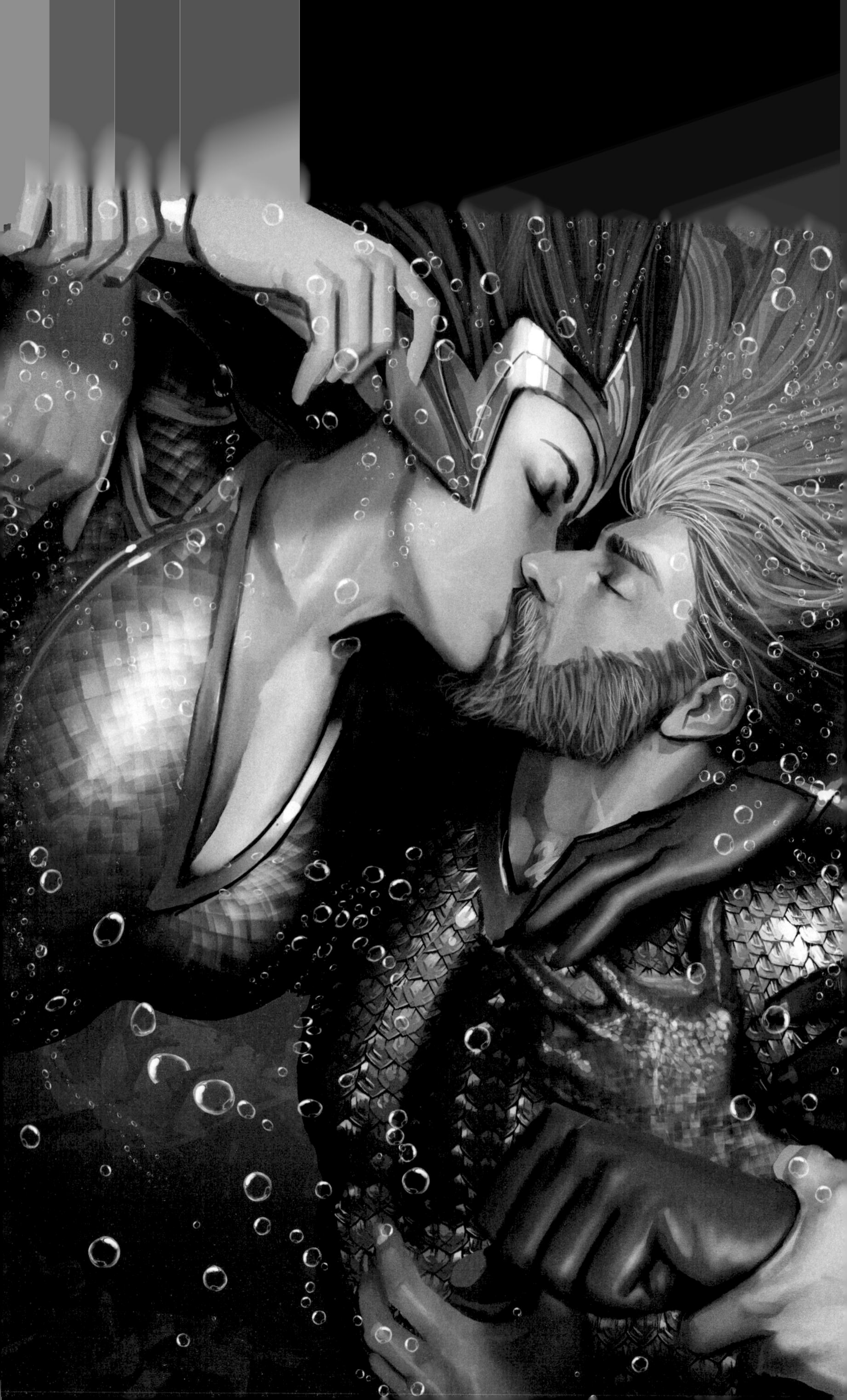

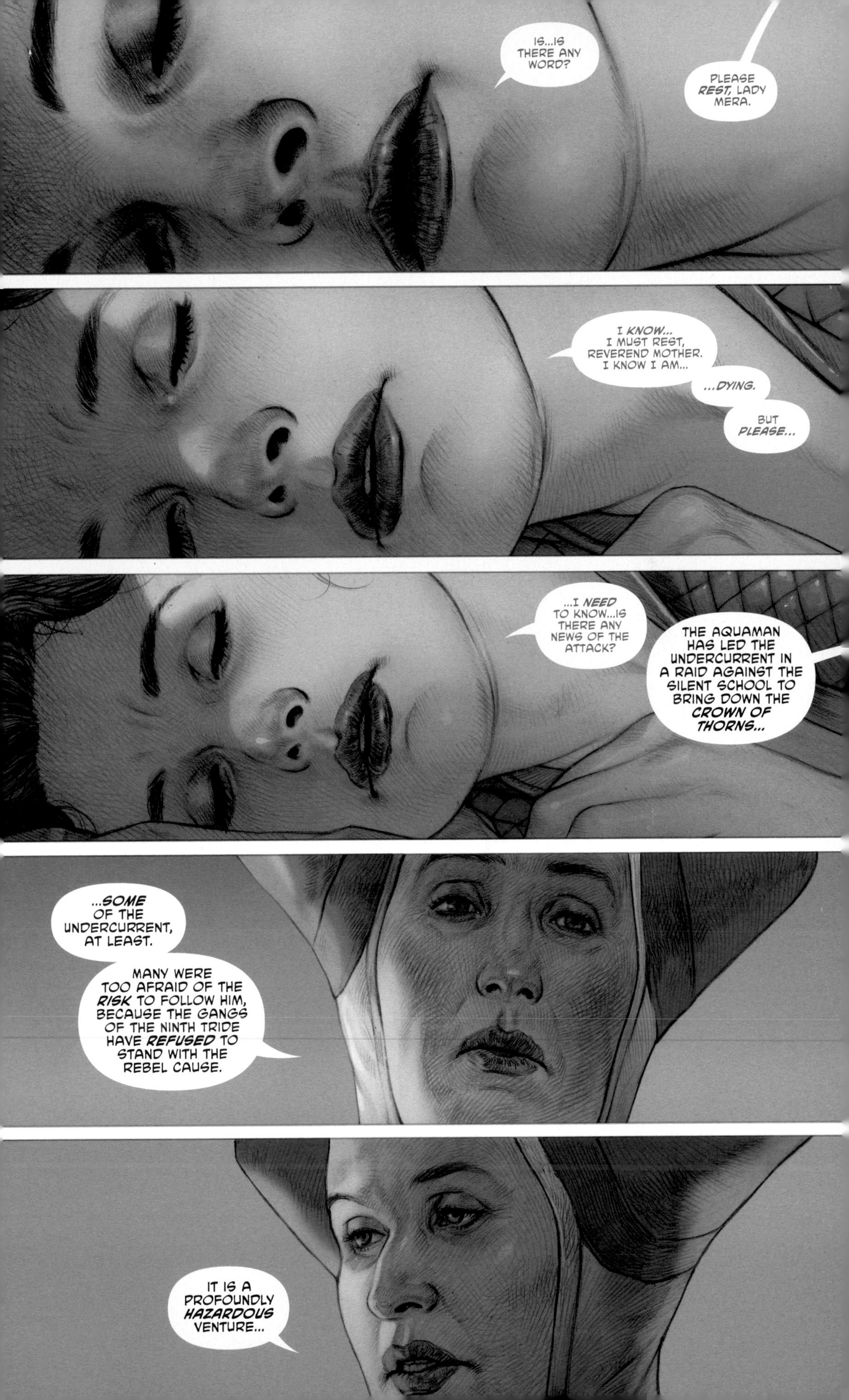
IS...IS THERE ANY WORD?
PLEASE *REST,* LADY MERA.
I *KNOW...* I MUST REST, REVEREND MOTHER. I KNOW I AM...
...DYING.
BUT *PLEASE...*
...I *NEED* TO KNOW...IS THERE ANY NEWS OF THE ATTACK?
THE AQUAMAN HAS LED THE UNDERCURRENT IN A RAID AGAINST THE SILENT SCHOOL TO BRING DOWN THE *CROWN OF THORNS...*
...SOME OF THE UNDERCURRENT, AT LEAST.
MANY WERE TOO AFRAID OF THE *RISK* TO FOLLOW HIM, BECAUSE THE GANGS OF THE NINTH TRIDE HAVE *REFUSED* TO STAND WITH THE REBEL CAUSE.
IT IS A PROFOUNDLY *HAZARDOUS* VENTURE...

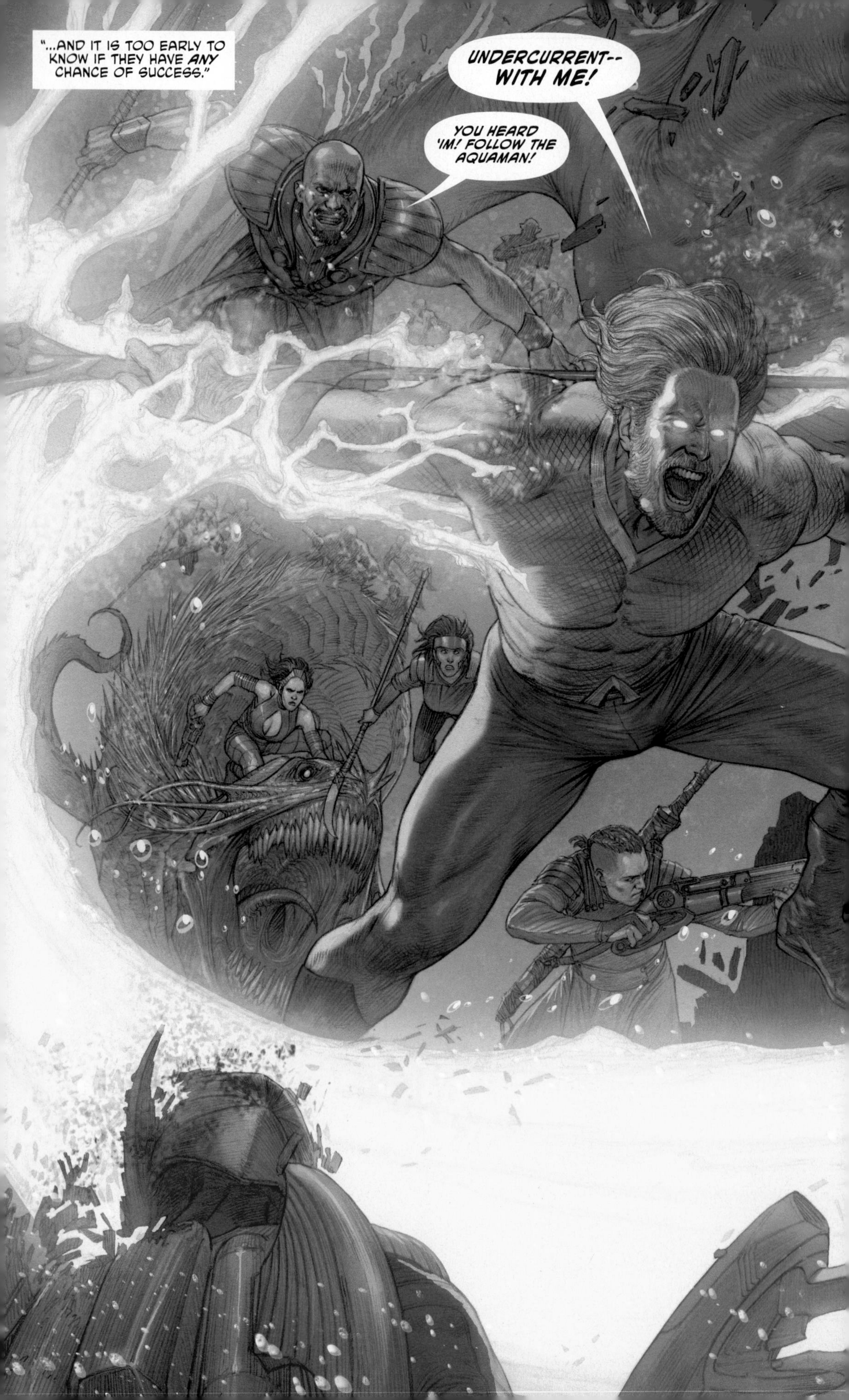
"...AND IT IS TOO EARLY TO KNOW IF THEY HAVE *ANY* CHANCE OF SUCCESS."
UNDERCURRENT-- WITH ME!
YOU HEARD 'IM! FOLLOW THE AQUAMAN!

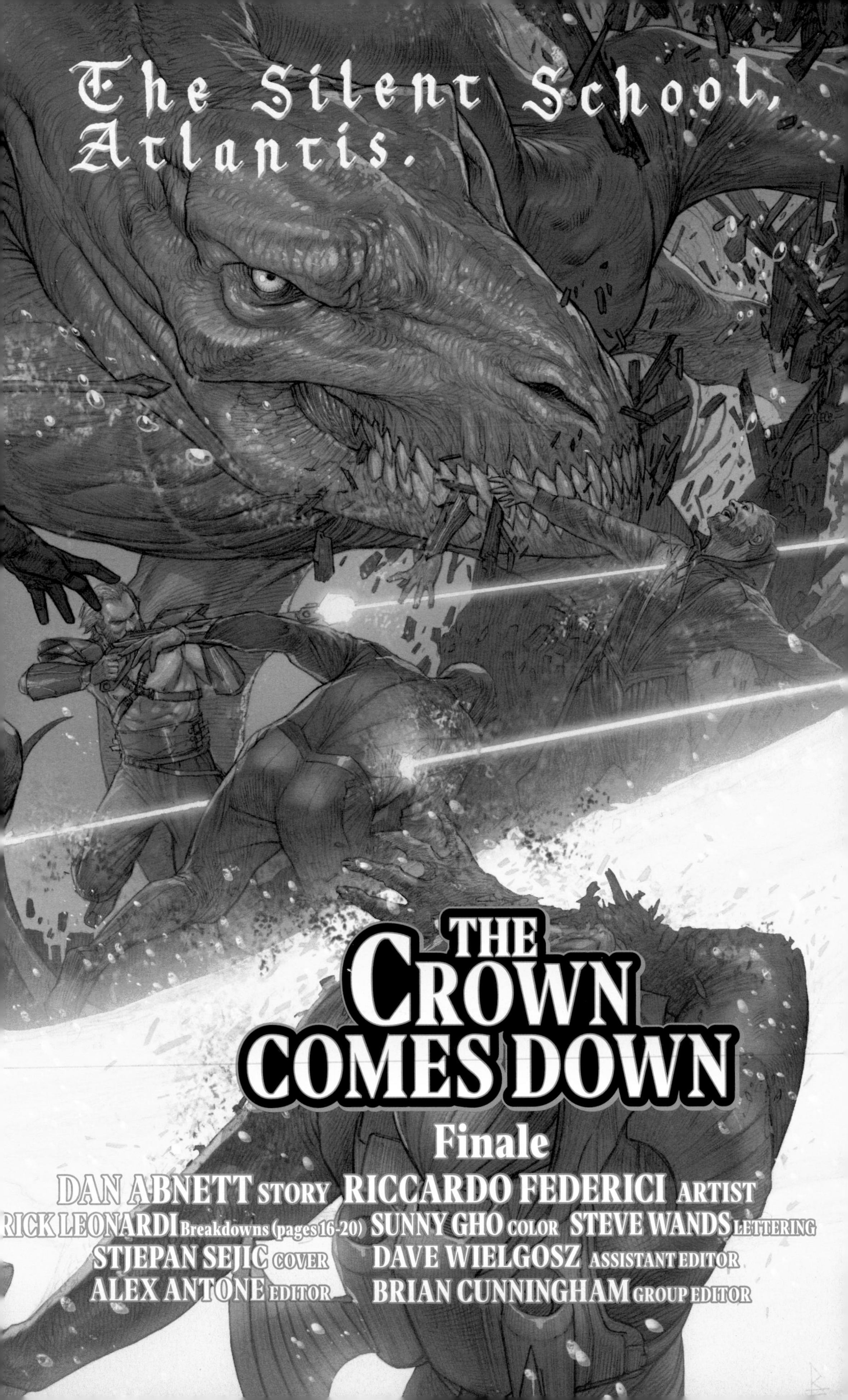
The Silent School, Atlantis.
THE CROWN COMES DOWN
Finale
DAN ABNETT STORY RICCARDO FEDERICI ARTIST
RICK LEONARDI Breakdowns (pages 16-20) SUNNY GHO COLOR STEVE WANDS LETTERING
STJEPAN SEJIC COVER DAVE WIELGOSZ ASSISTANT EDITOR
ALEX ANTONE EDITOR BRIAN CUNNINGHAM GROUP EDITOR

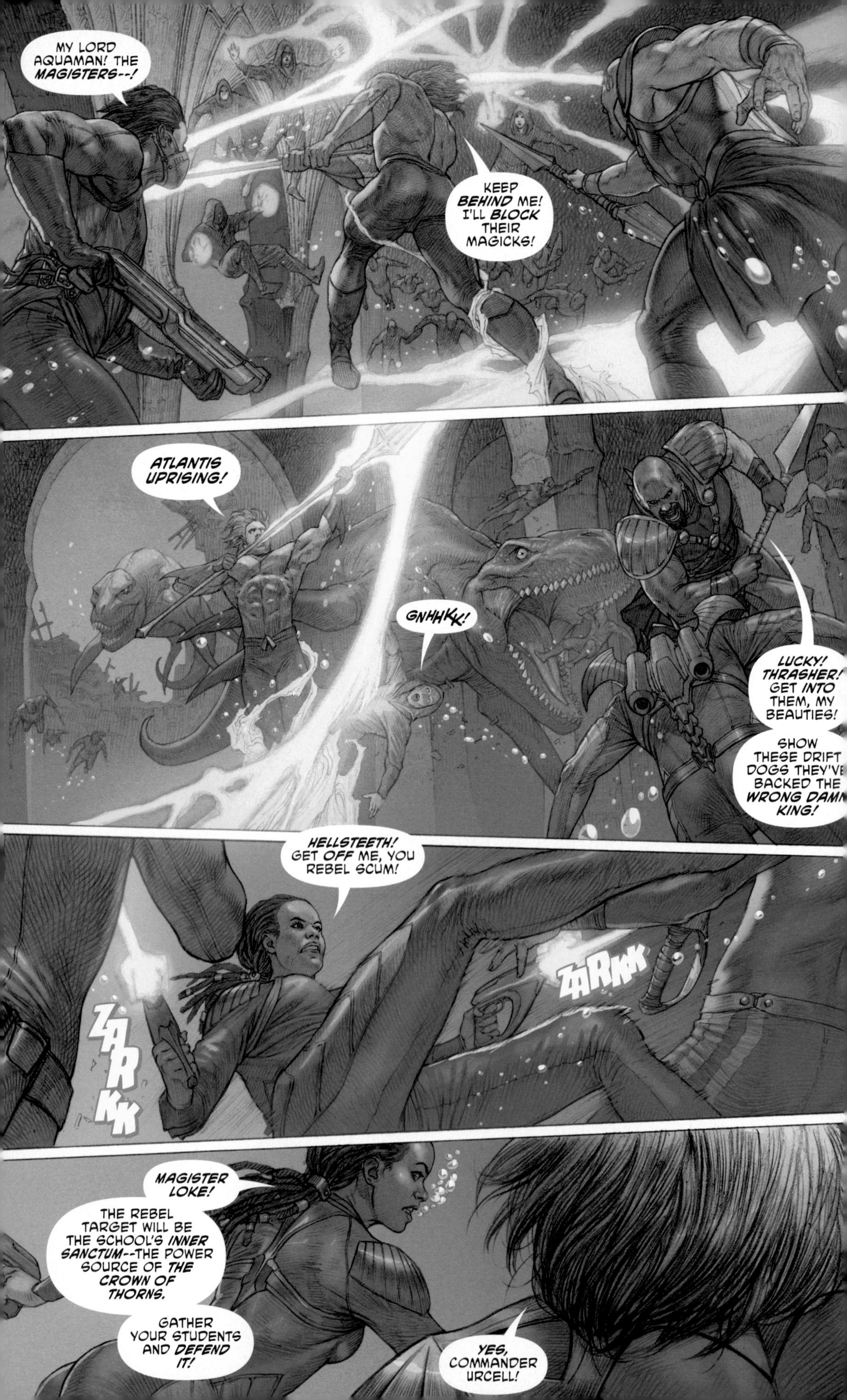
MY LORD AQUAMAN! THE MAGISTERS--!
KEEP BEHIND ME! I'LL BLOCK THEIR MAGICKS!
ATLANTIS UPRISING!
GNHHKK!
LUCKY! THRASHER! GET INTO THEM, MY BEAUTIES!
SHOW THESE DRIFT DOGS THEY'VE BACKED THE WRONG DAMN KING!
HELLSTEETH! GET OFF ME, YOU REBEL SCUM!
ZARKK
ZARKK
MAGISTER LOKE!
THE REBEL TARGET WILL BE THE SCHOOL'S INNER SANCTUM--THE POWER SOURCE OF THE CROWN OF THORNS.
GATHER YOUR STUDENTS AND DEFEND IT!
YES, COMMANDER URCELL!

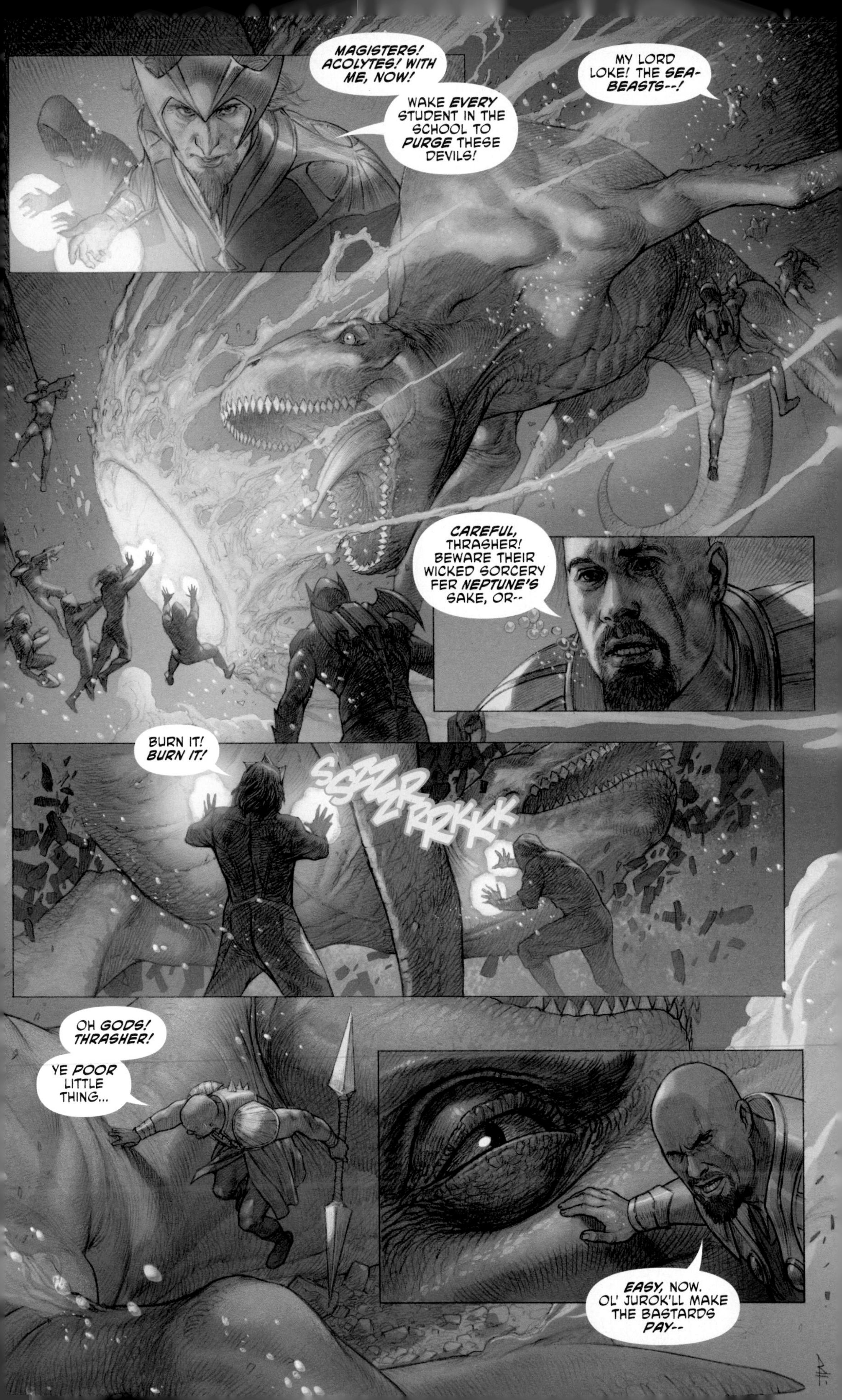

MAGISTERS! ACOLYTES! WITH ME, NOW!
WAKE EVERY STUDENT IN THE SCHOOL TO PURGE THESE DEVILS!
MY LORD LOKE! THE SEA-BEASTS--!
CAREFUL, THRASHER! BEWARE THEIR WICKED SORCERY FER NEPTUNE'S SAKE, OR--
BURN IT! BURN IT!
SSZZZRRRKKKK
OH GODS! THRASHER!
YE POOR LITTLE THING...
EASY, NOW. OL' JUROK'LL MAKE THE BASTARDS PAY--

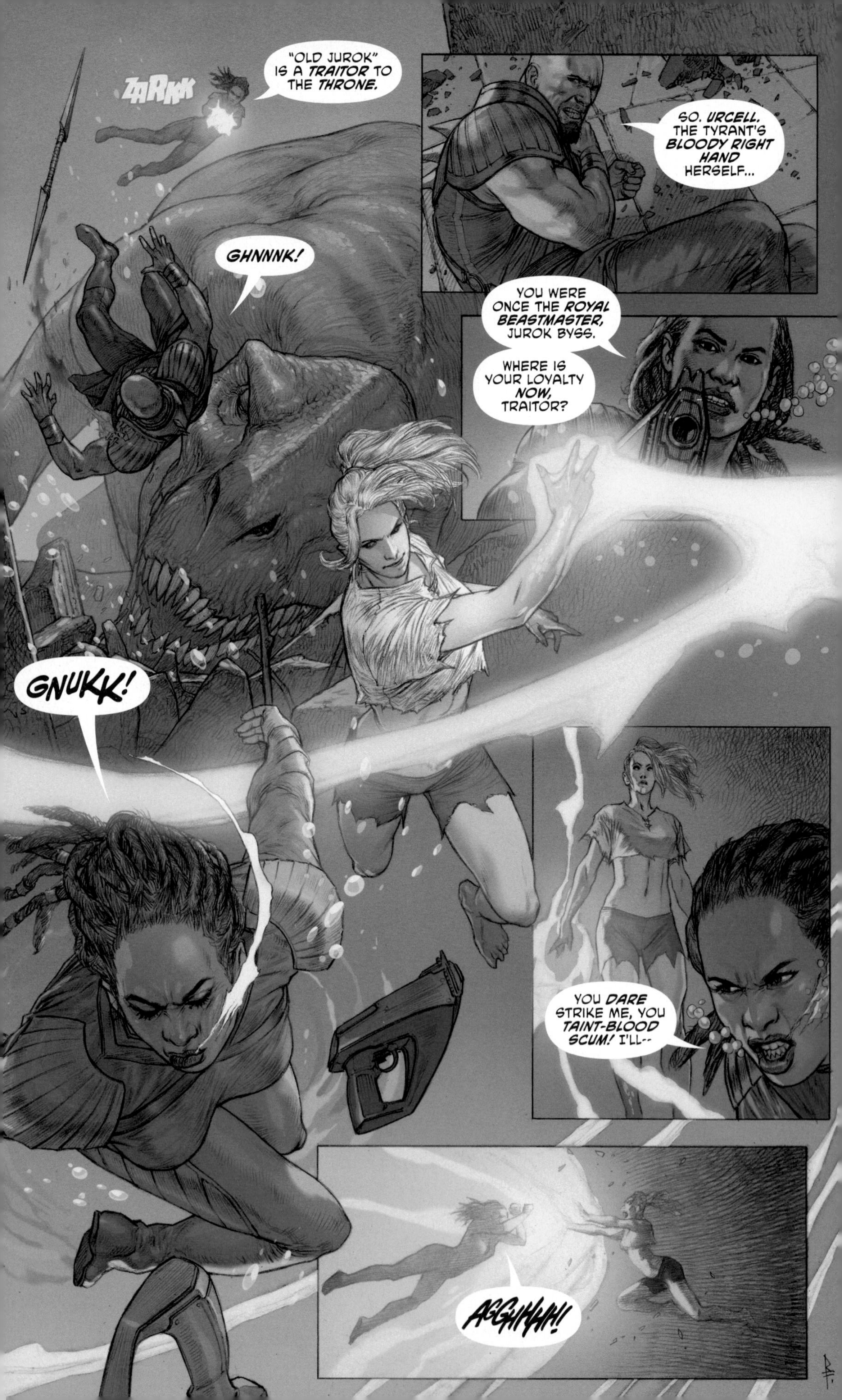
ZARKK
"OLD JUROK" IS A TRAITOR TO THE THRONE.
SO. URCELL. THE TYRANT'S BLOODY RIGHT HAND HERSELF...
GHNNNK!
YOU WERE ONCE THE ROYAL BEASTMASTER, JUROK BYSS.
WHERE IS YOUR LOYALTY NOW, TRAITOR?
GNUKK!
YOU DARE STRIKE ME, YOU TAINT-BLOOD SCUM! I'LL--
AGGHHHH!

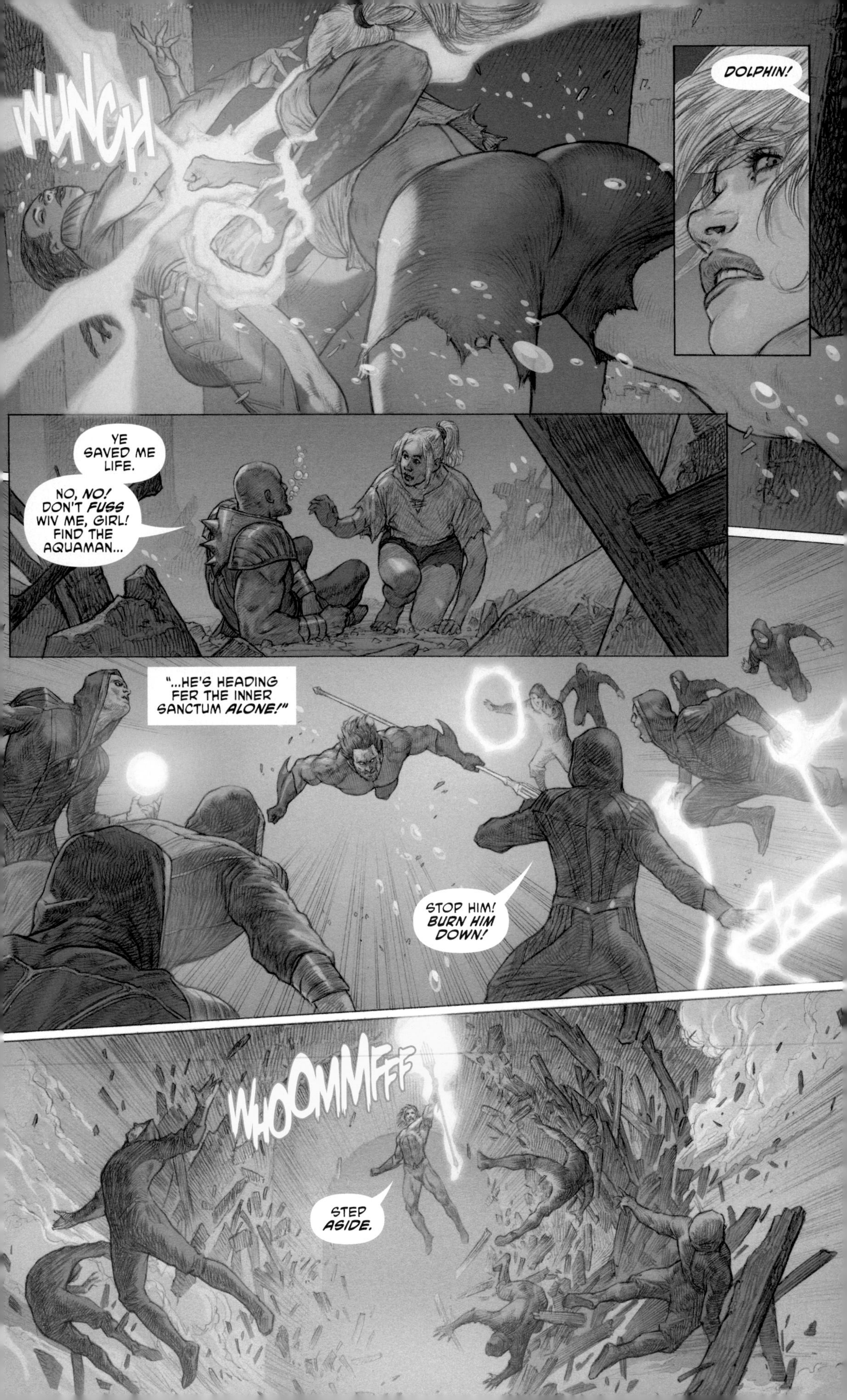
WUNCH
DOLPHIN!
YE SAVED ME LIFE.
NO, NO! DON'T FUSS WIV ME, GIRL! FIND THE AQUAMAN...
"...HE'S HEADING FER THE INNER SANCTUM ALONE!"
STOP HIM! BURN HIM DOWN!
WHOOMMFFF
STEP ASIDE.

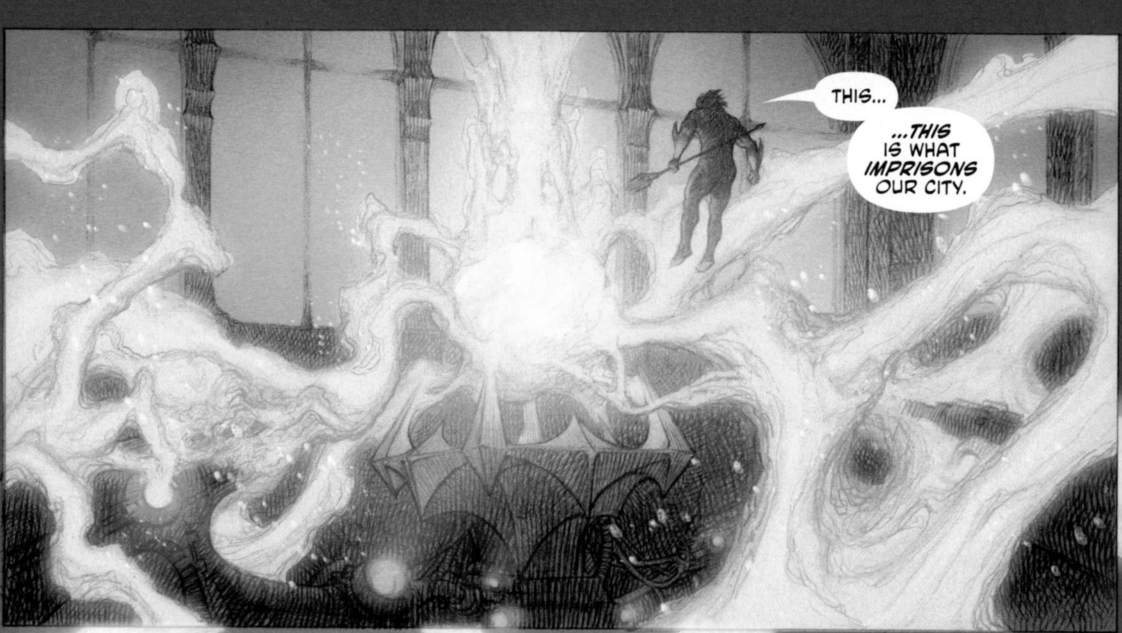
THIS...
...THIS IS WHAT IMPRISONS OUR CITY.

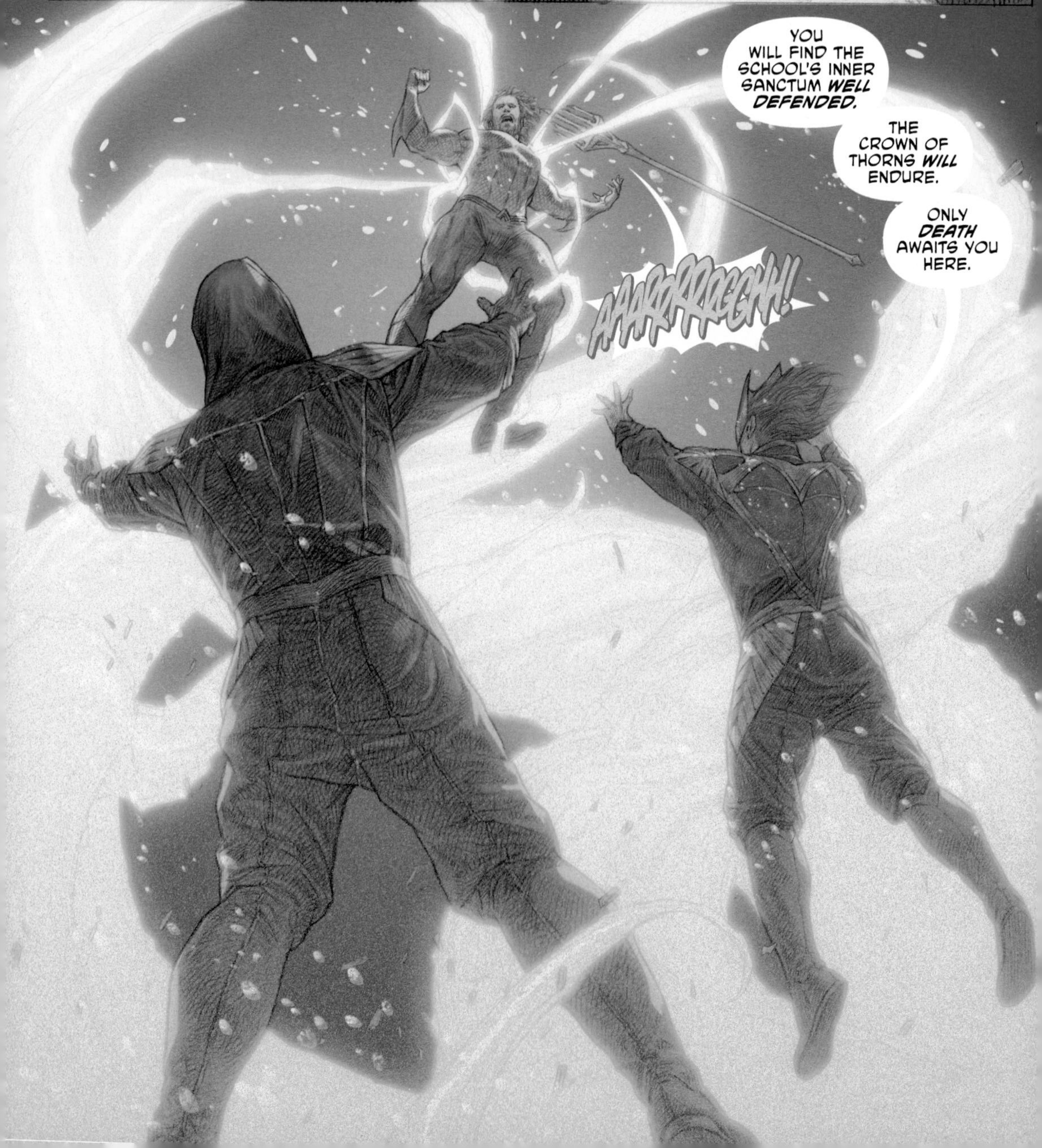
YOU WILL FIND THE SCHOOL'S INNER SANCTUM WELL DEFENDED.
THE CROWN OF THORNS WILL ENDURE.
ONLY DEATH AWAITS YOU HERE.
AAARRRRRGGHH!

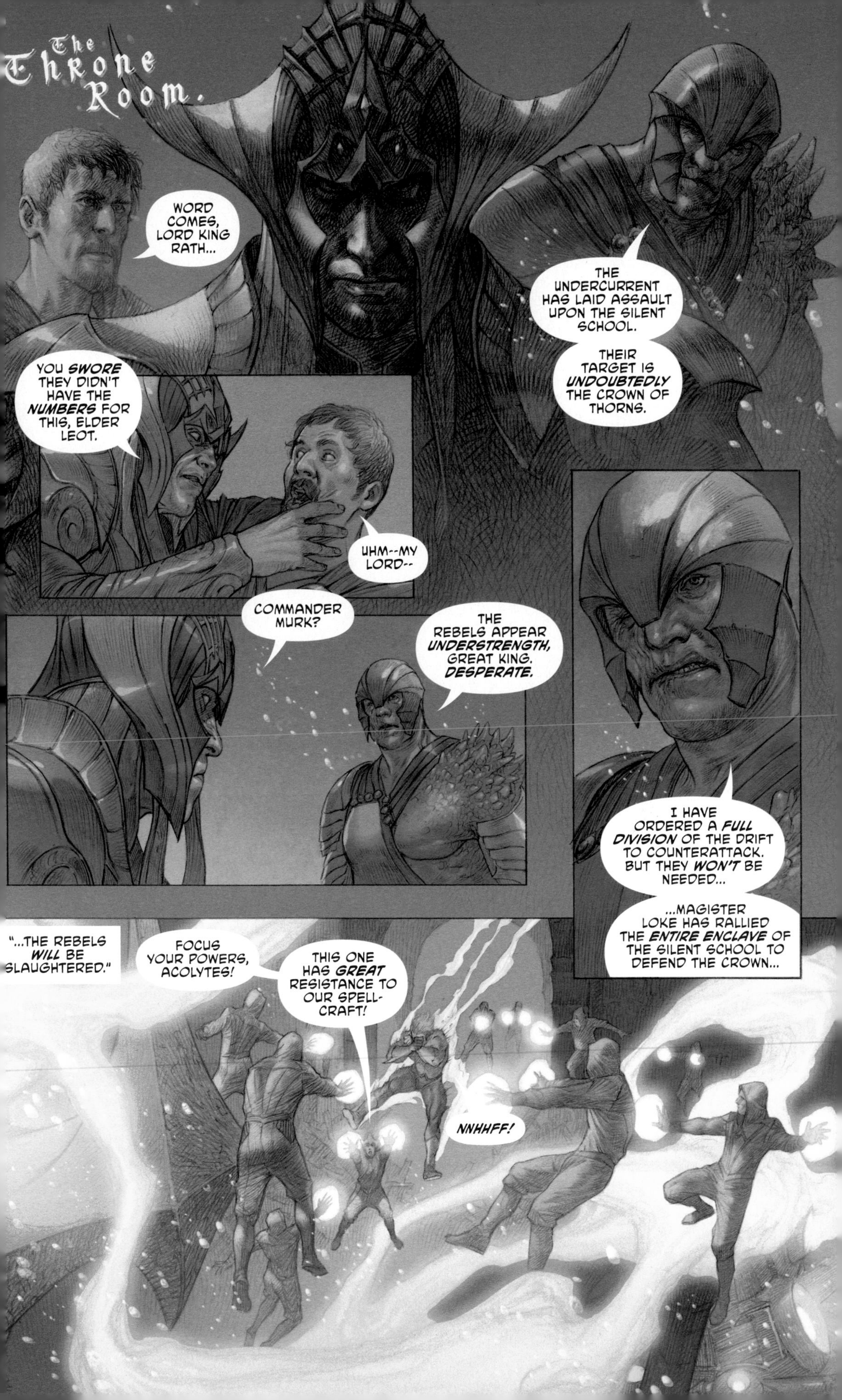

The Throne Room.
WORD COMES, LORD KING RATH...
THE UNDERCURRENT HAS LAID ASSAULT UPON THE SILENT SCHOOL.
THEIR TARGET IS UNDOUBTEDLY THE CROWN OF THORNS.
YOU SWORE THEY DIDN'T HAVE THE NUMBERS FOR THIS, ELDER LEOT.
UHM--MY LORD--
COMMANDER MURK?
THE REBELS APPEAR UNDERSTRENGTH, GREAT KING. DESPERATE.
I HAVE ORDERED A FULL DIVISION OF THE DRIFT TO COUNTERATTACK. BUT THEY WON'T BE NEEDED...
...MAGISTER LOKE HAS RALLIED THE ENTIRE ENCLAVE OF THE SILENT SCHOOL TO DEFEND THE CROWN...
"...THE REBELS WILL BE SLAUGHTERED."
FOCUS YOUR POWERS, ACOLYTES!
THIS ONE HAS GREAT RESISTANCE TO OUR SPELL-CRAFT!
NNHHFF!

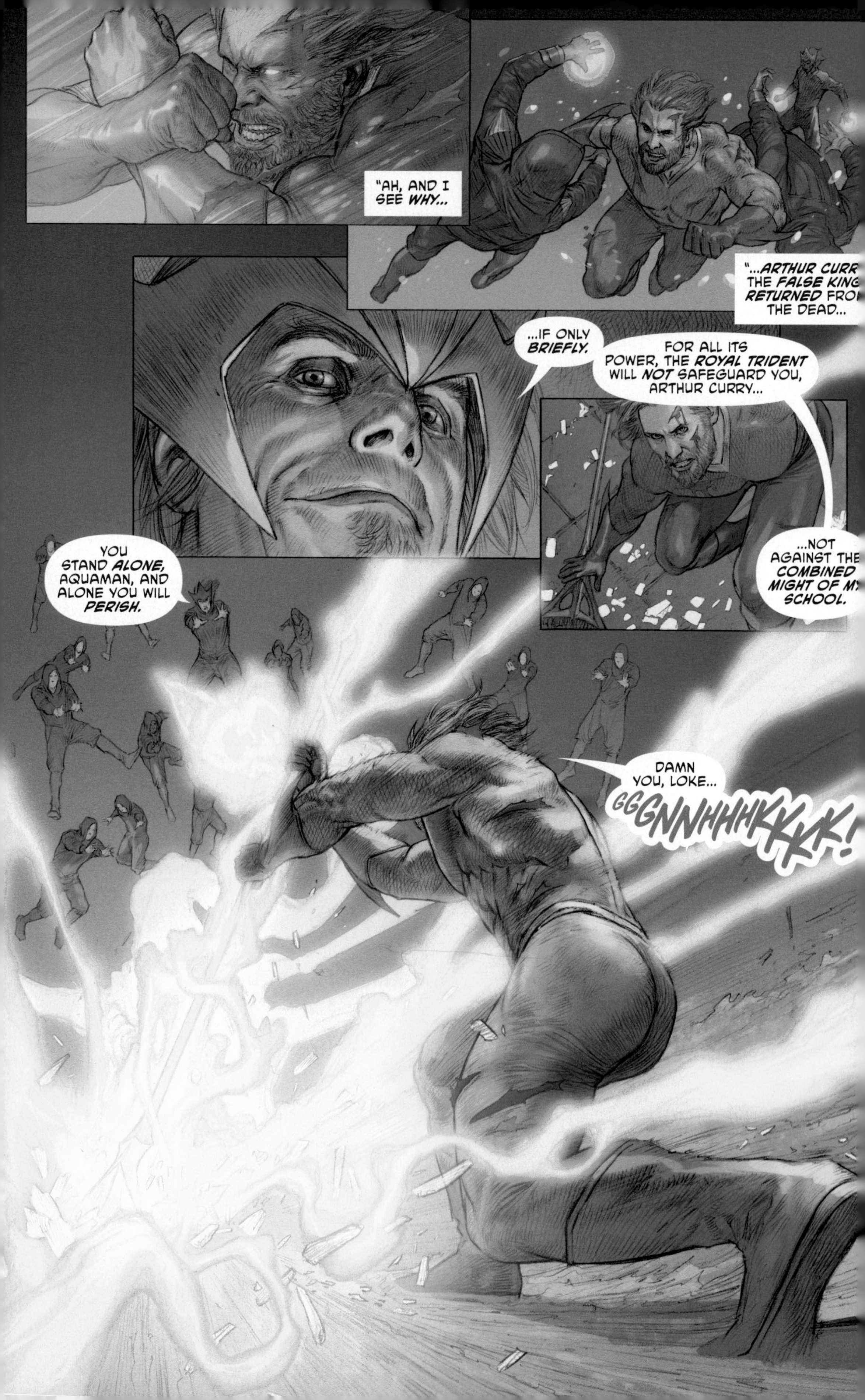
"AH, AND I SEE WHY...
"...ARTHUR CURR THE FALSE KING RETURNED FRO THE DEAD...
...IF ONLY BRIEFLY.
FOR ALL ITS POWER, THE ROYAL TRIDENT WILL NOT SAFEGUARD YOU, ARTHUR CURRY...
...NOT AGAINST THE COMBINED MIGHT OF MY SCHOOL.
YOU STAND ALONE, AQUAMAN, AND ALONE YOU WILL PERISH.
DAMN YOU, LOKE...
GGGNNHHHKKKK!

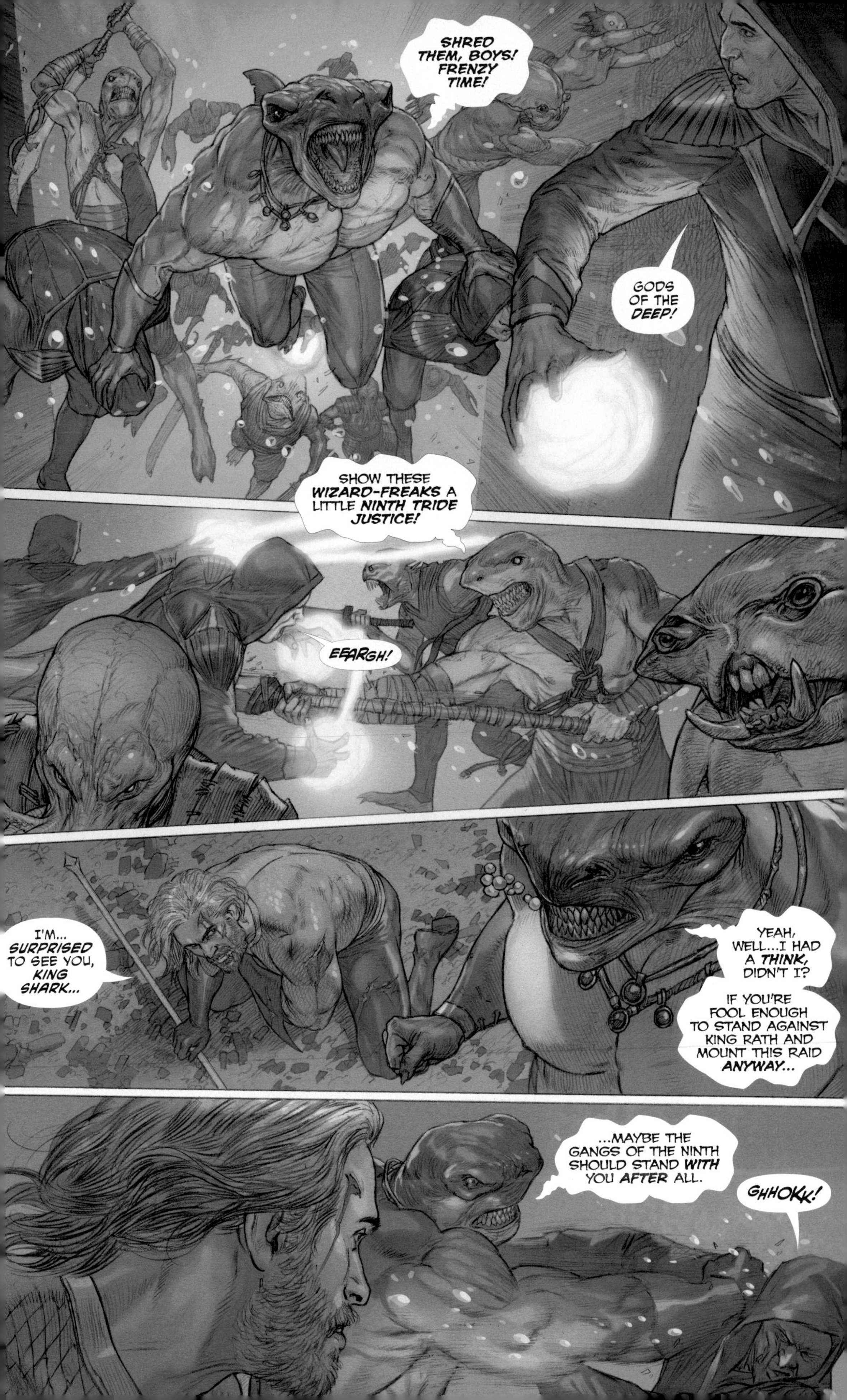
SHRED THEM, BOYS! FRENZY TIME!
GODS OF THE DEEP!
SHOW THESE WIZARD-FREAKS A LITTLE NINTH TRIDE JUSTICE!
EEARGH!
I'M... SURPRISED TO SEE YOU, KING SHARK...
YEAH, WELL...I HAD A THINK, DIDN'T I?
IF YOU'RE FOOL ENOUGH TO STAND AGAINST KING RATH AND MOUNT THIS RAID ANYWAY...
...MAYBE THE GANGS OF THE NINTH SHOULD STAND WITH YOU AFTER ALL.
GHHOKK!

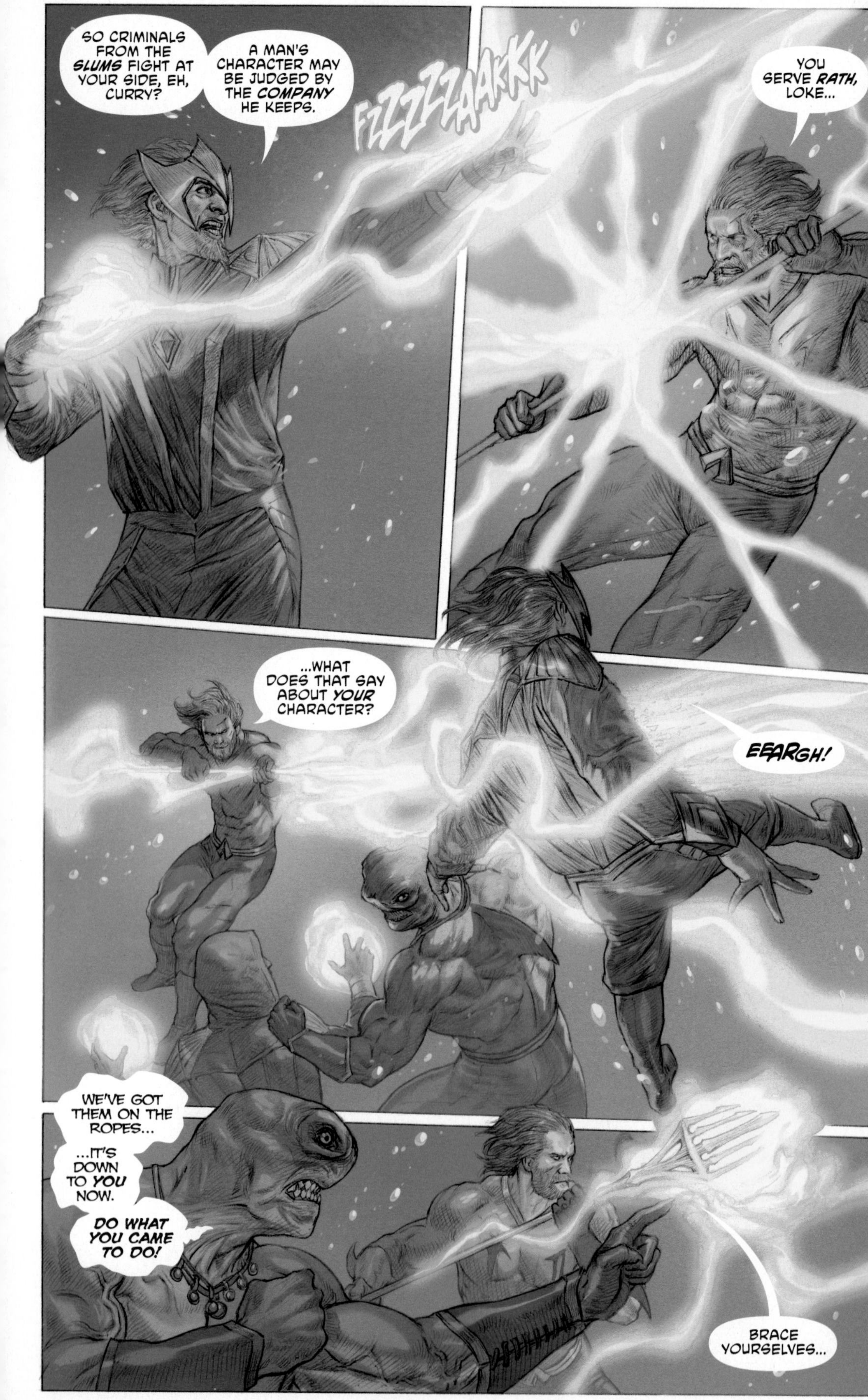
SO CRIMINALS FROM THE SLUMS FIGHT AT YOUR SIDE, EH, CURRY?
A MAN'S CHARACTER MAY BE JUDGED BY THE COMPANY HE KEEPS.
FZZZZZAAKKK
YOU SERVE RATH, LOKE...
...WHAT DOES THAT SAY ABOUT YOUR CHARACTER?
EEARGH!
WE'VE GOT THEM ON THE ROPES...
...IT'S DOWN TO YOU NOW.
DO WHAT YOU CAME TO DO!
BRACE YOURSELVES...

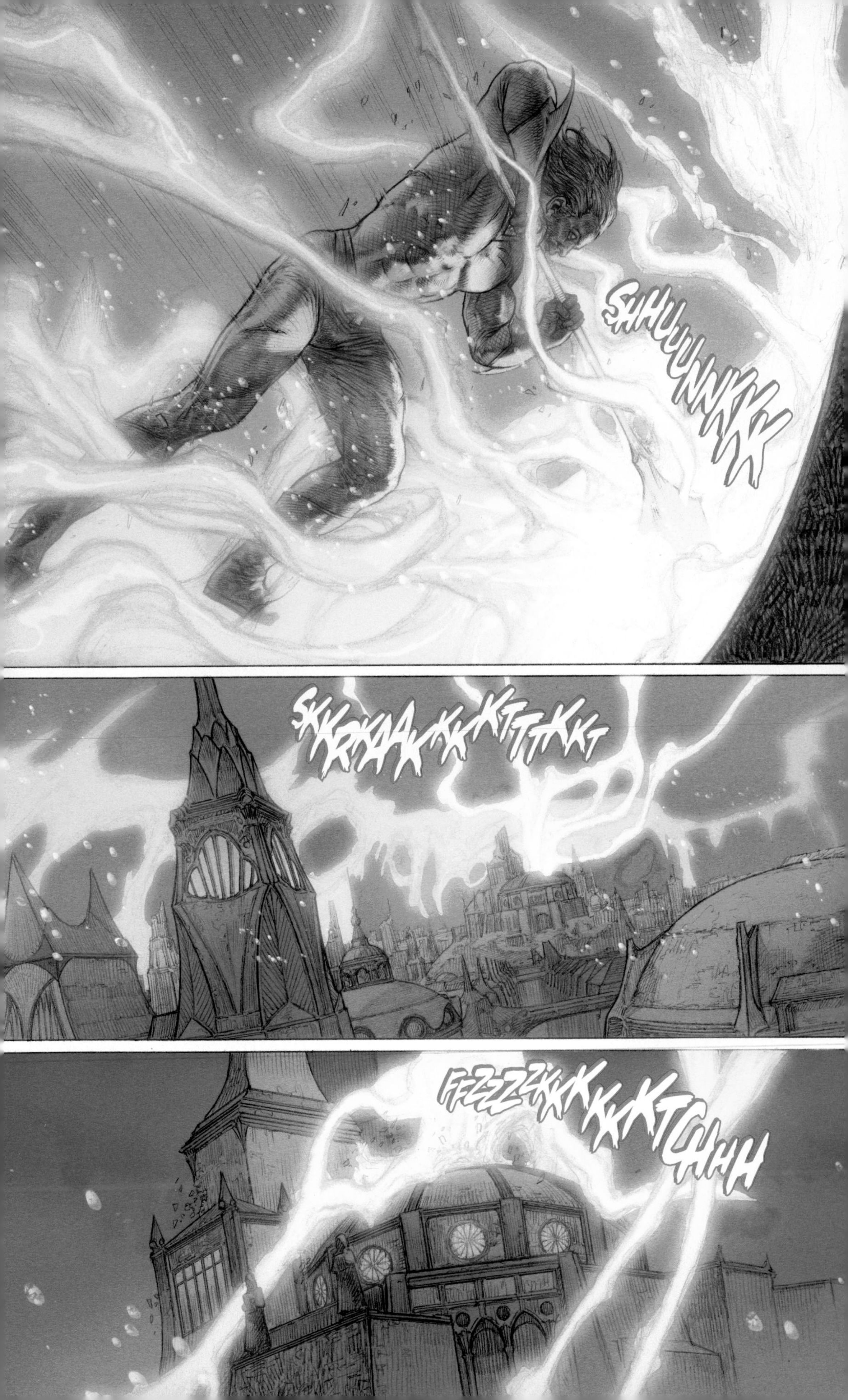
SHHUUNNKKK
SKKRKAAKKKKTTTKKT
FFZZZZKKKKKKTCHHH

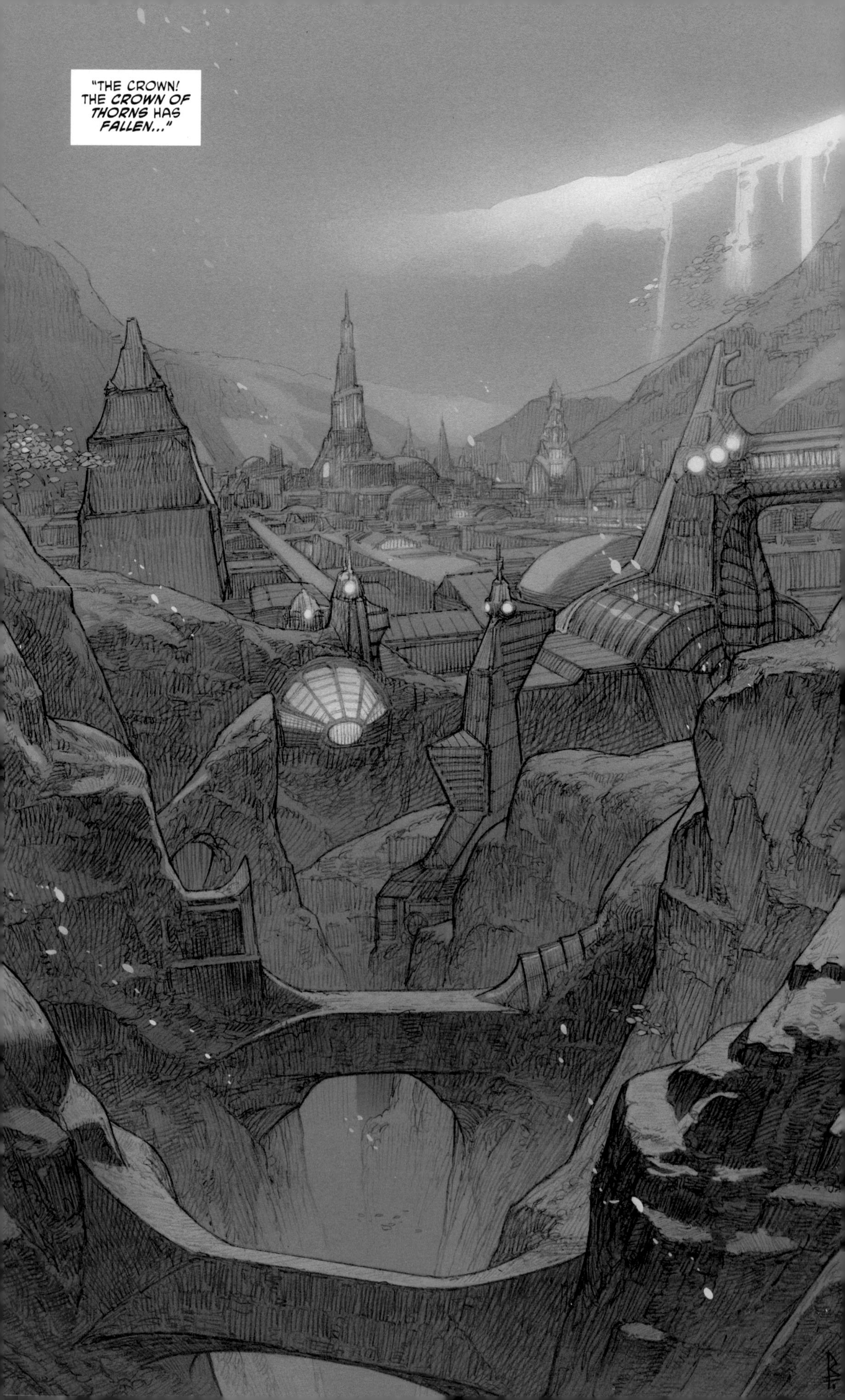
"THE CROWN! THE *CROWN OF THORNS* HAS *FALLEN...*"

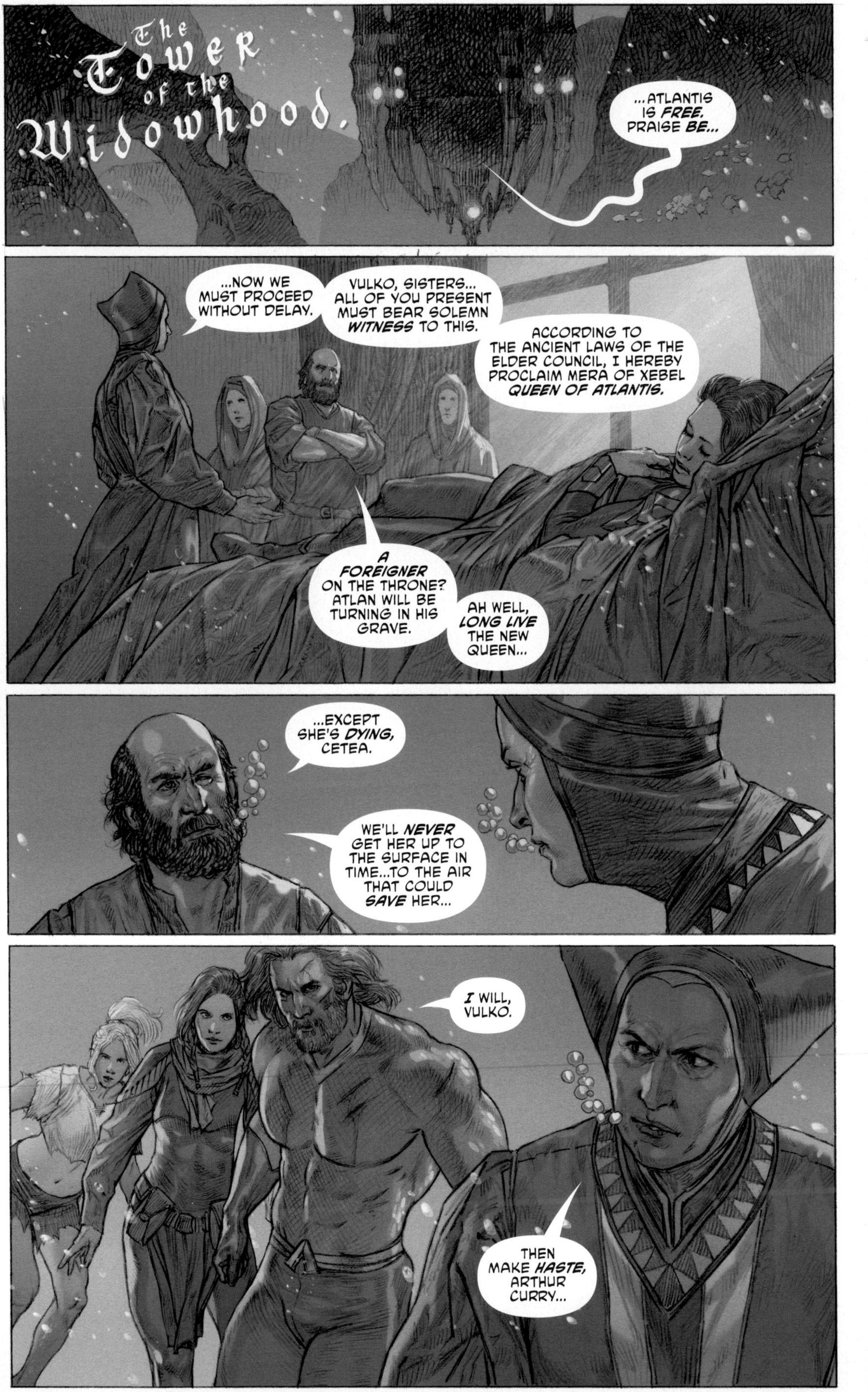

The Tower of the Widowhood.
...ATLANTIS IS FREE. PRAISE BE...
...NOW WE MUST PROCEED WITHOUT DELAY.
VULKO, SISTERS... ALL OF YOU PRESENT MUST BEAR SOLEMN WITNESS TO THIS.
ACCORDING TO THE ANCIENT LAWS OF THE ELDER COUNCIL, I HEREBY PROCLAIM MERA OF XEBEL QUEEN OF ATLANTIS.
A FOREIGNER ON THE THRONE? ATLAN WILL BE TURNING IN HIS GRAVE.
AH WELL, LONG LIVE THE NEW QUEEN...
...EXCEPT SHE'S DYING, CETEA.
WE'LL NEVER GET HER UP TO THE SURFACE IN TIME...TO THE AIR THAT COULD SAVE HER...
I WILL, VULKO.
THEN MAKE HASTE, ARTHUR CURRY...

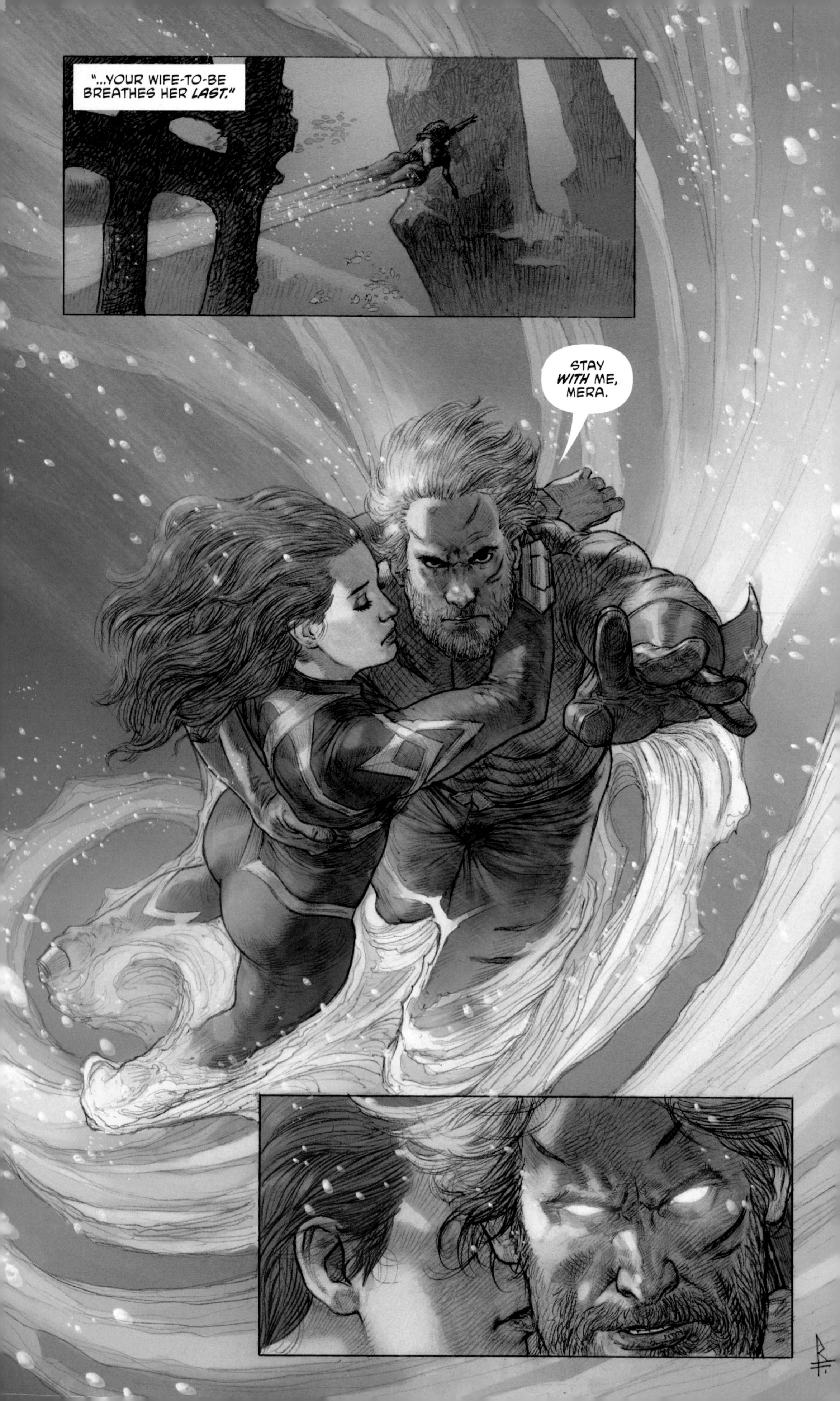
"...YOUR WIFE-TO-BE BREATHES HER *LAST.*"
STAY *WITH* ME, MERA.

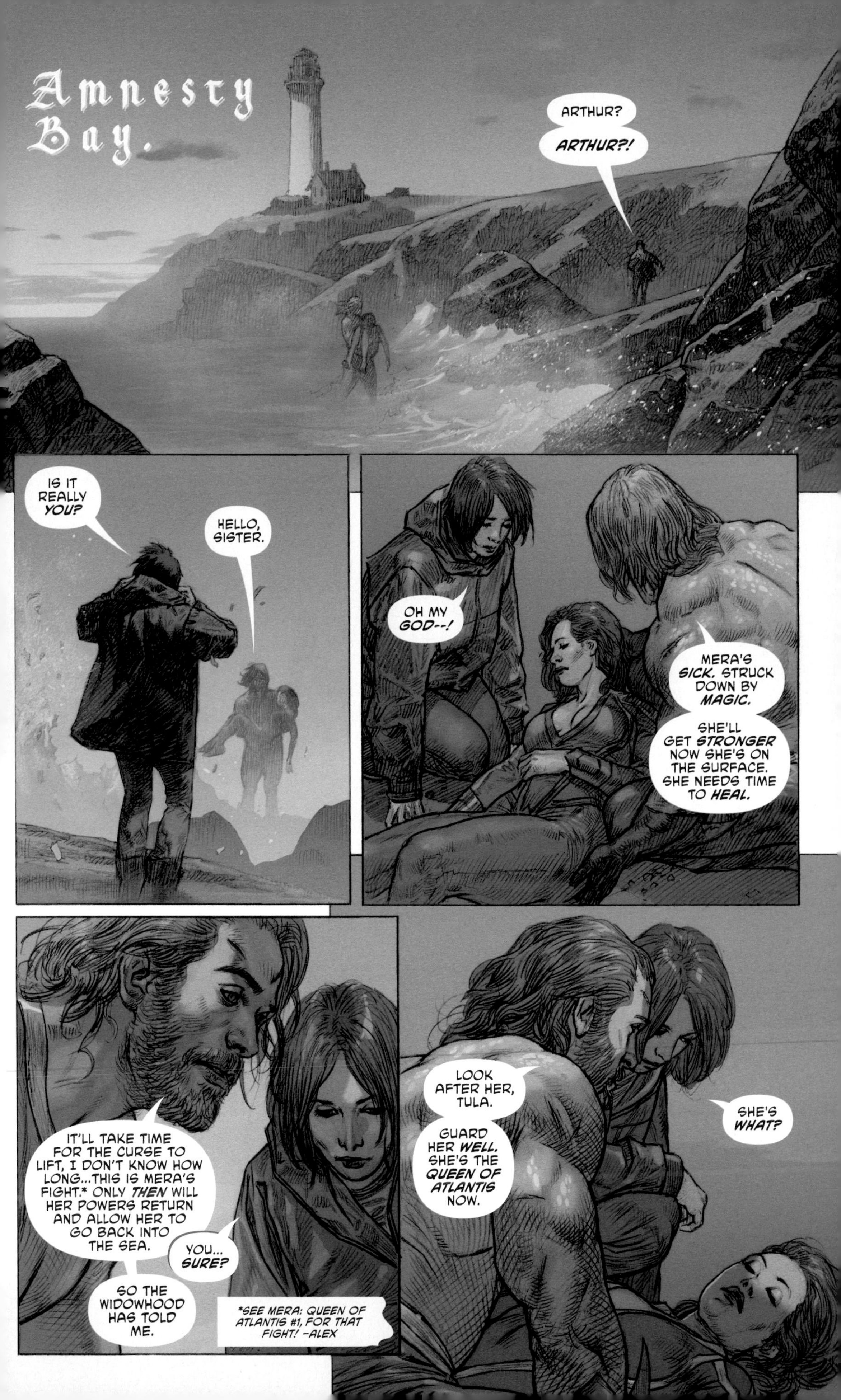

Amnesty Bay.
ARTHUR?
ARTHUR?!
IS IT REALLY YOU?
HELLO, SISTER.
OH MY GOD--!
MERA'S SICK. STRUCK DOWN BY MAGIC.
SHE'LL GET STRONGER NOW SHE'S ON THE SURFACE. SHE NEEDS TIME TO HEAL.
IT'LL TAKE TIME FOR THE CURSE TO LIFT, I DON'T KNOW HOW LONG...THIS IS MERA'S FIGHT.* ONLY THEN WILL HER POWERS RETURN AND ALLOW HER TO GO BACK INTO THE SEA.
YOU... SURE?
SO THE WIDOWHOOD HAS TOLD ME.
*SEE MERA: QUEEN OF ATLANTIS #1, FOR THAT FIGHT! -ALEX
LOOK AFTER HER, TULA.
GUARD HER WELL. SHE'S THE QUEEN OF ATLANTIS NOW.
SHE'S WHAT?

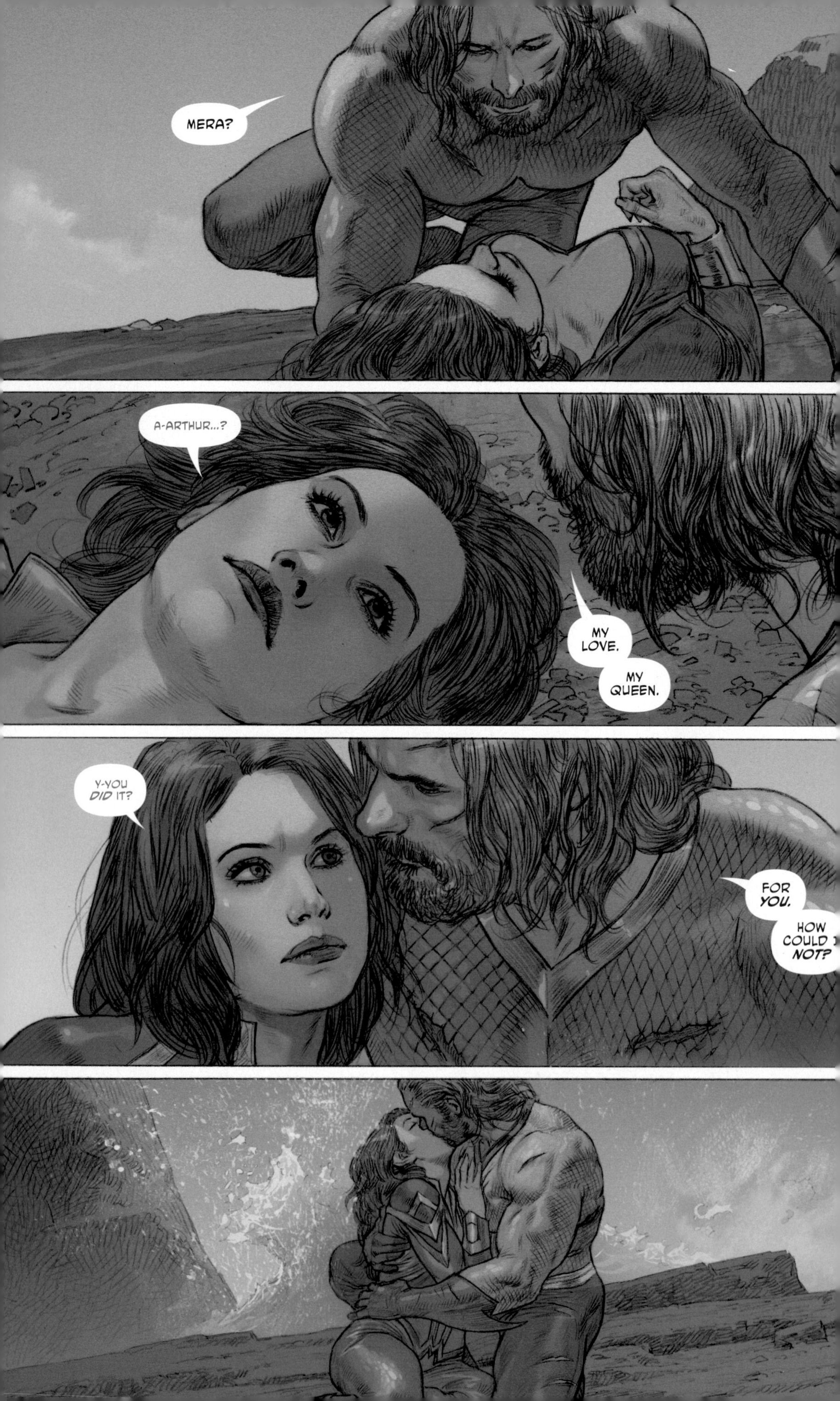
MERA?
A-ARTHUR...?
MY LOVE.
MY QUEEN.
Y-YOU DID IT?
FOR YOU.
HOW COULD I NOT?

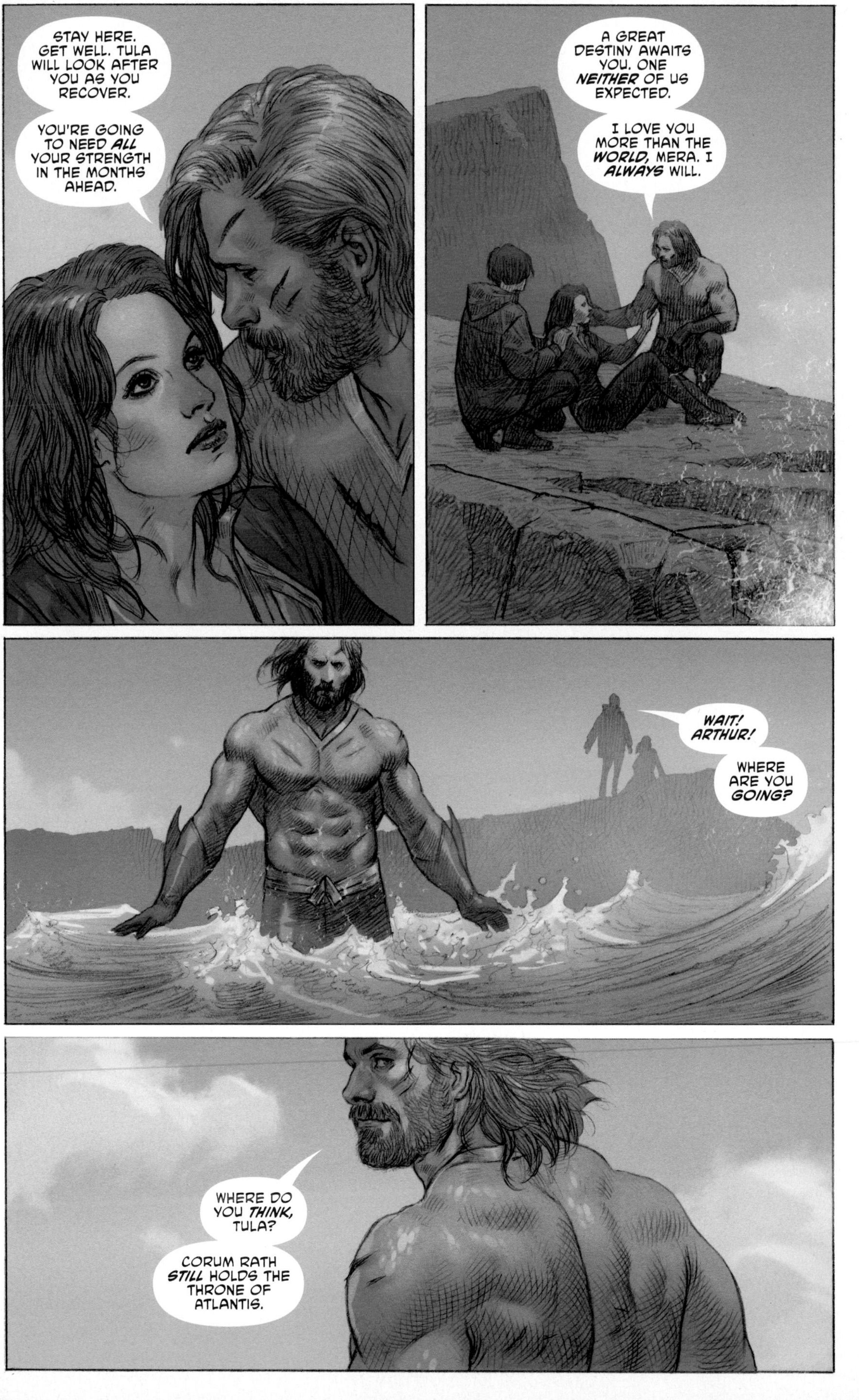
STAY HERE. GET WELL. TULA WILL LOOK AFTER YOU AS YOU RECOVER.
YOU'RE GOING TO NEED *ALL* YOUR STRENGTH IN THE MONTHS AHEAD.
A GREAT DESTINY AWAITS YOU. ONE *NEITHER* OF US EXPECTED.
I LOVE YOU MORE THAN THE *WORLD,* MERA. I *ALWAYS* WILL.
WAIT! ARTHUR!
WHERE ARE YOU *GOING?*
WHERE DO YOU *THINK,* TULA?
CORUM RATH *STILL* HOLDS THE THRONE OF ATLANTIS.

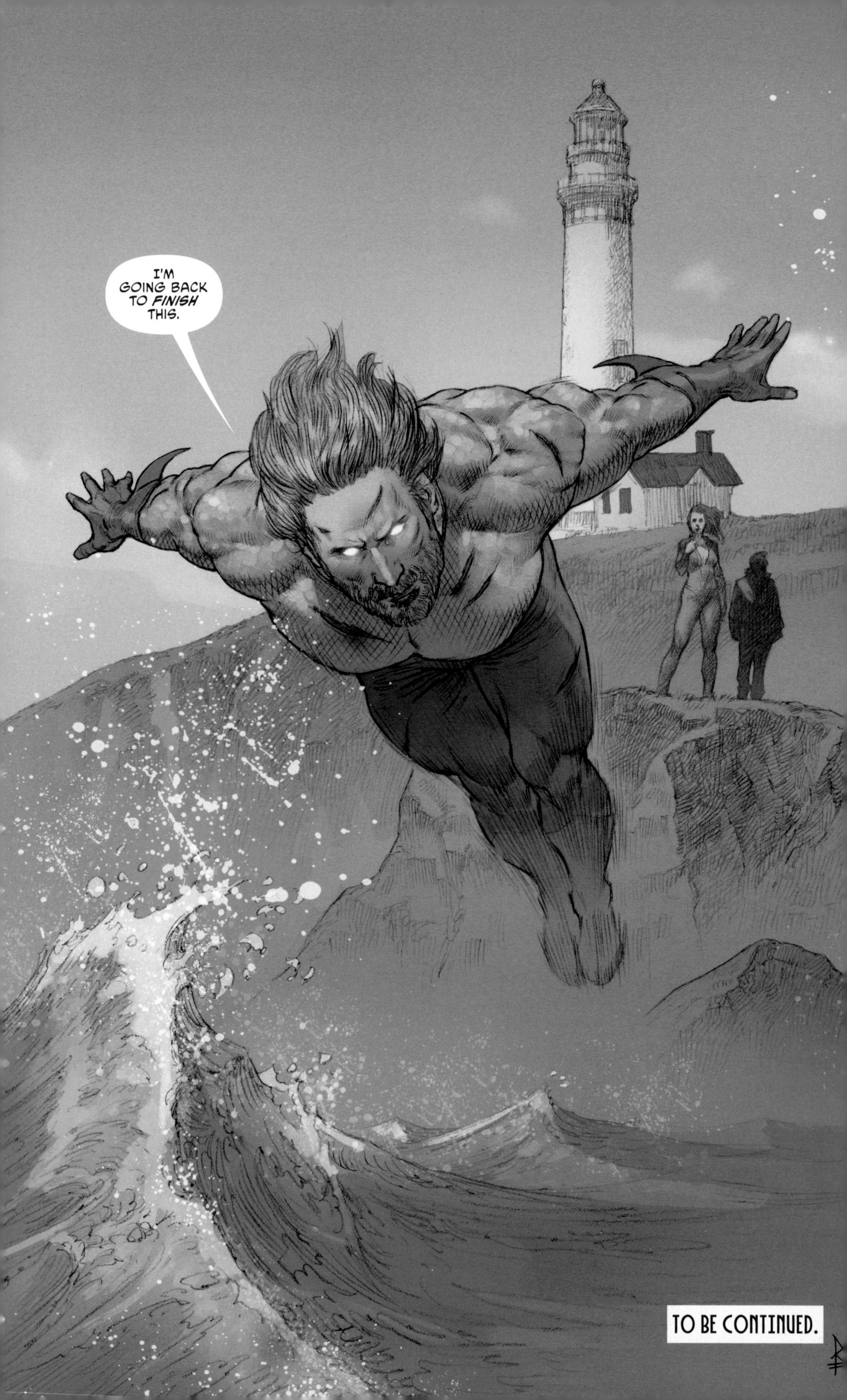
I'M GOING BACK TO *FINISH* THIS.
TO BE CONTINUED.

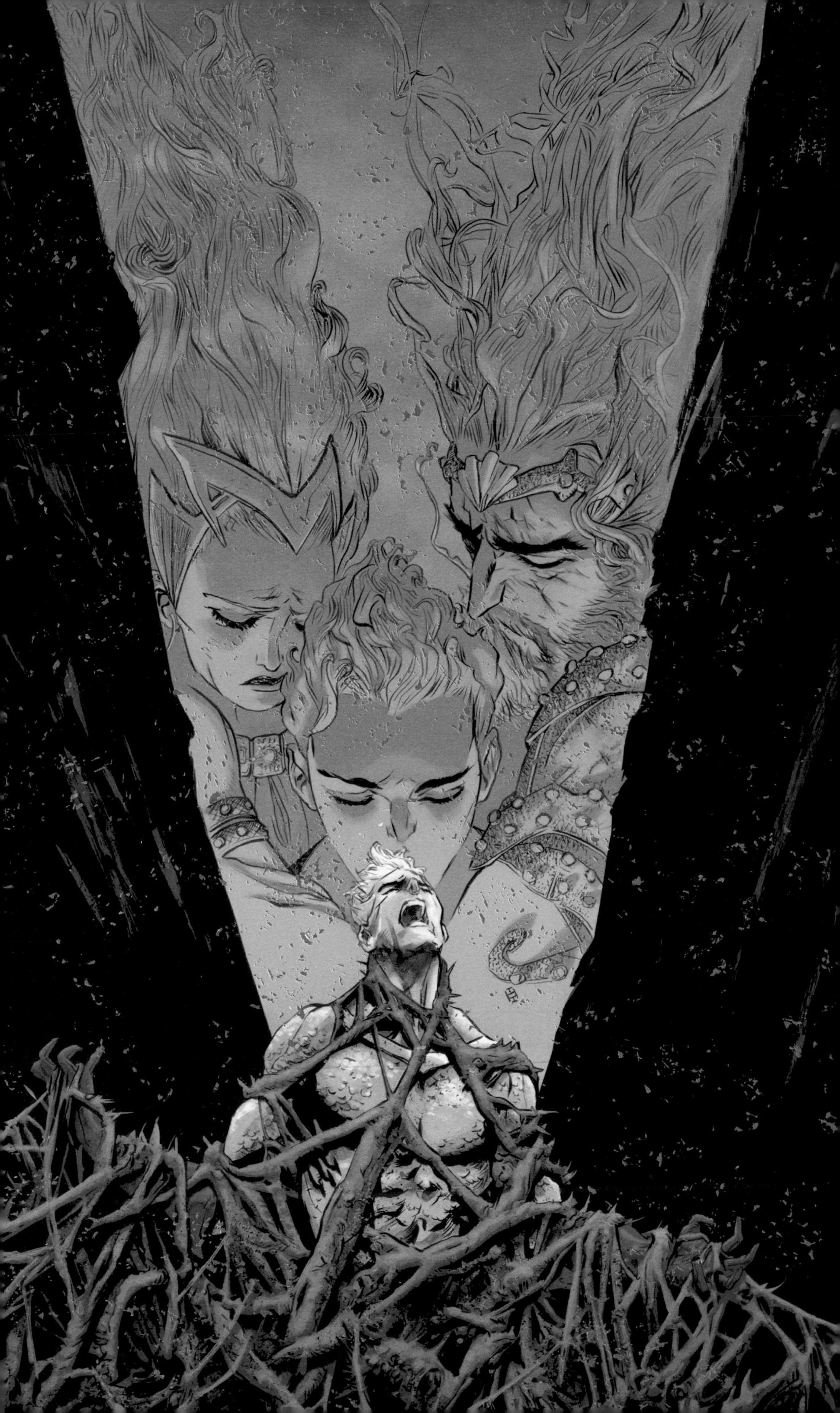

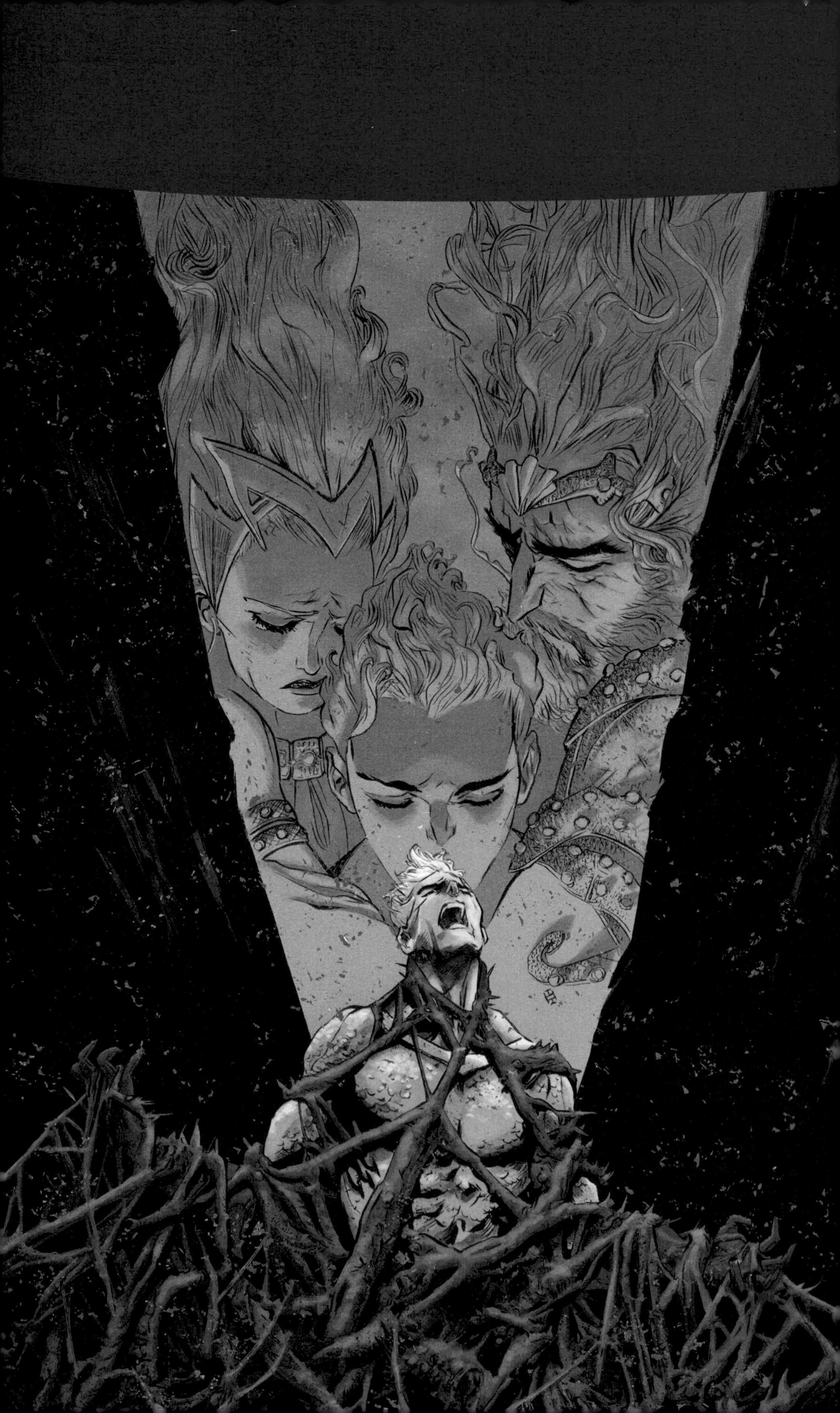

PROLOGUE

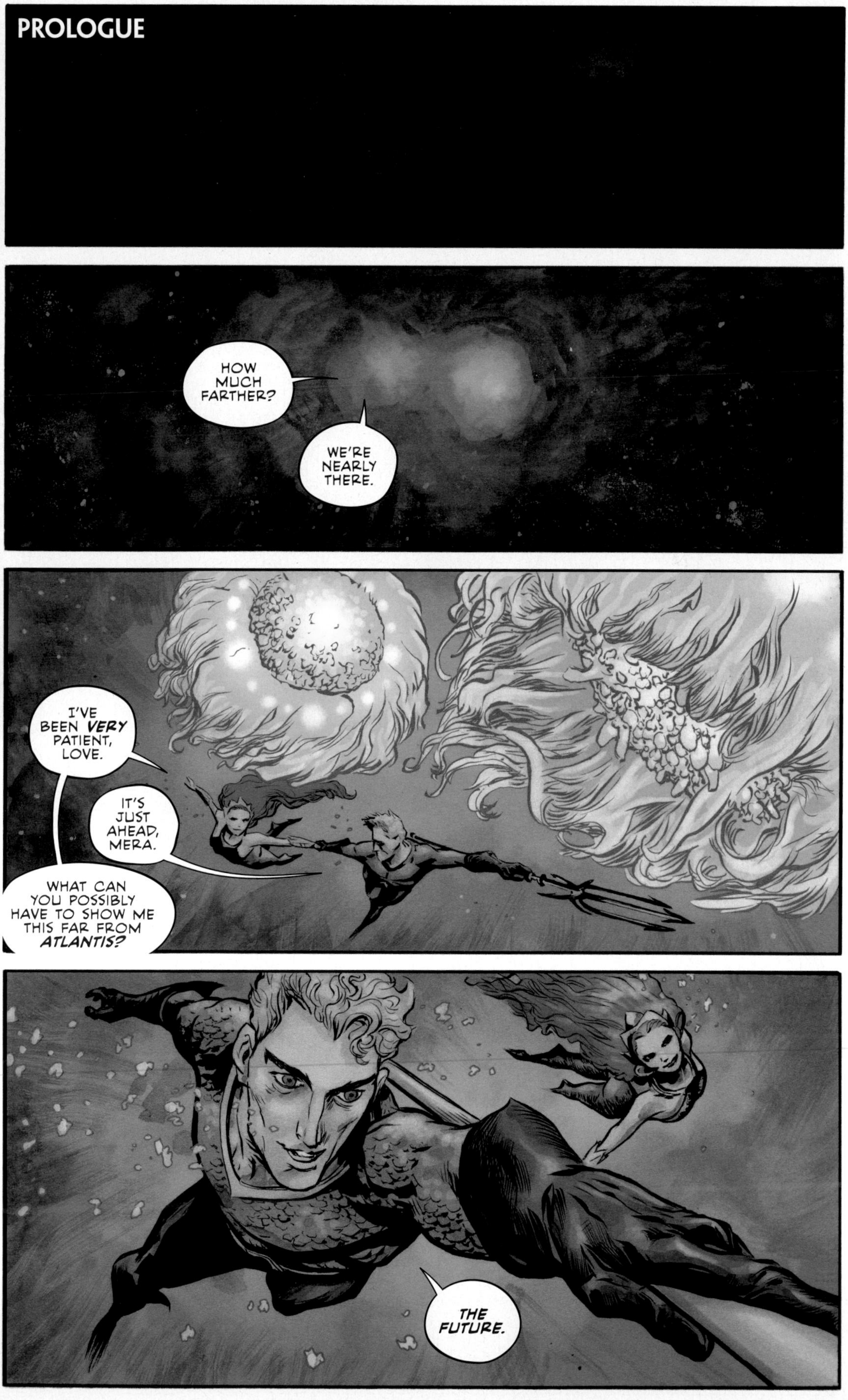
HOW MUCH FARTHER?
WE'RE NEARLY THERE.
I'VE BEEN *VERY* PATIENT, LOVE.
IT'S JUST AHEAD, MERA.
WHAT CAN YOU POSSIBLY HAVE TO SHOW ME THIS FAR FROM *ATLANTIS?*
THE FUTURE.

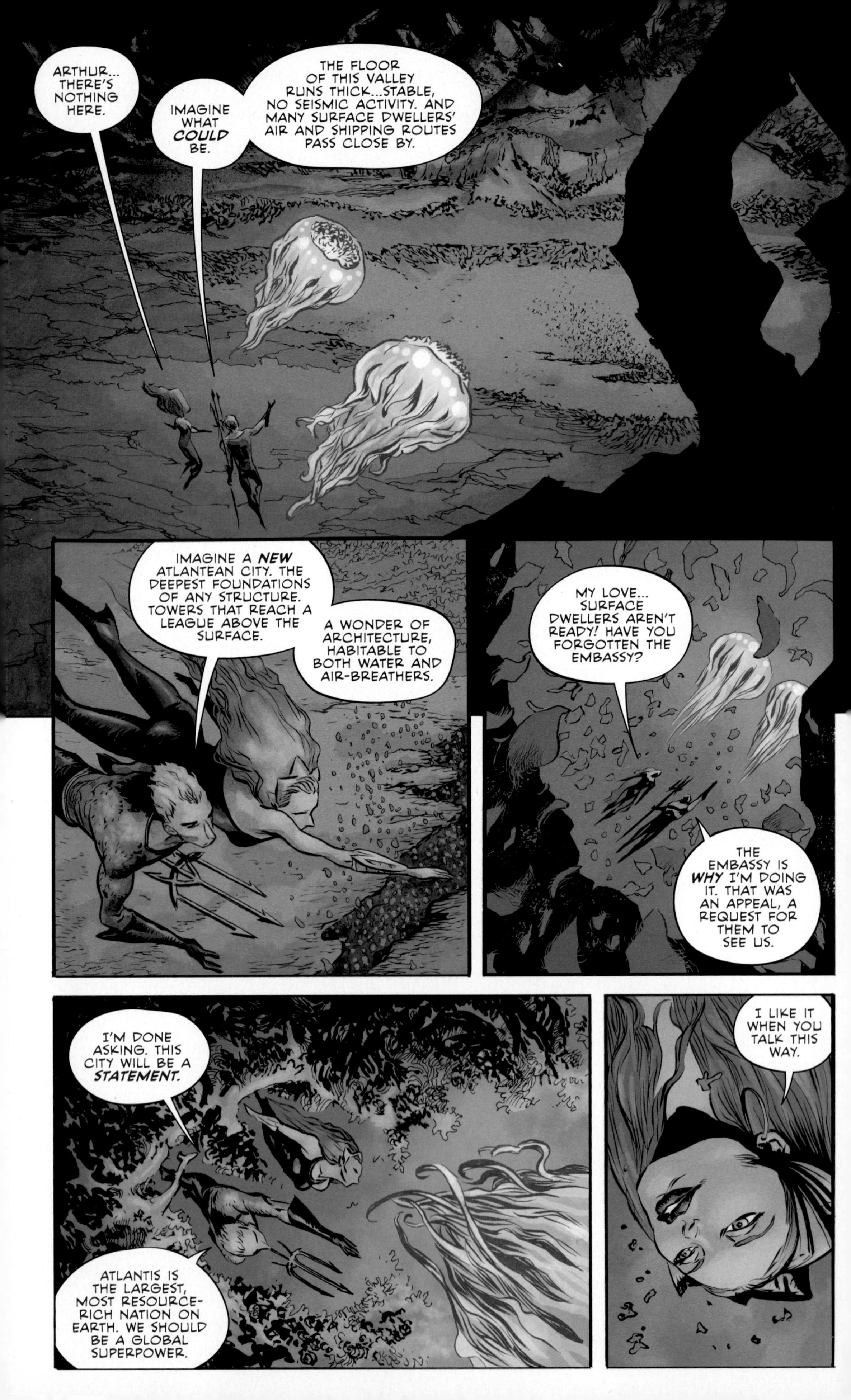
ARTHUR... THERE'S NOTHING HERE.
IMAGINE WHAT COULD BE.
THE FLOOR OF THIS VALLEY RUNS THICK...STABLE, NO SEISMIC ACTIVITY. AND MANY SURFACE DWELLERS' AIR AND SHIPPING ROUTES PASS CLOSE BY.
IMAGINE A NEW ATLANTEAN CITY. THE DEEPEST FOUNDATIONS OF ANY STRUCTURE. TOWERS THAT REACH A LEAGUE ABOVE THE SURFACE.
A WONDER OF ARCHITECTURE, HABITABLE TO BOTH WATER AND AIR-BREATHERS.
MY LOVE... SURFACE DWELLERS AREN'T READY! HAVE YOU FORGOTTEN THE EMBASSY?
THE EMBASSY IS WHY I'M DOING IT. THAT WAS AN APPEAL, A REQUEST FOR THEM TO SEE US.
I'M DONE ASKING. THIS CITY WILL BE A STATEMENT.
ATLANTIS IS THE LARGEST, MOST RESOURCE-RICH NATION ON EARTH. WE SHOULD BE A GLOBAL SUPERPOWER.
I LIKE IT WHEN YOU TALK THIS WAY.

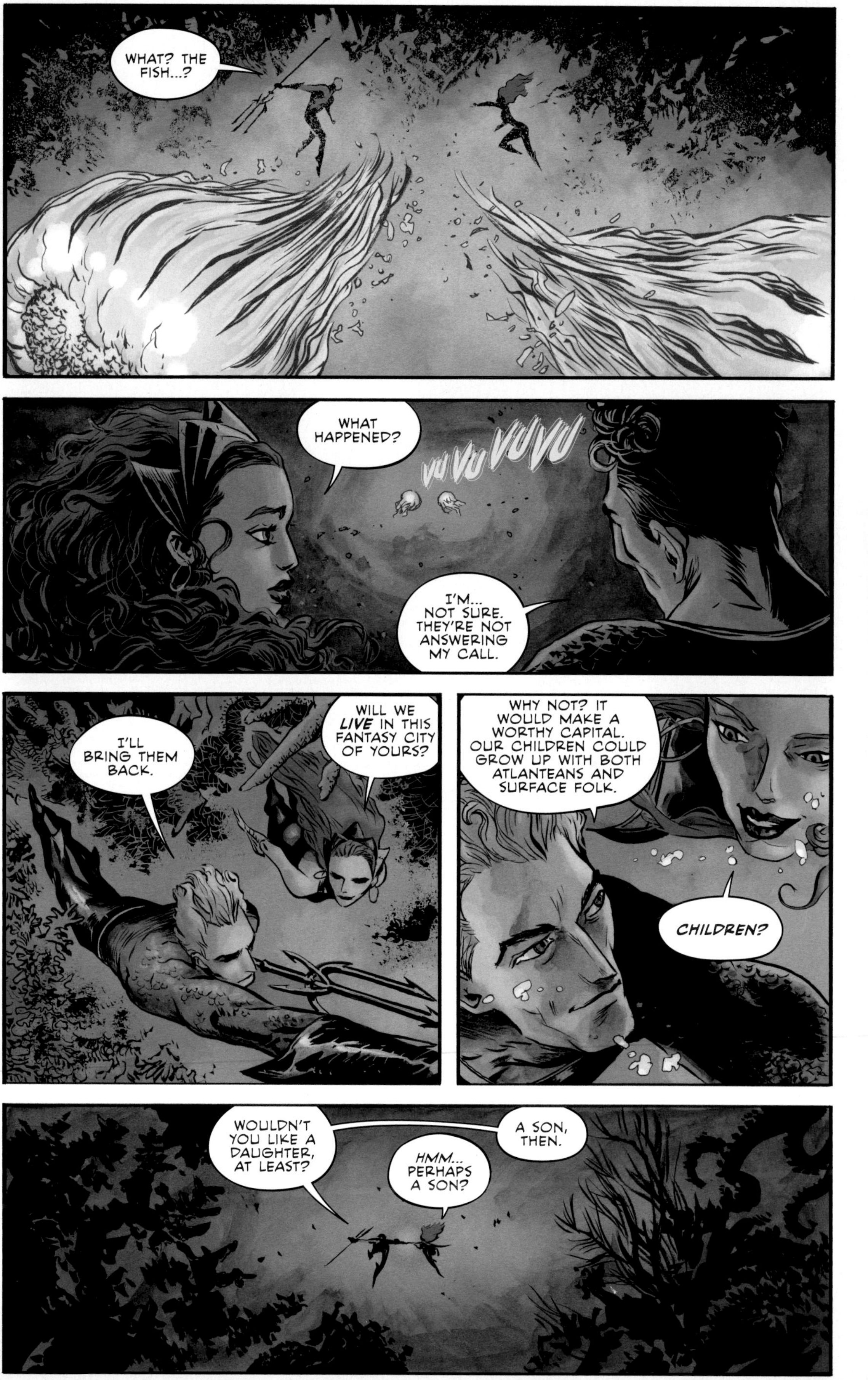
WHAT? THE FISH...?
WHAT HAPPENED?
VU VU VUVU
I'M... NOT SURE. THEY'RE NOT ANSWERING MY CALL.
I'LL BRING THEM BACK.
WILL WE *LIVE* IN THIS FANTASY CITY OF YOURS?
WHY NOT? IT WOULD MAKE A WORTHY CAPITAL. OUR CHILDREN COULD GROW UP WITH BOTH ATLANTEANS AND SURFACE FOLK.
CHILDREN?
HMM... PERHAPS A SON?
WOULDN'T YOU LIKE A DAUGHTER, AT LEAST?
A SON, THEN.

CHAPTER 1

CROWNSPIRE

PHILLIP KENNEDY JOHNSON WRITER
MAX FIUMARA ARTIST
DAVE STEWART COLORIST
DERON BENNETT LETTERER
MAX FIUMARA COVER
DIEGO LOPEZ ASSISTANT EDITOR
AMEDEO TURTURRO ASSOCIATE EDITOR
BRIAN CUNNINGHAM EDITOR

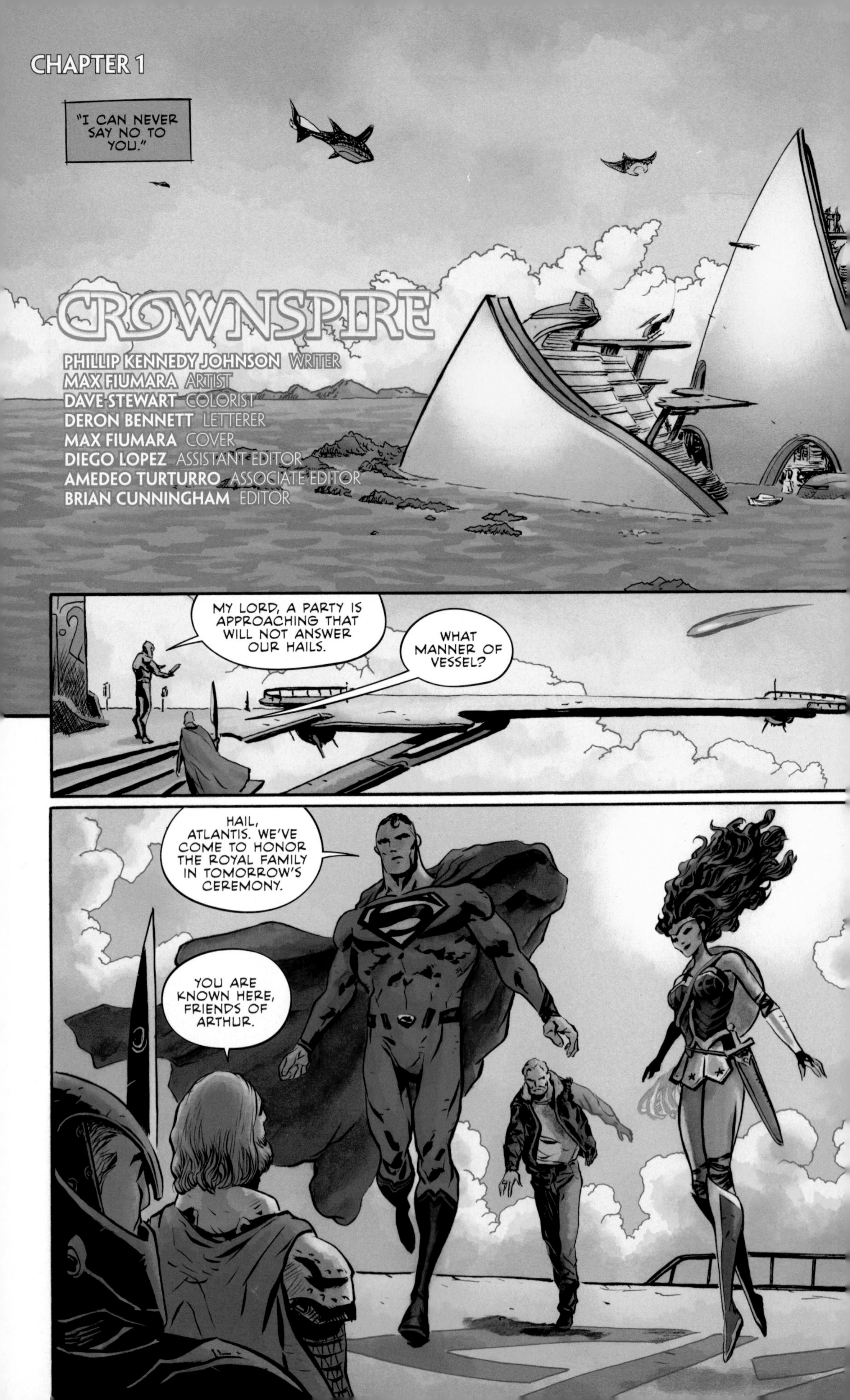
"I CAN NEVER SAY NO TO YOU."
MY LORD, A PARTY IS APPROACHING THAT WILL NOT ANSWER OUR HAILS.
WHAT MANNER OF VESSEL?
HAIL, ATLANTIS. WE'VE COME TO HONOR THE ROYAL FAMILY IN TOMORROW'S CEREMONY.
YOU ARE KNOWN HERE, FRIENDS OF ARTHUR.

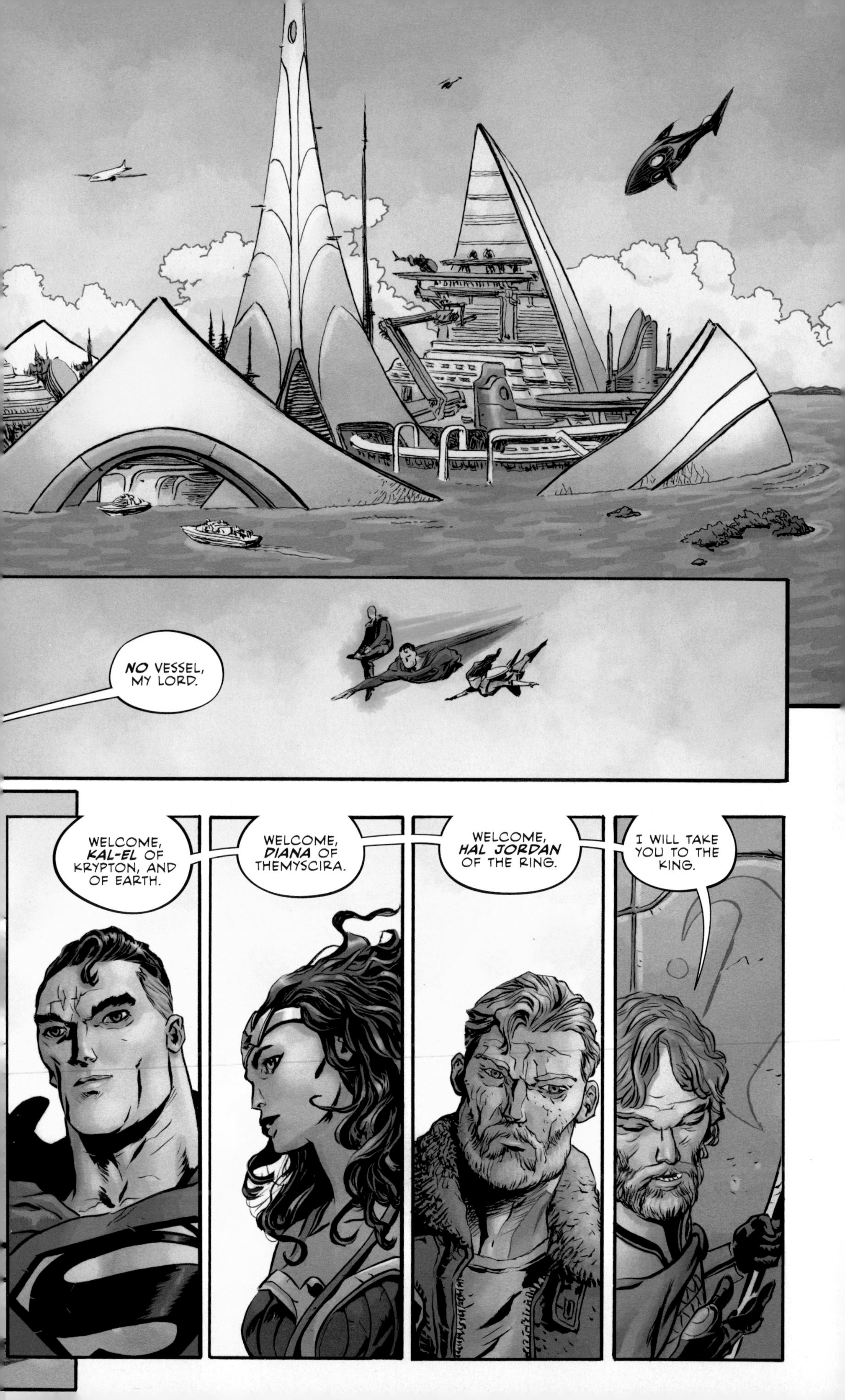
NO VESSEL, MY LORD.
WELCOME, KAL-EL OF KRYPTON, AND OF EARTH.
WELCOME, DIANA OF THEMYSCIRA.
WELCOME, HAL JORDAN OF THE RING.
I WILL TAKE YOU TO THE KING.

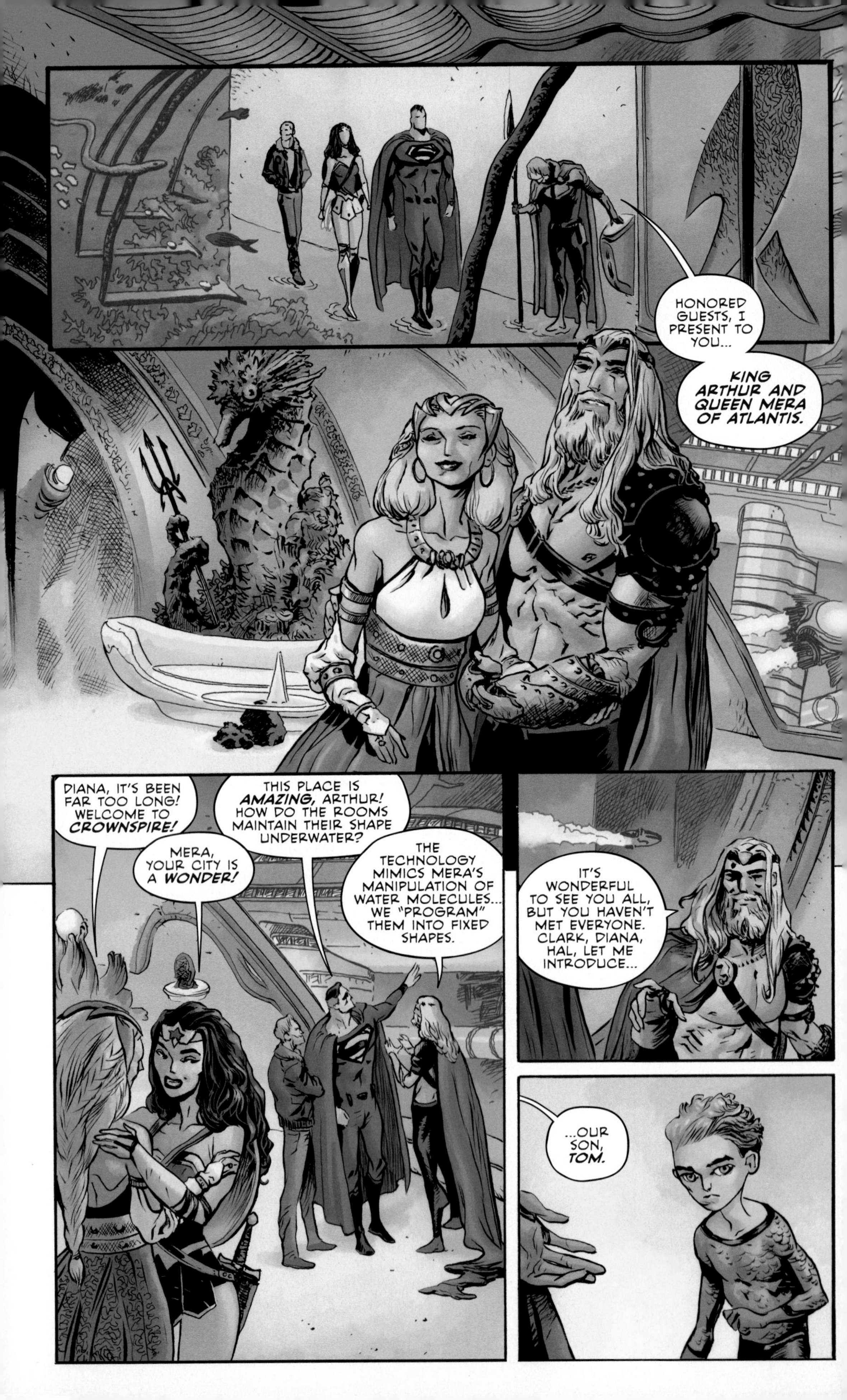
HONORED GUESTS, I PRESENT TO YOU...
KING ARTHUR AND QUEEN MERA OF ATLANTIS.
DIANA, IT'S BEEN FAR TOO LONG! WELCOME TO CROWNSPIRE!
MERA, YOUR CITY IS A WONDER!
THIS PLACE IS AMAZING, ARTHUR! HOW DO THE ROOMS MAINTAIN THEIR SHAPE UNDERWATER?
THE TECHNOLOGY MIMICS MERA'S MANIPULATION OF WATER MOLECULES... WE "PROGRAM" THEM INTO FIXED SHAPES.
IT'S WONDERFUL TO SEE YOU ALL, BUT YOU HAVEN'T MET EVERYONE. CLARK, DIANA, HAL, LET ME INTRODUCE...
...OUR SON, TOM.

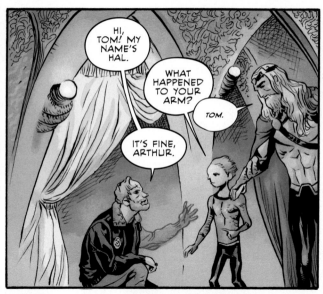

HI, TOM! MY NAME'S HAL.

WHAT HAPPENED TO YOUR ARM?

TOM.

IT'S FINE, ARTHUR.

I *LOST* IT, SO I MADE A NEW ONE.

WOULD YOU LIKE ONE, TOO?

YOU'VE GOT A BEAUTIFUL FAMILY, ARTHUR. HOW OLD IS TOM NOW?

TWELVE THIS WEEK. IT'S THE AGE WHEN MOST ATLANTEANS CHOOSE AN ANIMAL... WE'LL TAKE HIM TO THE LIGHTHOUSE, MAYBE FIND A DOLPHIN CALF FOR HIM.

BRUCE... SENDS HIS REGRETS HE COULDN'T COME.

BRUCE WAS NEVER ONE FOR SOCIAL CALLS. I DIDN'T EXPECT HIM TO COME FOR A SIMPLE COMING-OF-AGE CEREMONY.

I'M JUST HAPPY TO SEE THE REST OF--

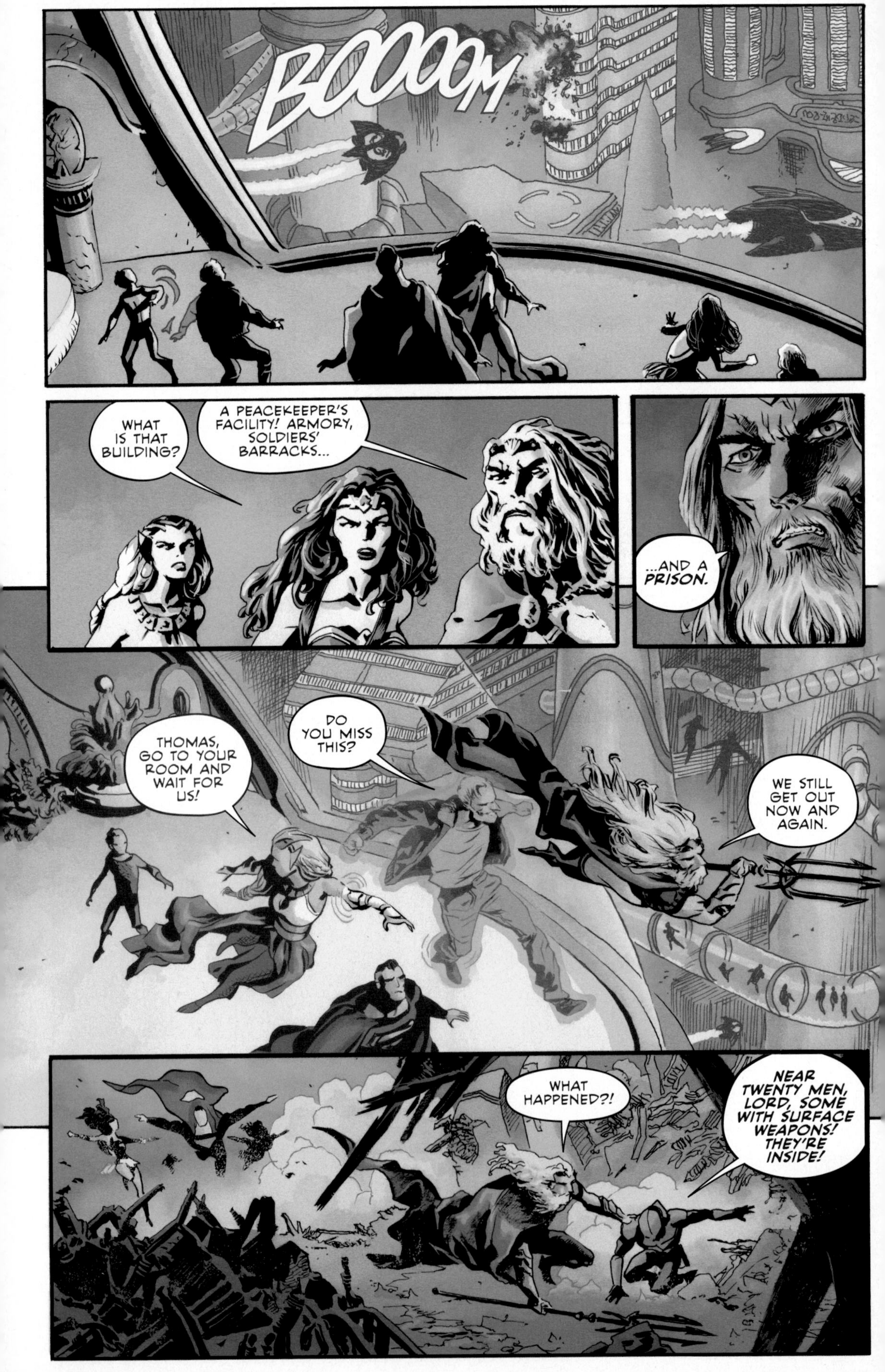
BOOOOM
WHAT IS THAT BUILDING?
A PEACEKEEPER'S FACILITY! ARMORY, SOLDIERS' BARRACKS...
...AND A PRISON.
THOMAS, GO TO YOUR ROOM AND WAIT FOR US!
DO YOU MISS THIS?
WE STILL GET OUT NOW AND AGAIN.
WHAT HAPPENED?!
NEAR TWENTY MEN, LORD, SOME WITH SURFACE WEAPONS! THEY'RE INSIDE!

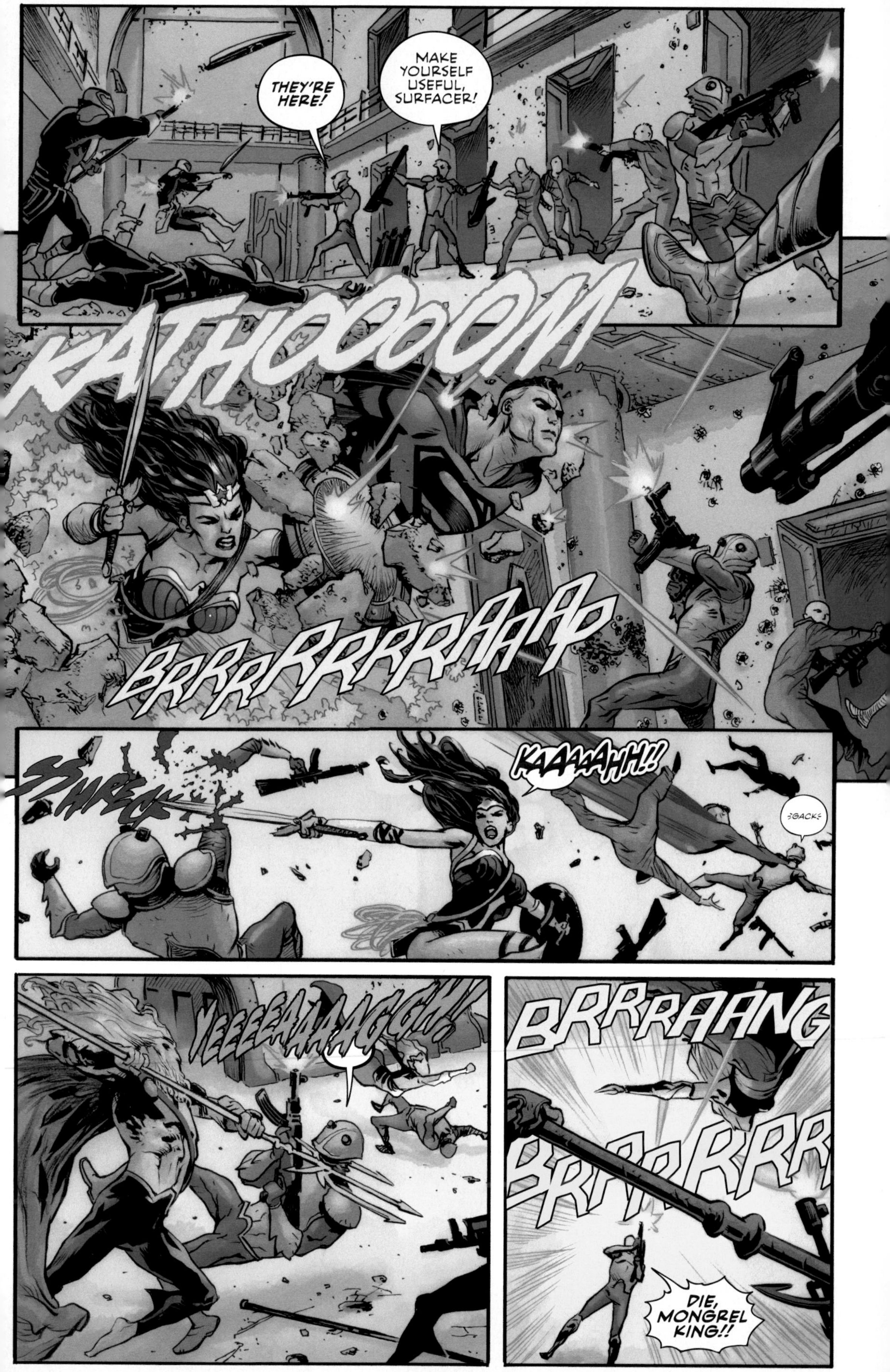
THEY'RE HERE!
MAKE YOURSELF USEFUL, SURFACER!
KATHOOOOM
BRRRRRRRAAAP
SHREK
KAAAAAHH!!
GACK
YEEEEAAAAGGH!
BRRRAANG
BRRRRRR
DIE, MONGREL KING!!

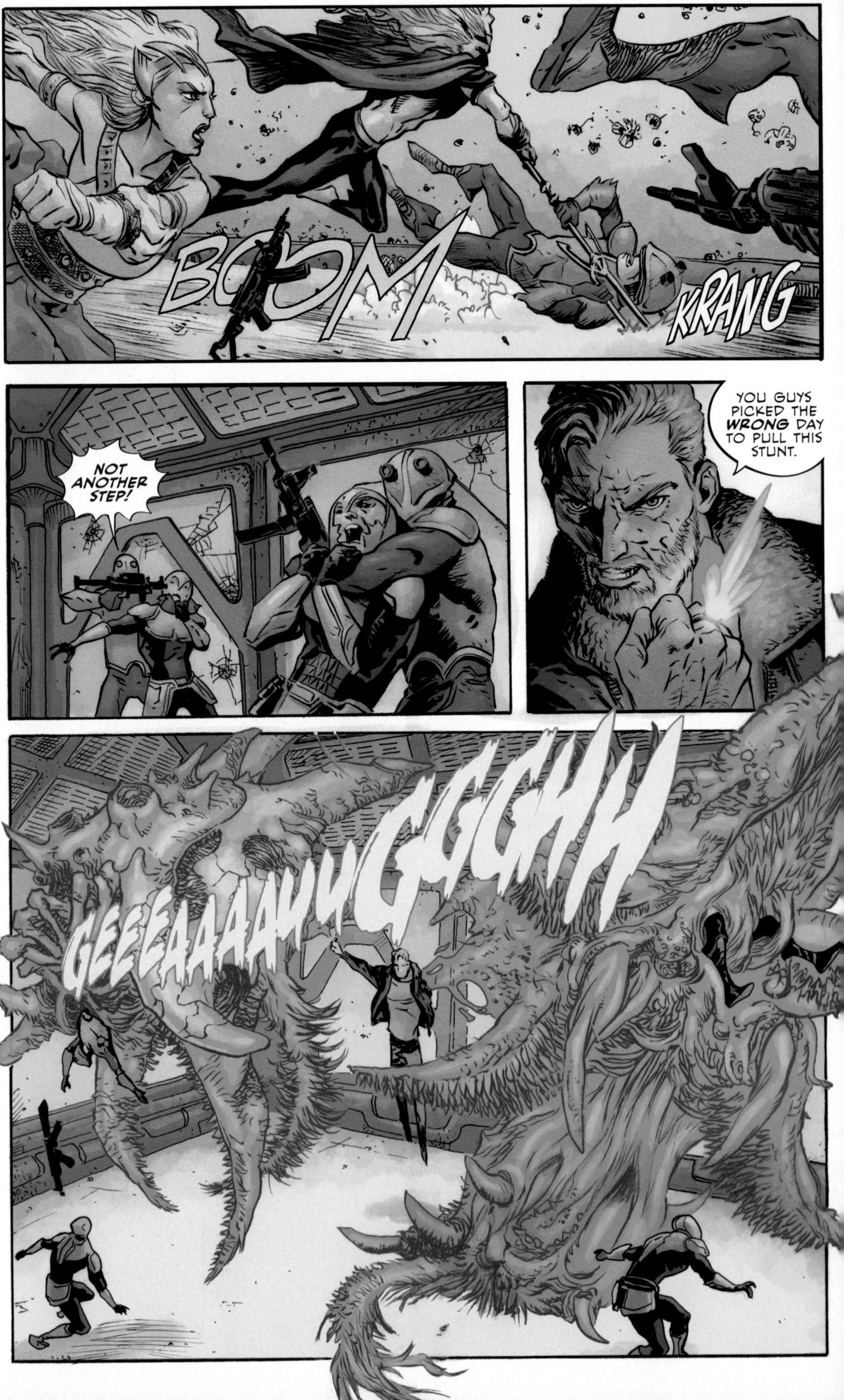
BOOM
KRANG
NOT ANOTHER STEP!
YOU GUYS PICKED THE **WRONG** DAY TO PULL THIS STUNT.
GEEEAAAAUUGGGHH

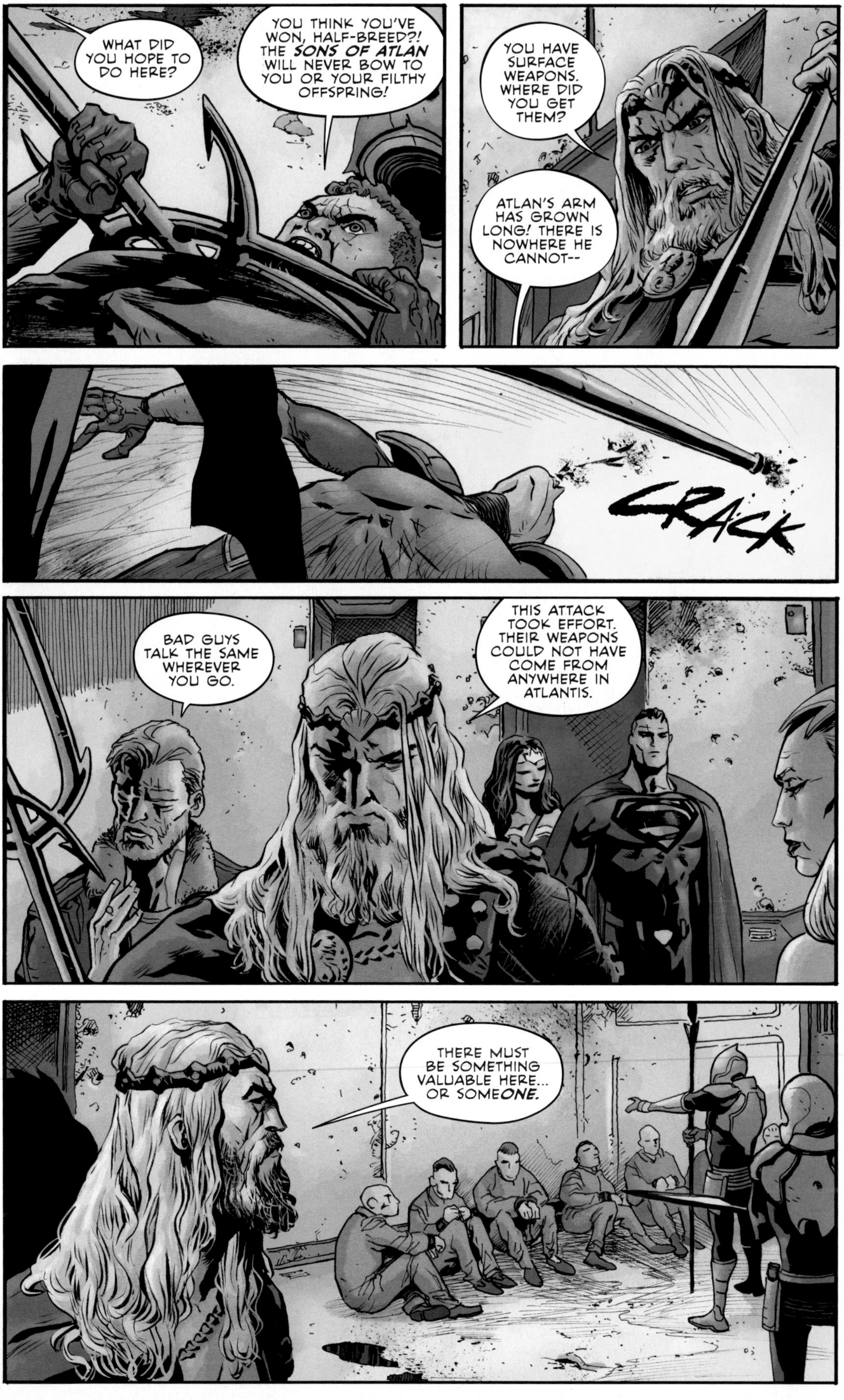
WHAT DID YOU HOPE TO DO HERE?
YOU THINK YOU'VE WON, HALF-BREED?! THE ***SONS OF ATLAN*** WILL NEVER BOW TO YOU OR YOUR FILTHY OFFSPRING!
YOU HAVE SURFACE WEAPONS. WHERE DID YOU GET THEM?
ATLAN'S ARM HAS GROWN LONG! THERE IS NOWHERE HE CANNOT--
CRACK
BAD GUYS TALK THE SAME WHEREVER YOU GO.
THIS ATTACK TOOK EFFORT. THEIR WEAPONS COULD NOT HAVE COME FROM ANYWHERE IN ATLANTIS.
THERE MUST BE SOMETHING VALUABLE HERE... OR SOME***ONE.***

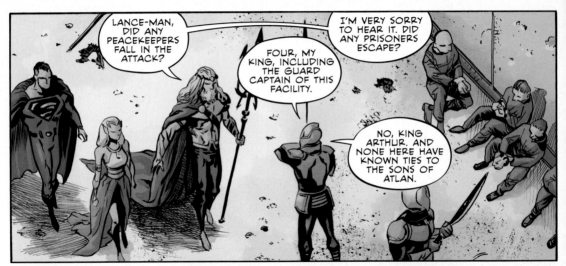

LANCE-MAN, DID ANY PEACEKEEPERS FALL IN THE ATTACK?

I'M VERY SORRY TO HEAR IT. DID ANY PRISONERS ESCAPE?

FOUR, MY KING, INCLUDING THE GUARD CAPTAIN OF THIS FACILITY.

NO, KING ARTHUR. AND NONE HERE HAVE KNOWN TIES TO THE SONS OF ATLAN.

NOTHING ELSE THEY MIGHT HAVE BEEN AFTER?

NOT THAT WE KNOW, MY KING.

LANCE-MAN?

WHERE DOES *THIS* LEAD?

JUST A STORAGE CLOSET, MY QUEEN. I'VE NEVER SEEN IT OPEN--ONLY THE GUARD CAPTAIN HAD ACCESS TO...

TO...

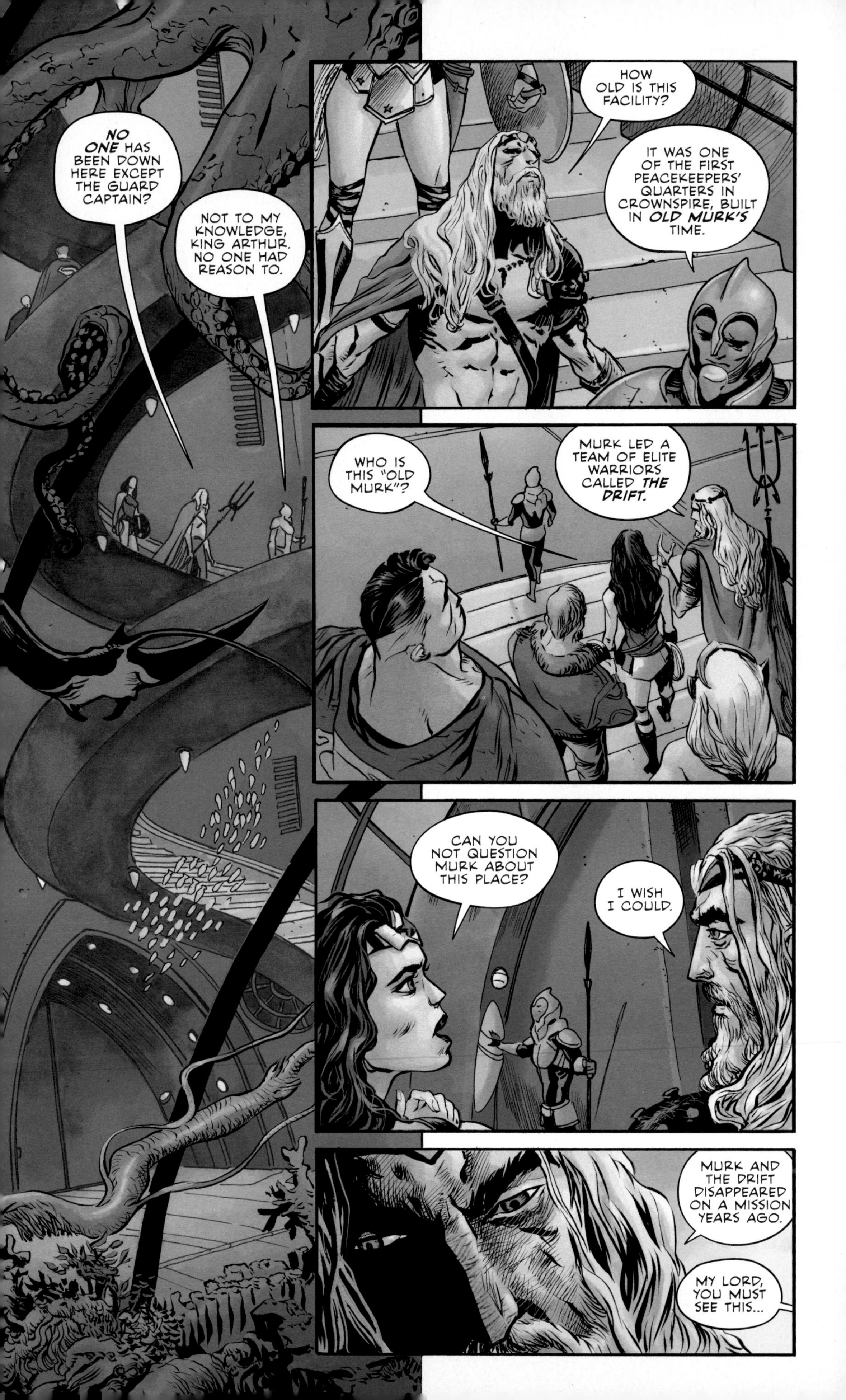
NO ONE HAS BEEN DOWN HERE EXCEPT THE GUARD CAPTAIN?
NOT TO MY KNOWLEDGE, KING ARTHUR. NO ONE HAD REASON TO.
HOW OLD IS THIS FACILITY?
IT WAS ONE OF THE FIRST PEACEKEEPERS' QUARTERS IN CROWNSPIRE, BUILT IN OLD MURK'S TIME.
WHO IS THIS "OLD MURK"?
MURK LED A TEAM OF ELITE WARRIORS CALLED THE DRIFT.
CAN YOU NOT QUESTION MURK ABOUT THIS PLACE?
I WISH I COULD.
MURK AND THE DRIFT DISAPPEARED ON A MISSION YEARS AGO.
MY LORD, YOU MUST SEE THIS...

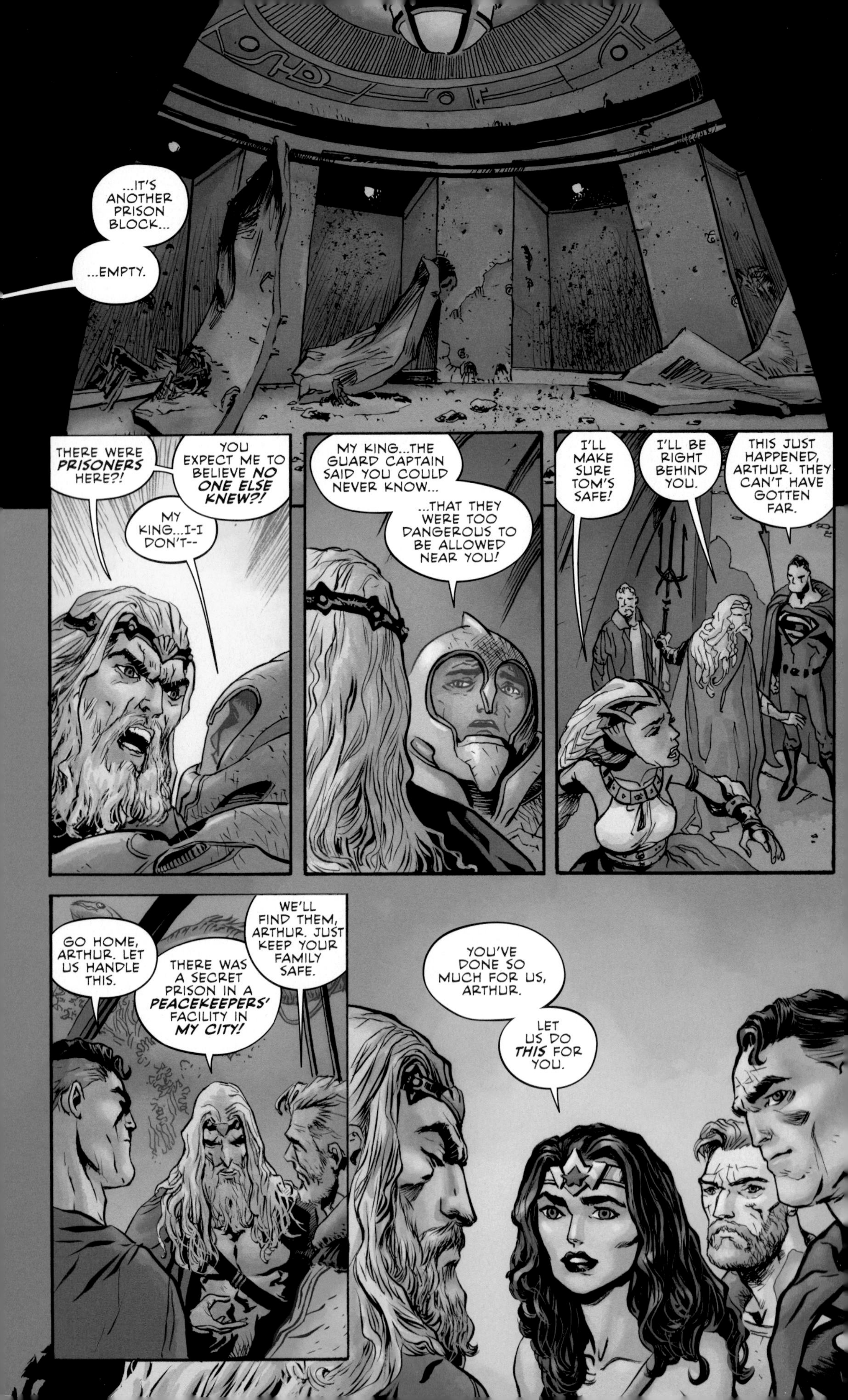
...IT'S ANOTHER PRISON BLOCK...
...EMPTY.
THERE WERE PRISONERS HERE?!
YOU EXPECT ME TO BELIEVE NO ONE ELSE KNEW?!
MY KING...I-I DON'T--
MY KING...THE GUARD CAPTAIN SAID YOU COULD NEVER KNOW...
...THAT THEY WERE TOO DANGEROUS TO BE ALLOWED NEAR YOU!
I'LL MAKE SURE TOM'S SAFE!
I'LL BE RIGHT BEHIND YOU.
THIS JUST HAPPENED, ARTHUR. THEY CAN'T HAVE GOTTEN FAR.
GO HOME, ARTHUR. LET US HANDLE THIS.
THERE WAS A SECRET PRISON IN A PEACEKEEPERS' FACILITY IN MY CITY!
WE'LL FIND THEM, ARTHUR. JUST KEEP YOUR FAMILY SAFE.
YOU'VE DONE SO MUCH FOR US, ARTHUR.
LET US DO THIS FOR YOU.

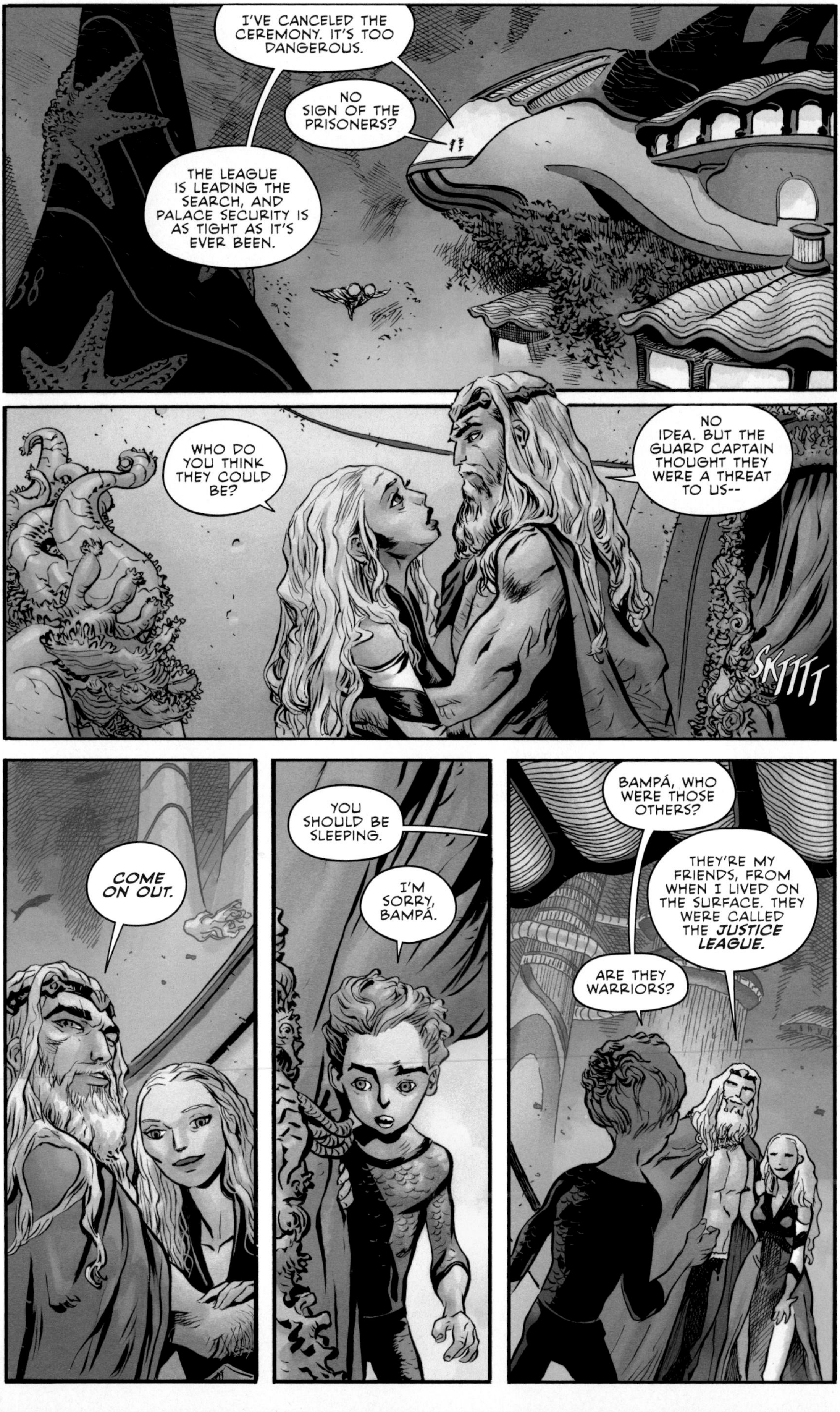

I'VE CANCELED THE CEREMONY. IT'S TOO DANGEROUS.
NO SIGN OF THE PRISONERS?
THE LEAGUE IS LEADING THE SEARCH, AND PALACE SECURITY IS AS TIGHT AS IT'S EVER BEEN.
WHO DO YOU THINK THEY COULD BE?
NO IDEA. BUT THE GUARD CAPTAIN THOUGHT THEY WERE A THREAT TO US--
SKTTTT
COME ON OUT.
YOU SHOULD BE SLEEPING.
I'M SORRY, BAMPÁ.
BAMPÁ, WHO WERE THOSE OTHERS?
THEY'RE MY FRIENDS, FROM WHEN I LIVED ON THE SURFACE. THEY WERE CALLED THE ***JUSTICE LEAGUE.***
ARE THEY WARRIORS?

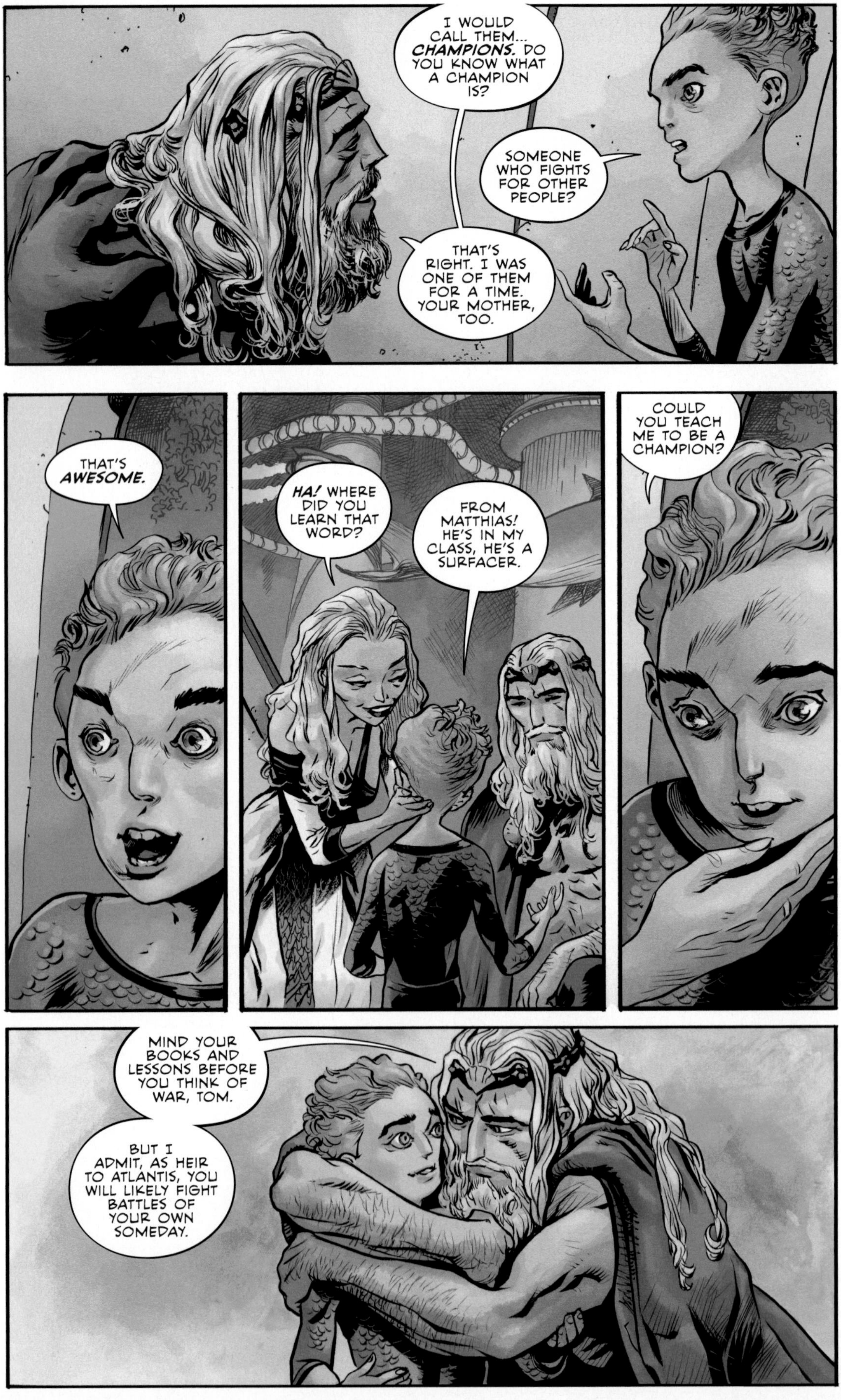
I WOULD CALL THEM... CHAMPIONS. DO YOU KNOW WHAT A CHAMPION IS?
SOMEONE WHO FIGHTS FOR OTHER PEOPLE?
THAT'S RIGHT. I WAS ONE OF THEM FOR A TIME. YOUR MOTHER, TOO.
THAT'S AWESOME.
HA! WHERE DID YOU LEARN THAT WORD?
FROM MATTHIAS! HE'S IN MY CLASS, HE'S A SURFACER.
COULD YOU TEACH ME TO BE A CHAMPION?
MIND YOUR BOOKS AND LESSONS BEFORE YOU THINK OF WAR, TOM.
BUT I ADMIT, AS HEIR TO ATLANTIS, YOU WILL LIKELY FIGHT BATTLES OF YOUR OWN SOMEDAY.

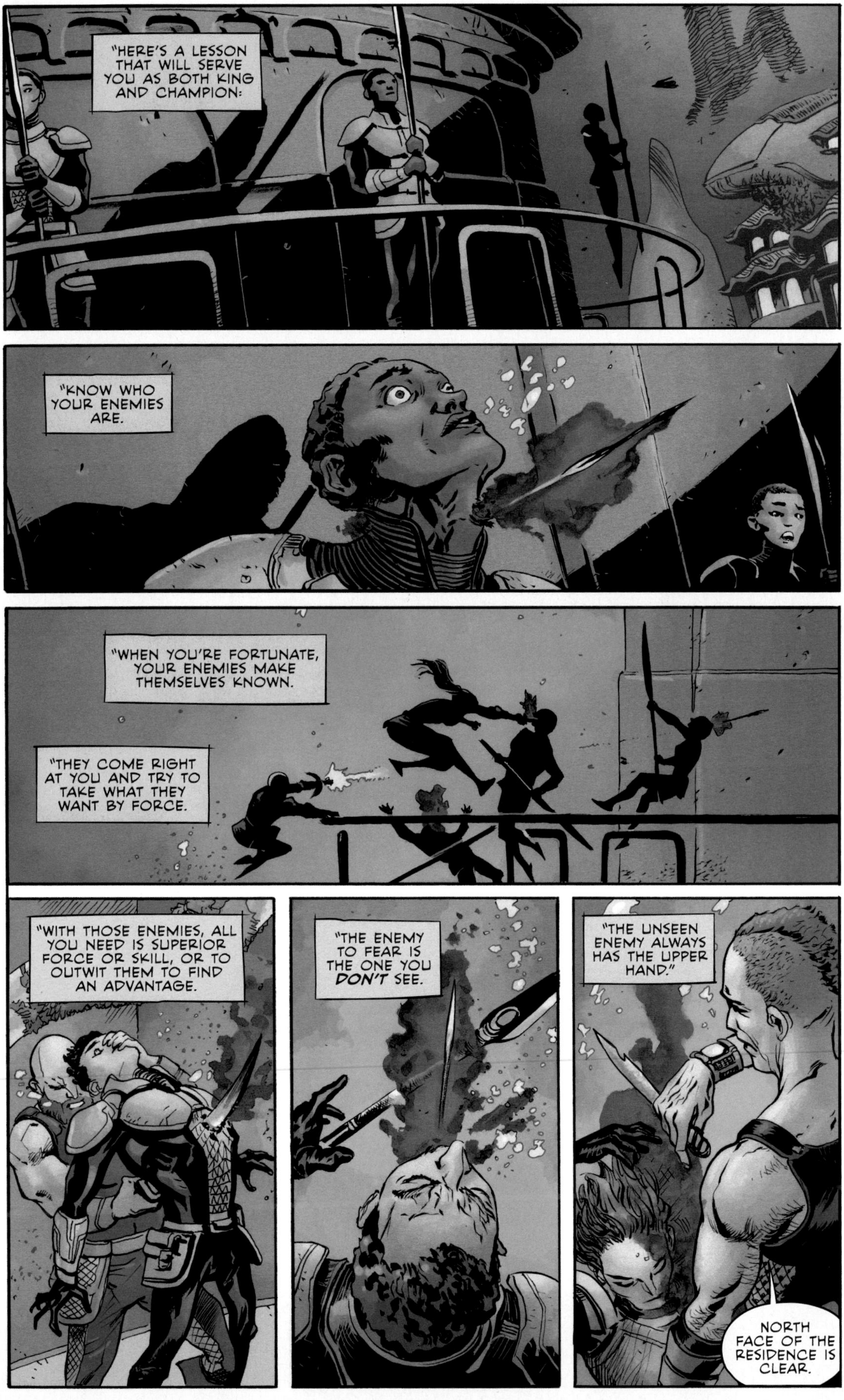
"HERE'S A LESSON THAT WILL SERVE YOU AS BOTH KING AND CHAMPION:
"KNOW WHO YOUR ENEMIES ARE.
"WHEN YOU'RE FORTUNATE, YOUR ENEMIES MAKE THEMSELVES KNOWN.
"THEY COME RIGHT AT YOU AND TRY TO TAKE WHAT THEY WANT BY FORCE.
"WITH THOSE ENEMIES, ALL YOU NEED IS SUPERIOR FORCE OR SKILL, OR TO OUTWIT THEM TO FIND AN ADVANTAGE.
"THE ENEMY TO FEAR IS THE ONE YOU *DON'T* SEE.
"THE UNSEEN ENEMY ALWAYS HAS THE UPPER HAND."
NORTH FACE OF THE RESIDENCE IS CLEAR.

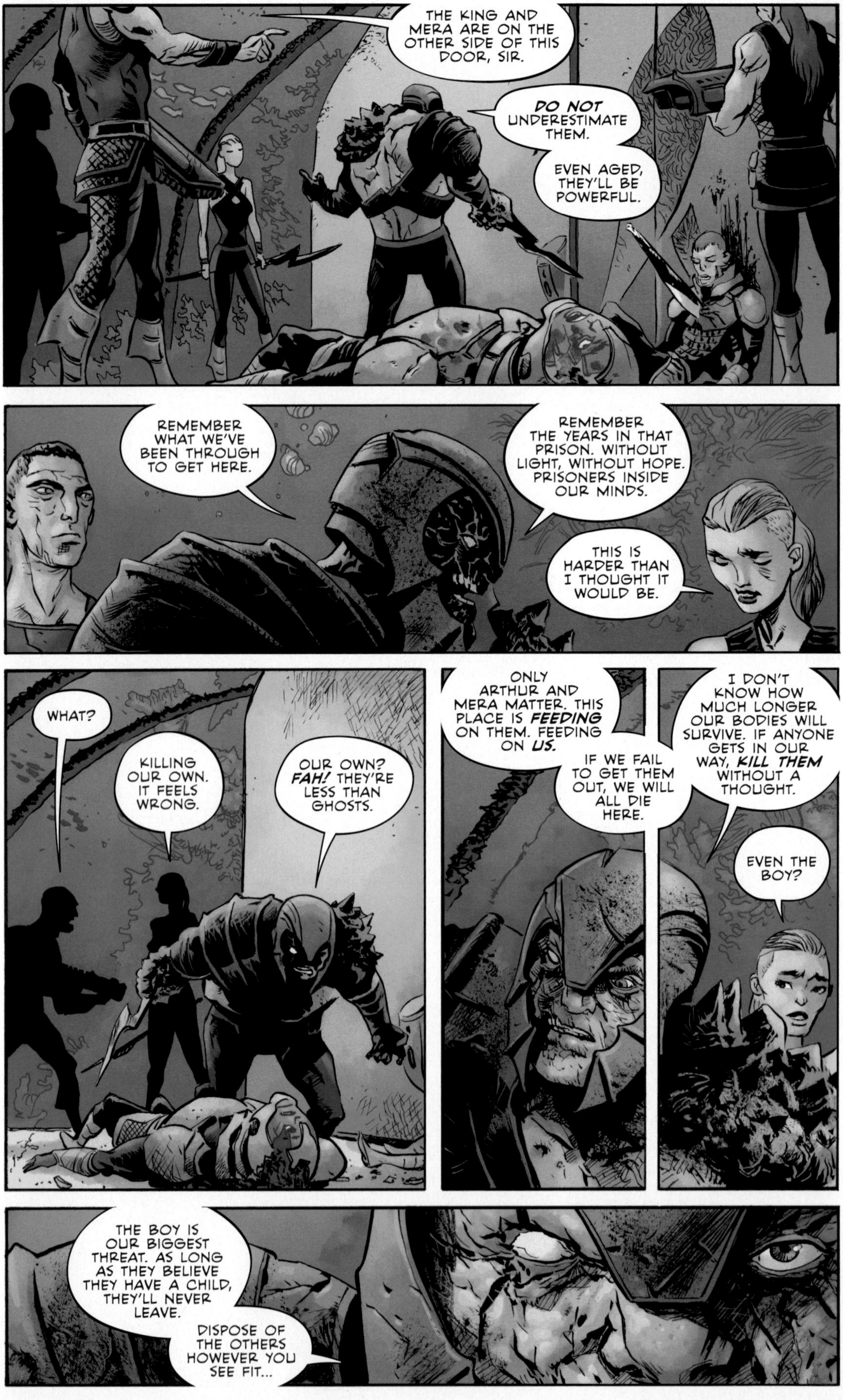
THE KING AND MERA ARE ON THE OTHER SIDE OF THIS DOOR, SIR.
DO NOT UNDERESTIMATE THEM.
EVEN AGED, THEY'LL BE POWERFUL.
REMEMBER WHAT WE'VE BEEN THROUGH TO GET HERE.
REMEMBER THE YEARS IN THAT PRISON. WITHOUT LIGHT, WITHOUT HOPE. PRISONERS INSIDE OUR MINDS.
THIS IS HARDER THAN I THOUGHT IT WOULD BE.
WHAT?
KILLING OUR OWN. IT FEELS WRONG.
OUR OWN? *FAH!* THEY'RE LESS THAN GHOSTS.
ONLY ARTHUR AND MERA MATTER. THIS PLACE IS *FEEDING* ON THEM. FEEDING ON *US.*
IF WE FAIL TO GET THEM OUT, WE WILL ALL DIE HERE.
I DON'T KNOW HOW MUCH LONGER OUR BODIES WILL SURVIVE. IF ANYONE GETS IN OUR WAY, *KILL THEM* WITHOUT A THOUGHT.
EVEN THE BOY?
THE BOY IS OUR BIGGEST THREAT. AS LONG AS THEY BELIEVE THEY HAVE A CHILD, THEY'LL NEVER LEAVE.
DISPOSE OF THE OTHERS HOWEVER YOU SEE FIT...

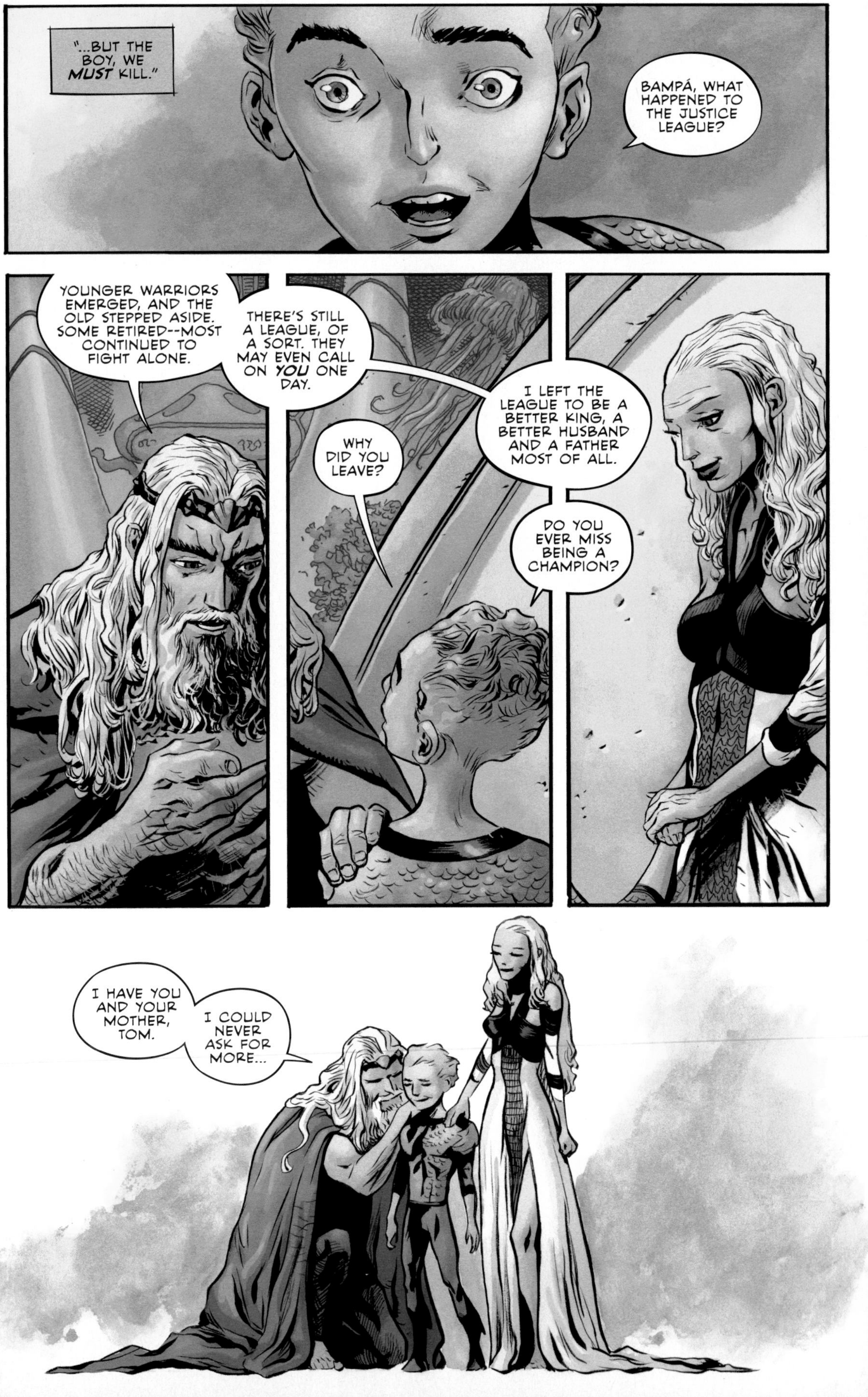
"...BUT THE BOY, WE *MUST* KILL."
BAMPÁ, WHAT HAPPENED TO THE JUSTICE LEAGUE?
YOUNGER WARRIORS EMERGED, AND THE OLD STEPPED ASIDE. SOME RETIRED--MOST CONTINUED TO FIGHT ALONE.
THERE'S STILL A LEAGUE, OF A SORT. THEY MAY EVEN CALL ON *YOU* ONE DAY.
WHY DID YOU LEAVE?
I LEFT THE LEAGUE TO BE A BETTER KING, A BETTER HUSBAND AND A FATHER MOST OF ALL.
DO YOU EVER MISS BEING A CHAMPION?
I HAVE YOU AND YOUR MOTHER, TOM.
I COULD NEVER ASK FOR MORE...

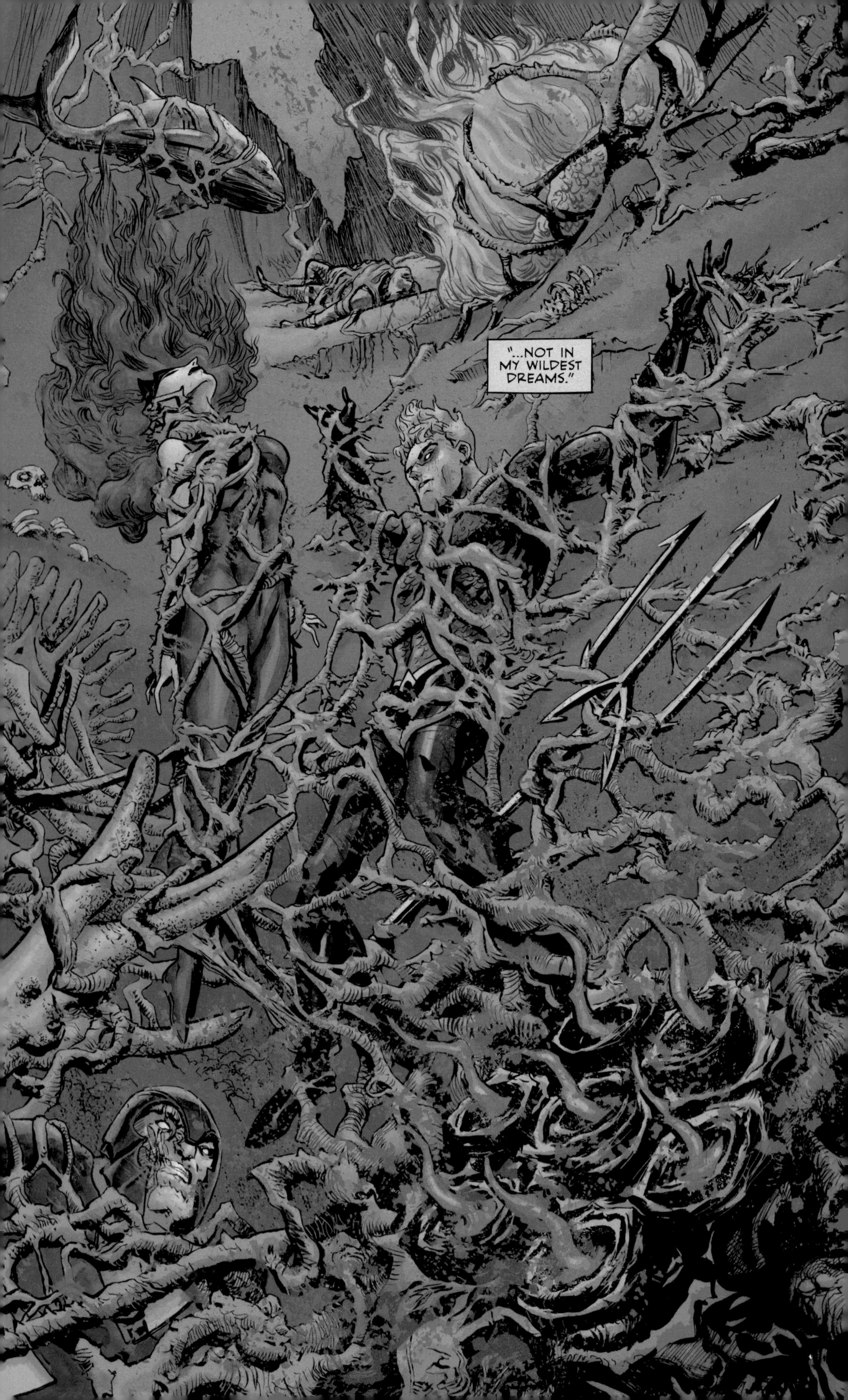
"...NOT IN MY WILDEST DREAMS."

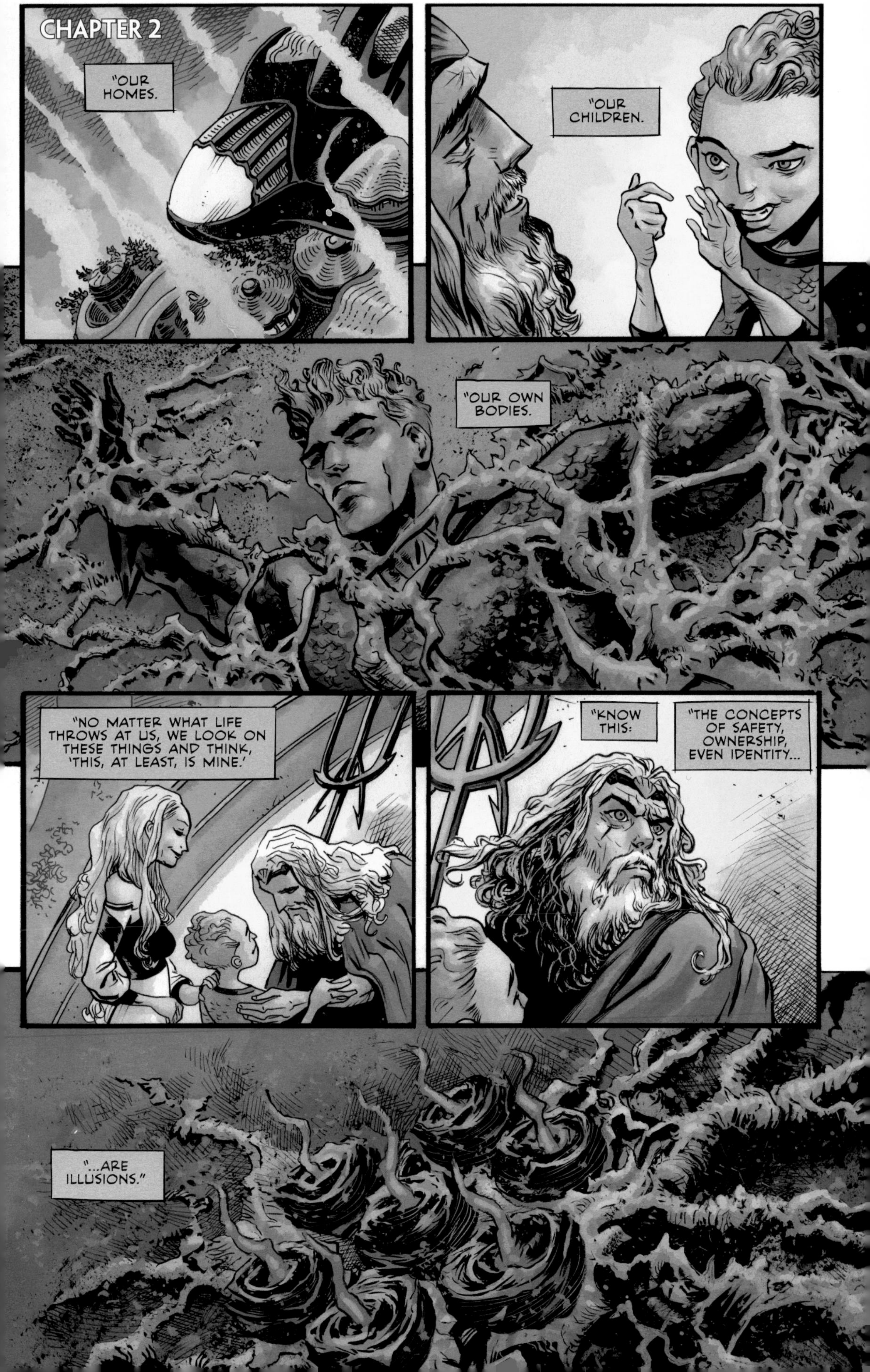
CHAPTER 2
"OUR HOMES.
"OUR CHILDREN.
"OUR OWN BODIES.
"NO MATTER WHAT LIFE THROWS AT US, WE LOOK ON THESE THINGS AND THINK, 'THIS, AT LEAST, IS MINE.'
"KNOW THIS:
"THE CONCEPTS OF SAFETY, OWNERSHIP, EVEN IDENTITY...
"...ARE ILLUSIONS."

"AND THEY ARE LOST AS EASILY AS A PASSING THOUGHT."

I DON'T KNOW HOW YOU GOT IN HERE...

SHRECK

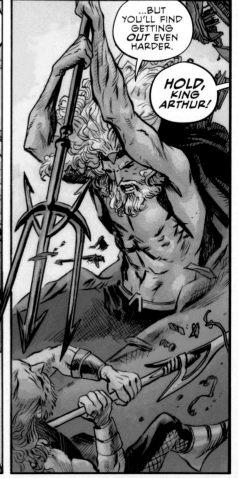

...BUT YOU'LL FIND GETTING *OUT* EVEN HARDER.

HOLD, KING ARTHUR!

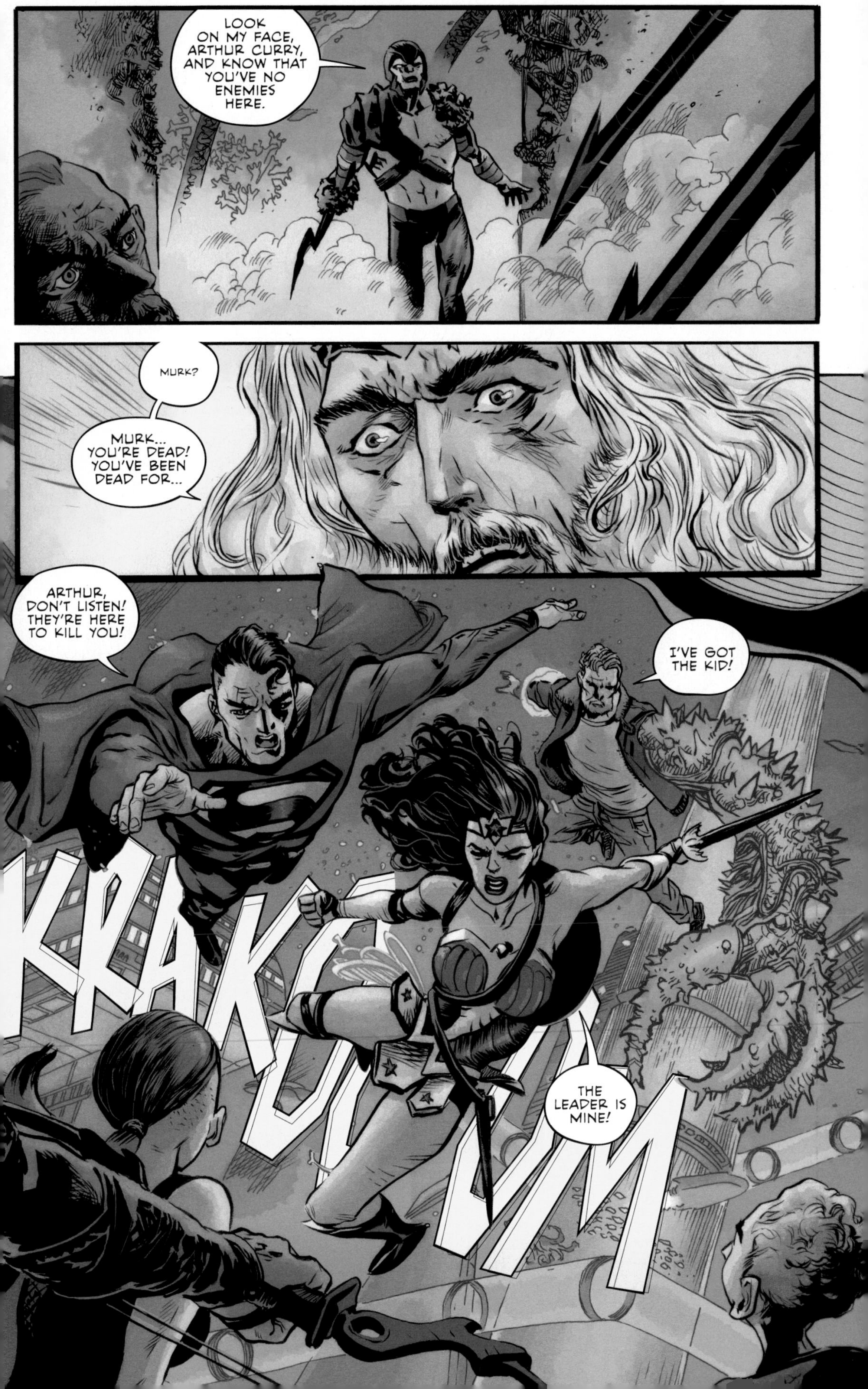
LOOK ON MY FACE, ARTHUR CURRY, AND KNOW THAT YOU'VE NO ENEMIES HERE.
MURK?
MURK... YOU'RE DEAD! YOU'VE BEEN DEAD FOR...
ARTHUR, DON'T LISTEN! THEY'RE HERE TO KILL YOU!
I'VE GOT THE KID!
KRAKOOOM
THE LEADER IS MINE!

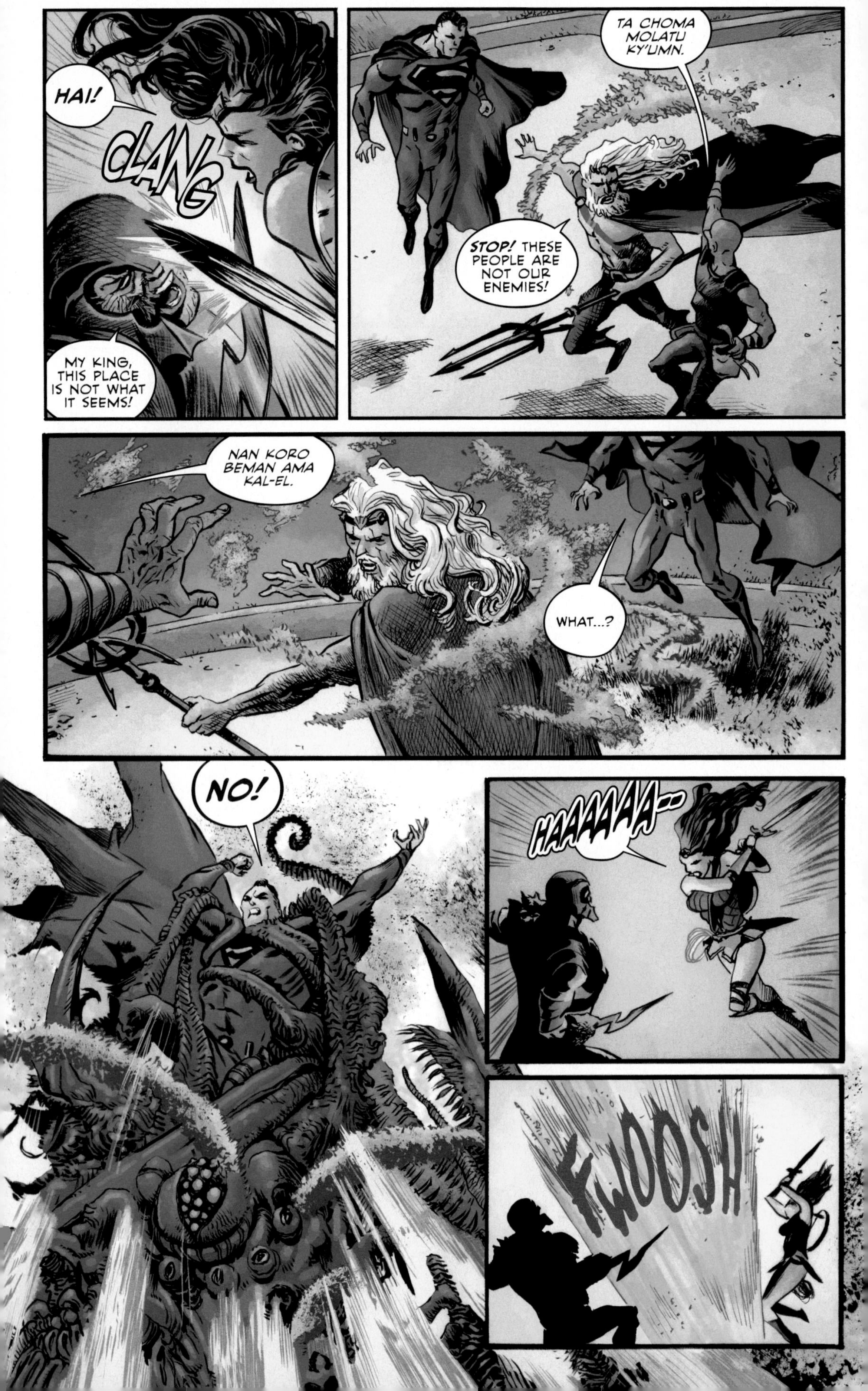

HAI!
CLANG
MY KING, THIS PLACE IS NOT WHAT IT SEEMS!
TA CHOMA MOLATU KY'UMN.
STOP! THESE PEOPLE ARE NOT OUR ENEMIES!
NAN KORO BEMAN AMA KAL-EL.
WHAT...?
NO!
HAAAAAA--
FWOOSH

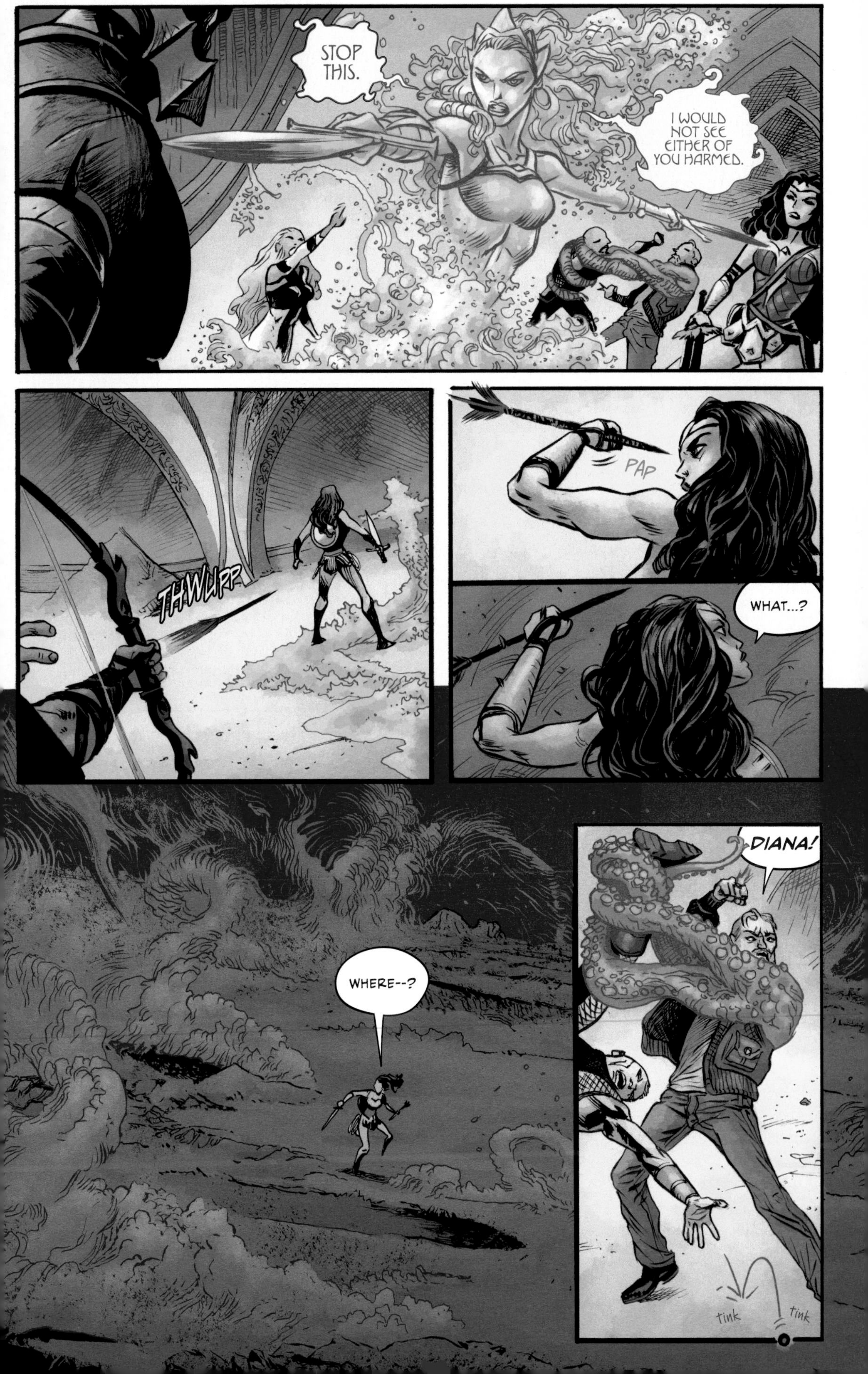
STOP THIS.
I WOULD NOT SEE EITHER OF YOU HARMED.
THWUPP
PAP
WHAT...?
WHERE--?
DIANA!
tink
tink

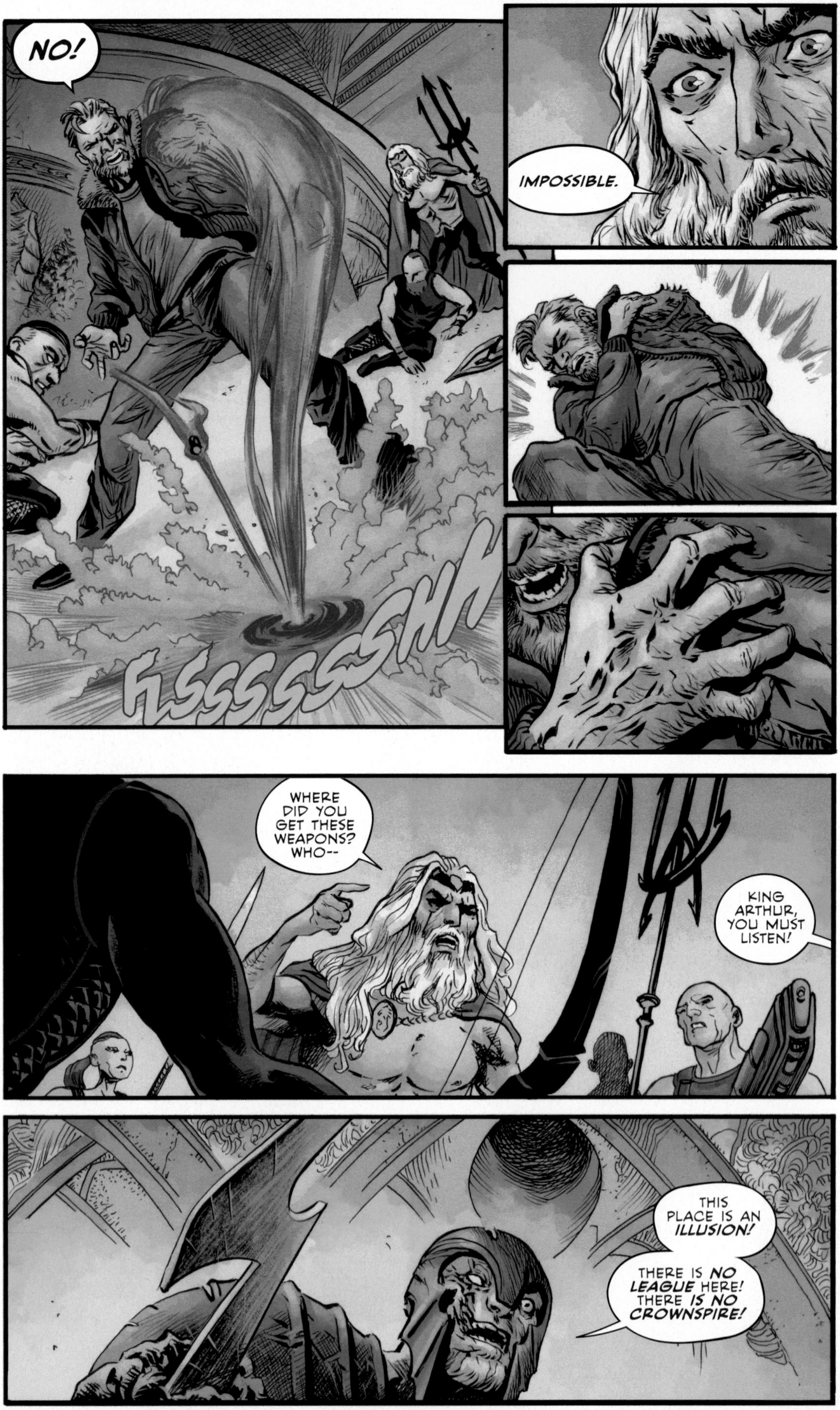
NO!
FSSSSSSSHH
IMPOSSIBLE.
WHERE DID YOU GET THESE WEAPONS? WHO--
KING ARTHUR, YOU MUST LISTEN!
THIS PLACE IS AN ILLUSION!
THERE IS NO LEAGUE HERE! THERE IS NO CROWNSPIRE!

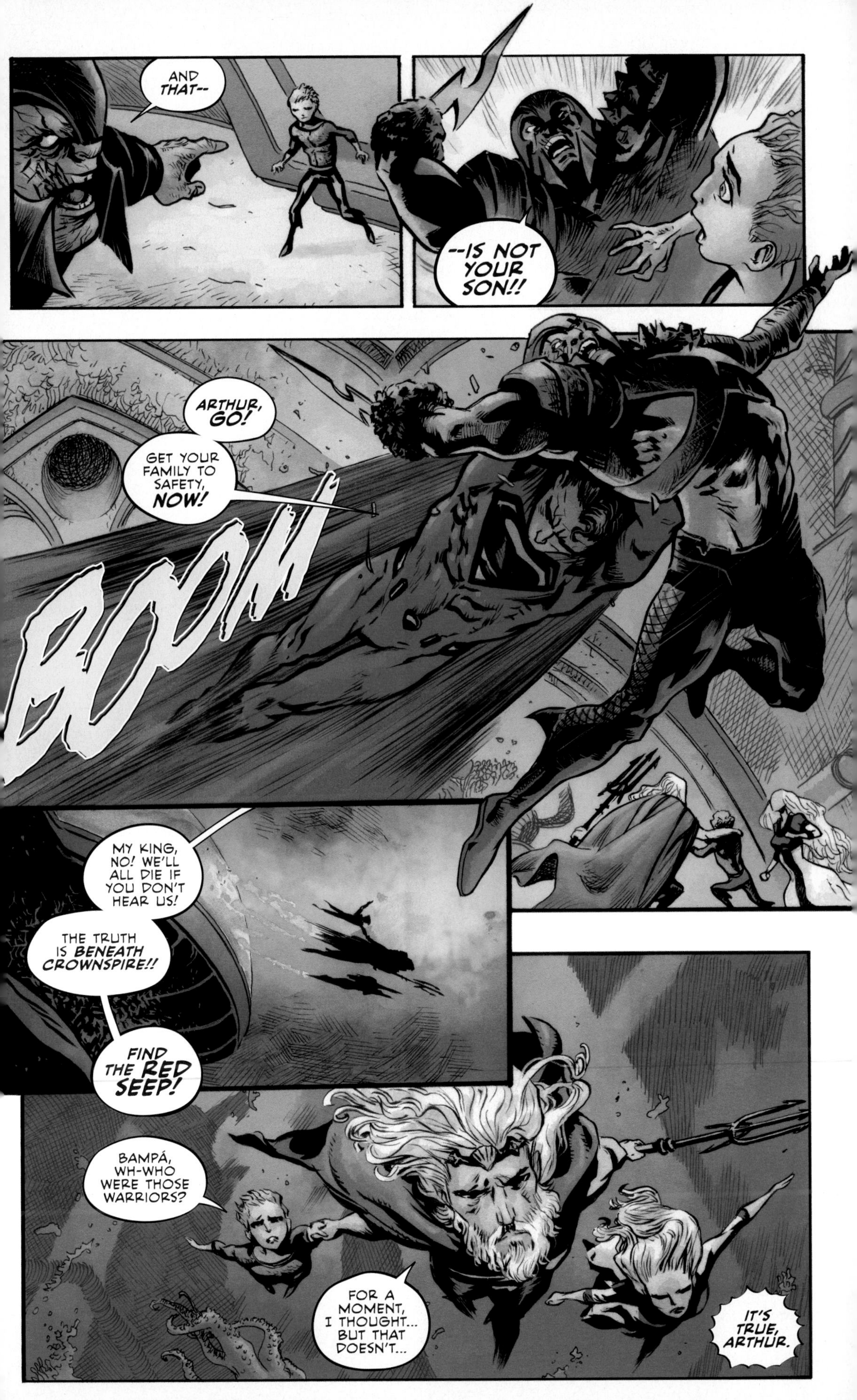
AND THAT--
--IS NOT YOUR SON!!
ARTHUR, GO!
GET YOUR FAMILY TO SAFETY, NOW!
BOOM
MY KING, NO! WE'LL ALL DIE IF YOU DON'T HEAR US!
THE TRUTH IS BENEATH CROWNSPIRE!!
FIND THE RED SEEP!
BAMPÁ, WH-WHO WERE THOSE WARRIORS?
FOR A MOMENT, I THOUGHT... BUT THAT DOESN'T...
IT'S TRUE, ARTHUR.

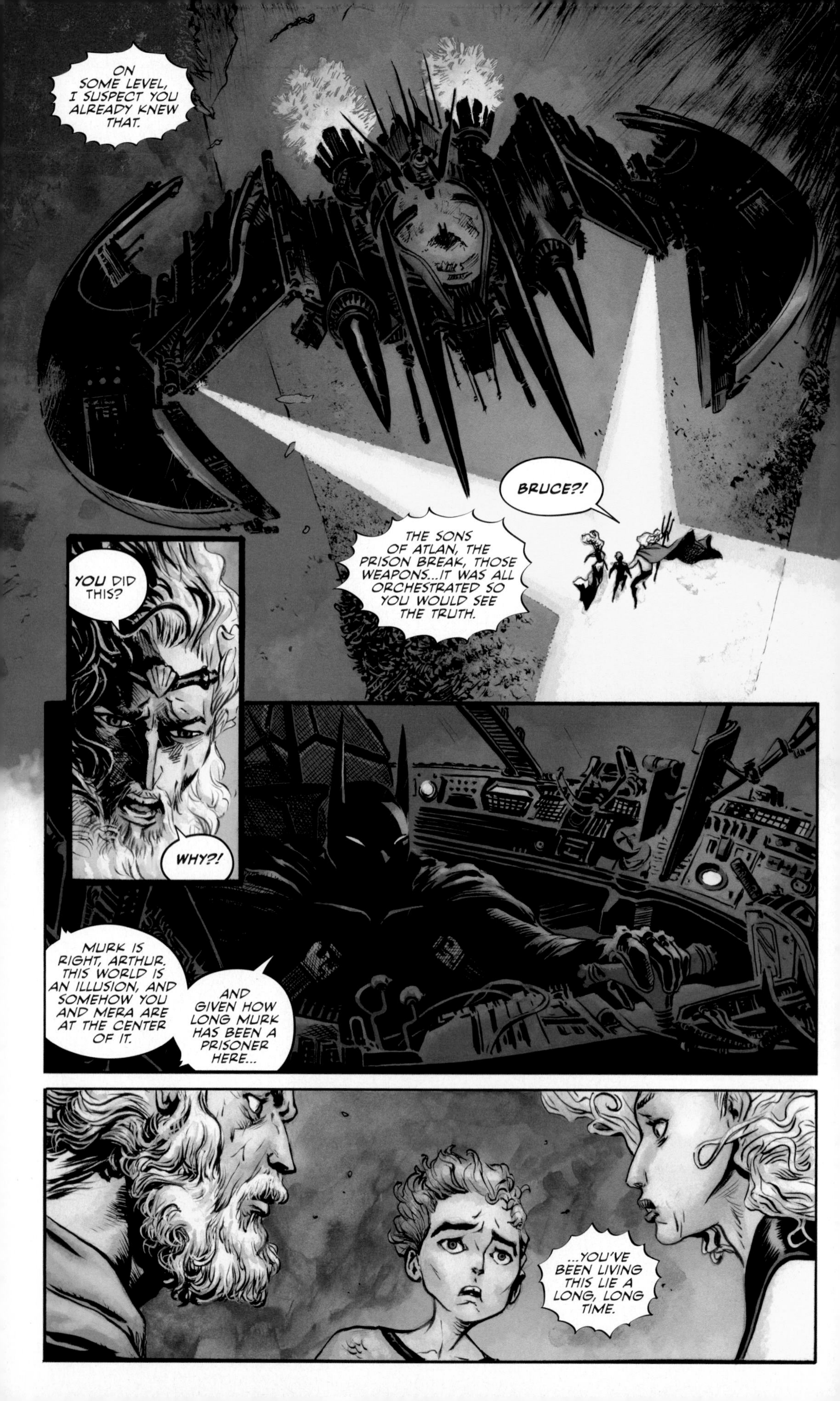

ON SOME LEVEL, I SUSPECT YOU ALREADY KNEW THAT.
BRUCE?!
THE SONS OF ATLAN, THE PRISON BREAK, THOSE WEAPONS...IT WAS ALL ORCHESTRATED SO YOU WOULD SEE THE TRUTH.
YOU DID THIS?
WHY?!
MURK IS RIGHT, ARTHUR. THIS WORLD IS AN ILLUSION, AND SOMEHOW YOU AND MERA ARE AT THE CENTER OF IT.
AND GIVEN HOW LONG MURK HAS BEEN A PRISONER HERE...
...YOU'VE BEEN LIVING THIS LIE A LONG, LONG TIME.

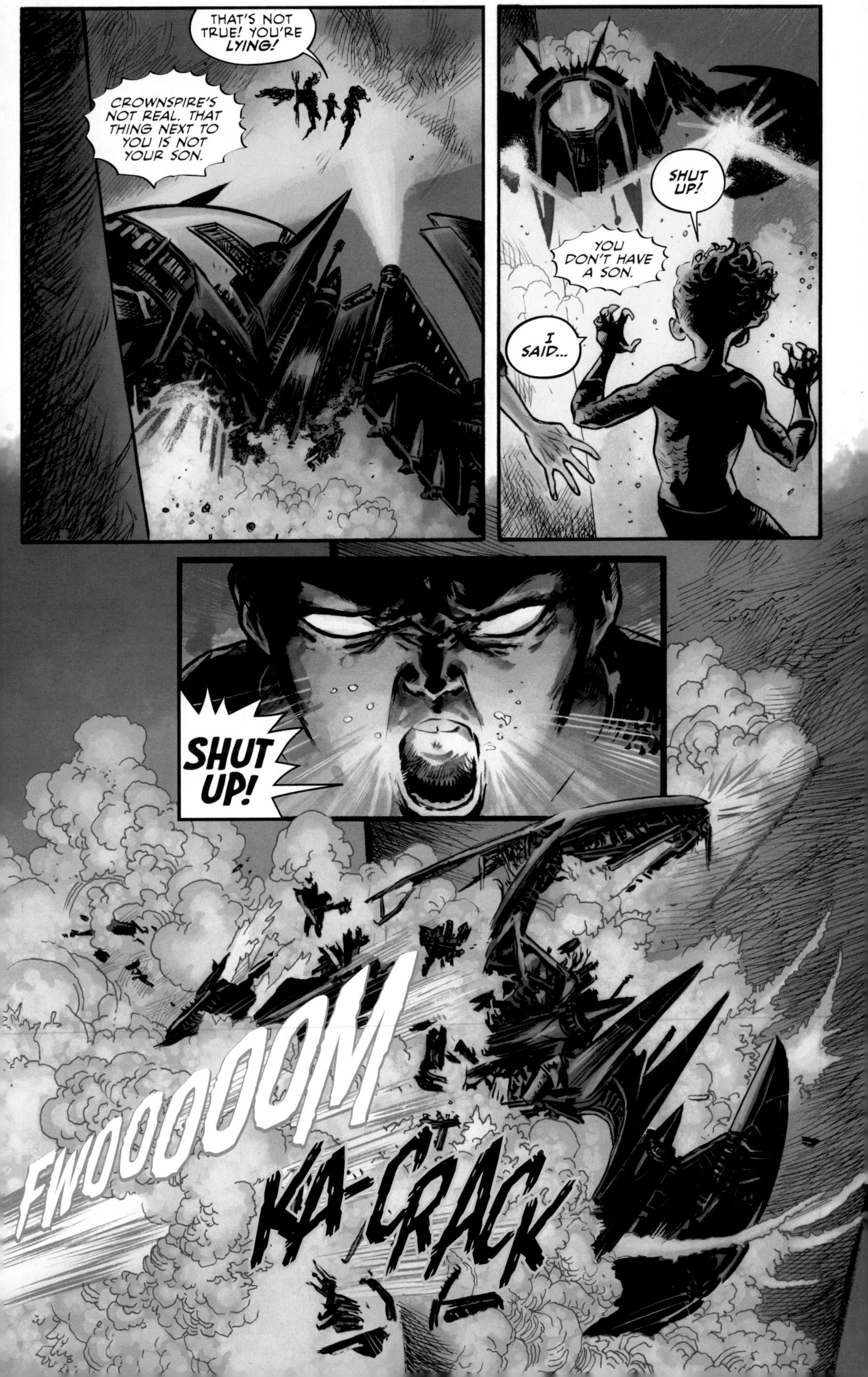

THAT'S NOT TRUE! YOU'RE LYING!
CROWNSPIRE'S NOT REAL. THAT THING NEXT TO YOU IS NOT YOUR SON.
SHUT UP!
YOU DON'T HAVE A SON.
I SAID...
SHUT UP!
FWOOOOOOM
KA-CRACK

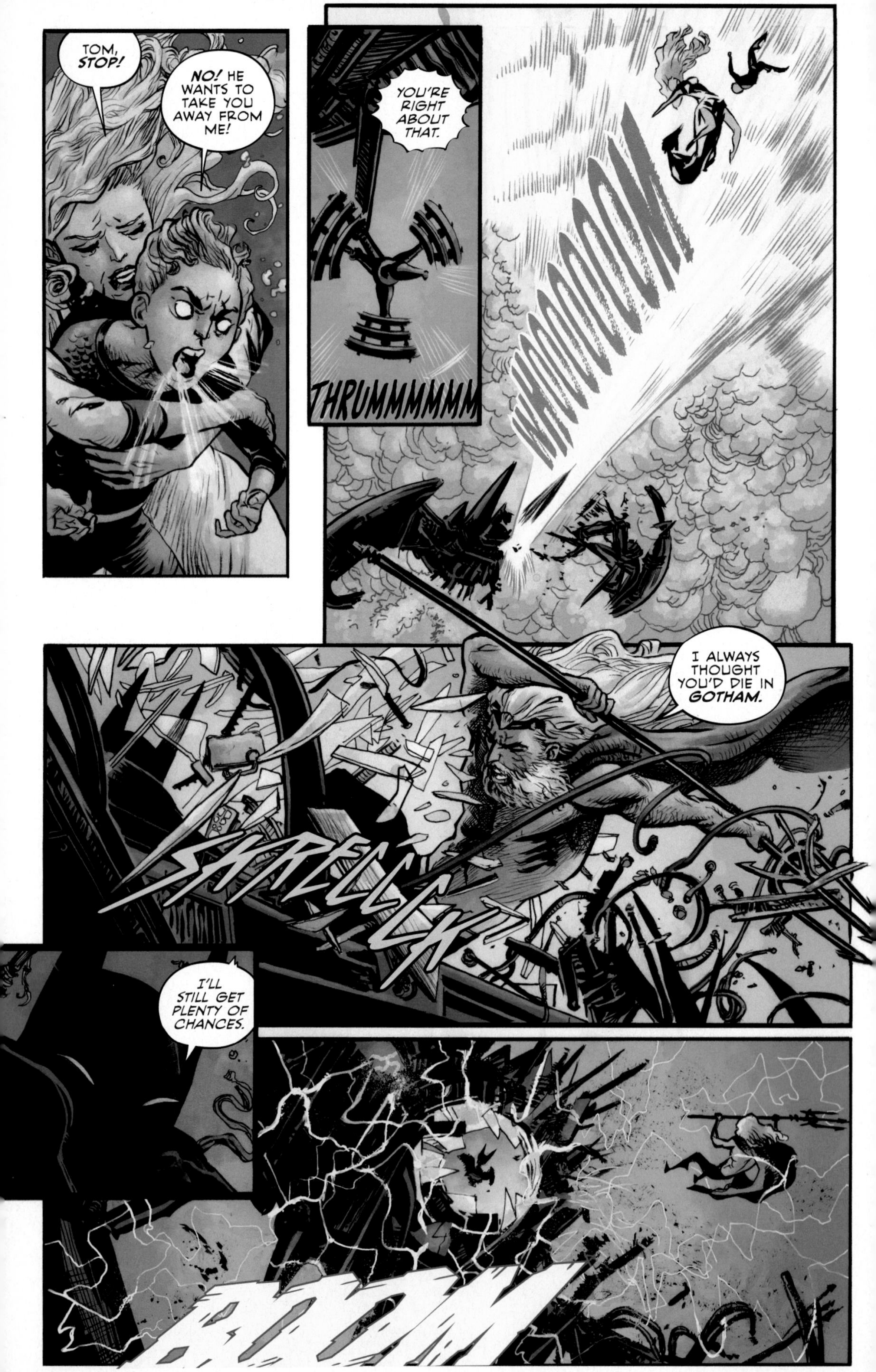
TOM, STOP!
NO! HE WANTS TO TAKE YOU AWAY FROM ME!
YOU'RE RIGHT ABOUT THAT.
THRUMMMMMM
WHOOOOOOM
I ALWAYS THOUGHT YOU'D DIE IN GOTHAM.
SKREEEEK
I'LL STILL GET PLENTY OF CHANCES.
BOOM

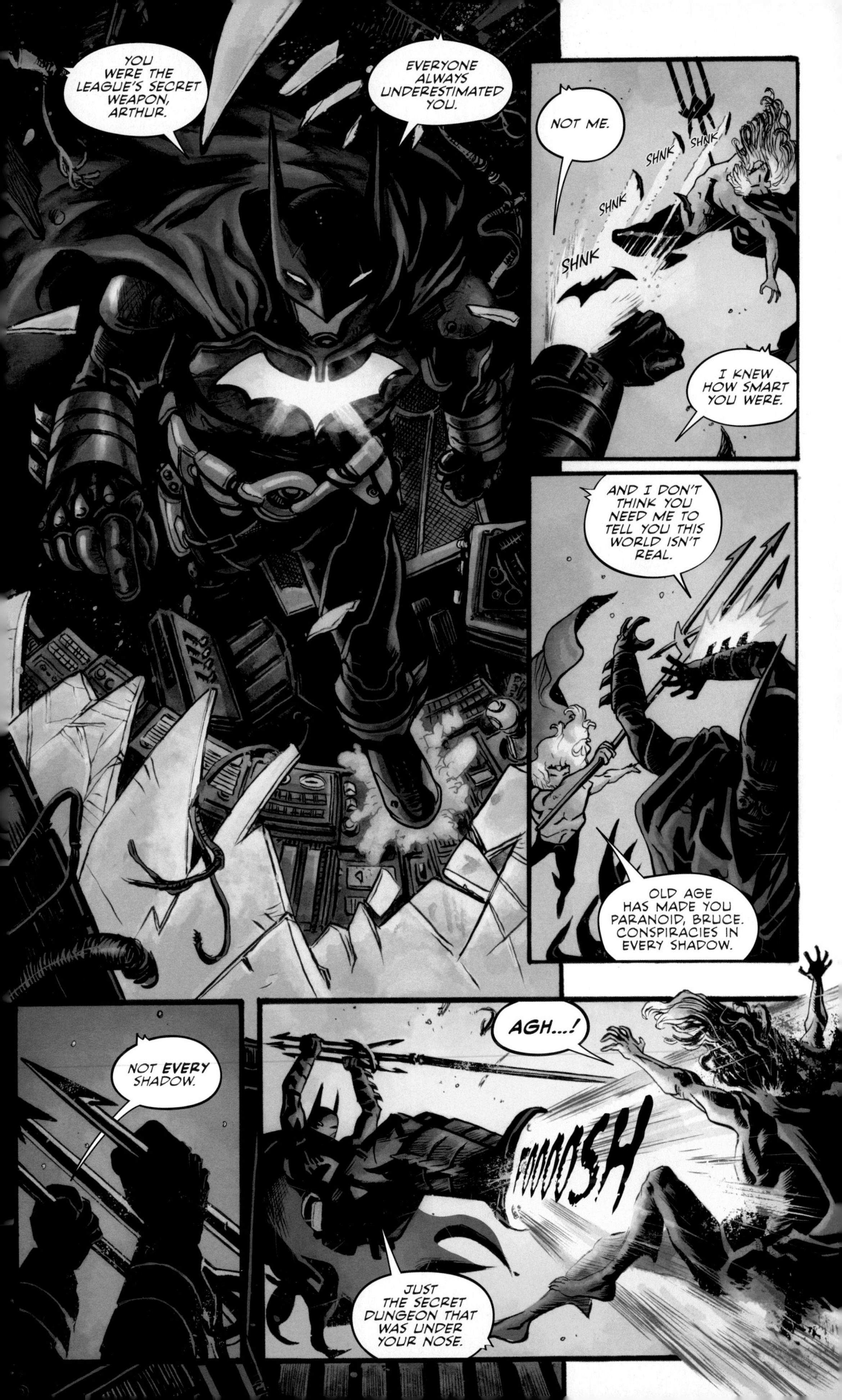
YOU WERE THE LEAGUE'S SECRET WEAPON, ARTHUR.
EVERYONE ALWAYS UNDERESTIMATED YOU.
NOT ME.
SHNK
SHNK
SHNK
SHNK
I KNEW HOW SMART YOU WERE.
AND I DON'T THINK YOU NEED ME TO TELL YOU THIS WORLD ISN'T REAL.
OLD AGE HAS MADE YOU PARANOID, BRUCE. CONSPIRACIES IN EVERY SHADOW.
NOT **EVERY** SHADOW.
AGH...!
FWOOOSH
JUST THE SECRET DUNGEON THAT WAS UNDER YOUR NOSE.

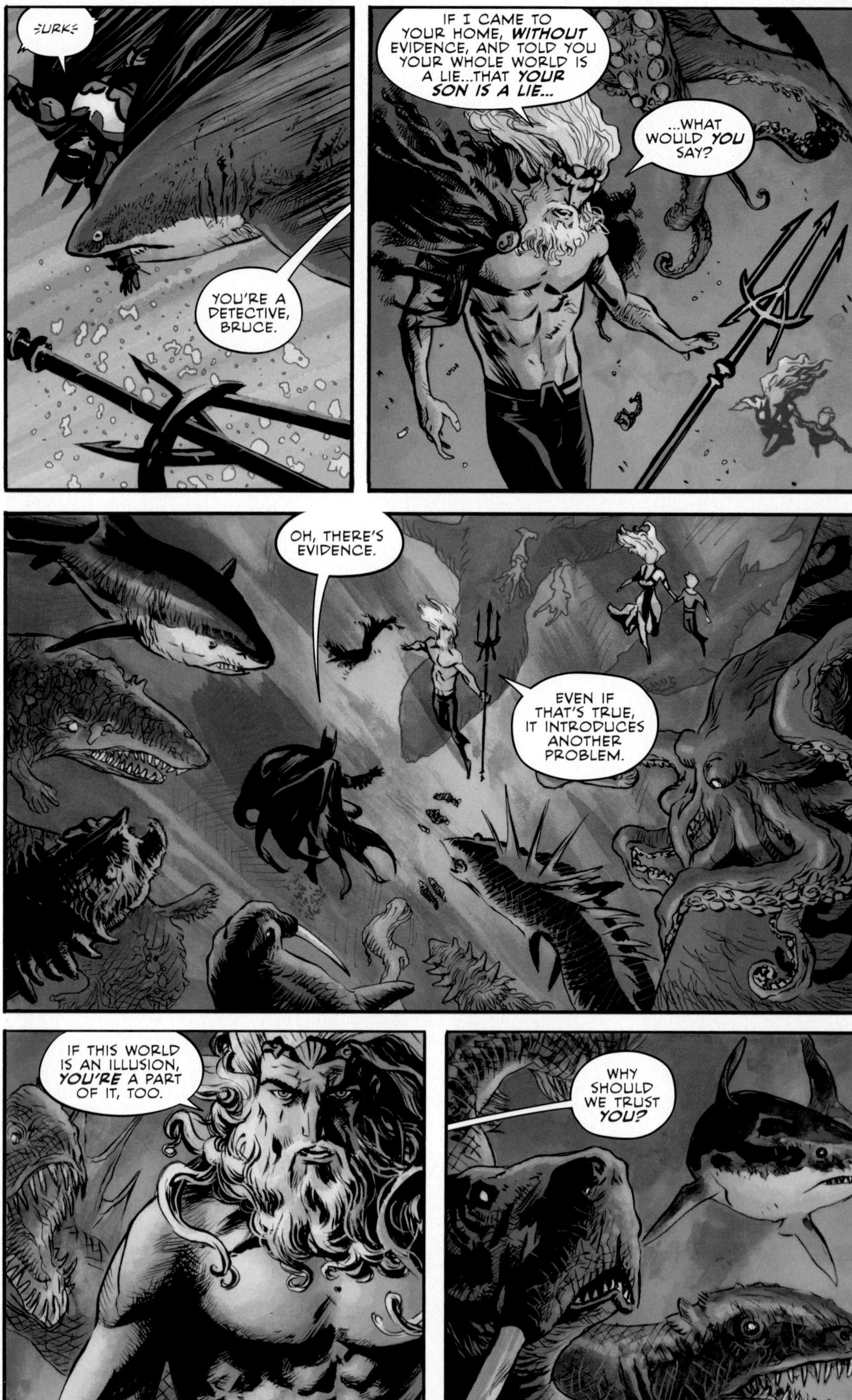

URK
YOU'RE A DETECTIVE, BRUCE.
IF I CAME TO YOUR HOME, WITHOUT EVIDENCE, AND TOLD YOU YOUR WHOLE WORLD IS A LIE...THAT YOUR SON IS A LIE...
...WHAT WOULD YOU SAY?
OH, THERE'S EVIDENCE.
EVEN IF THAT'S TRUE, IT INTRODUCES ANOTHER PROBLEM.
IF THIS WORLD IS AN ILLUSION, YOU'RE A PART OF IT, TOO.
WHY SHOULD WE TRUST YOU?

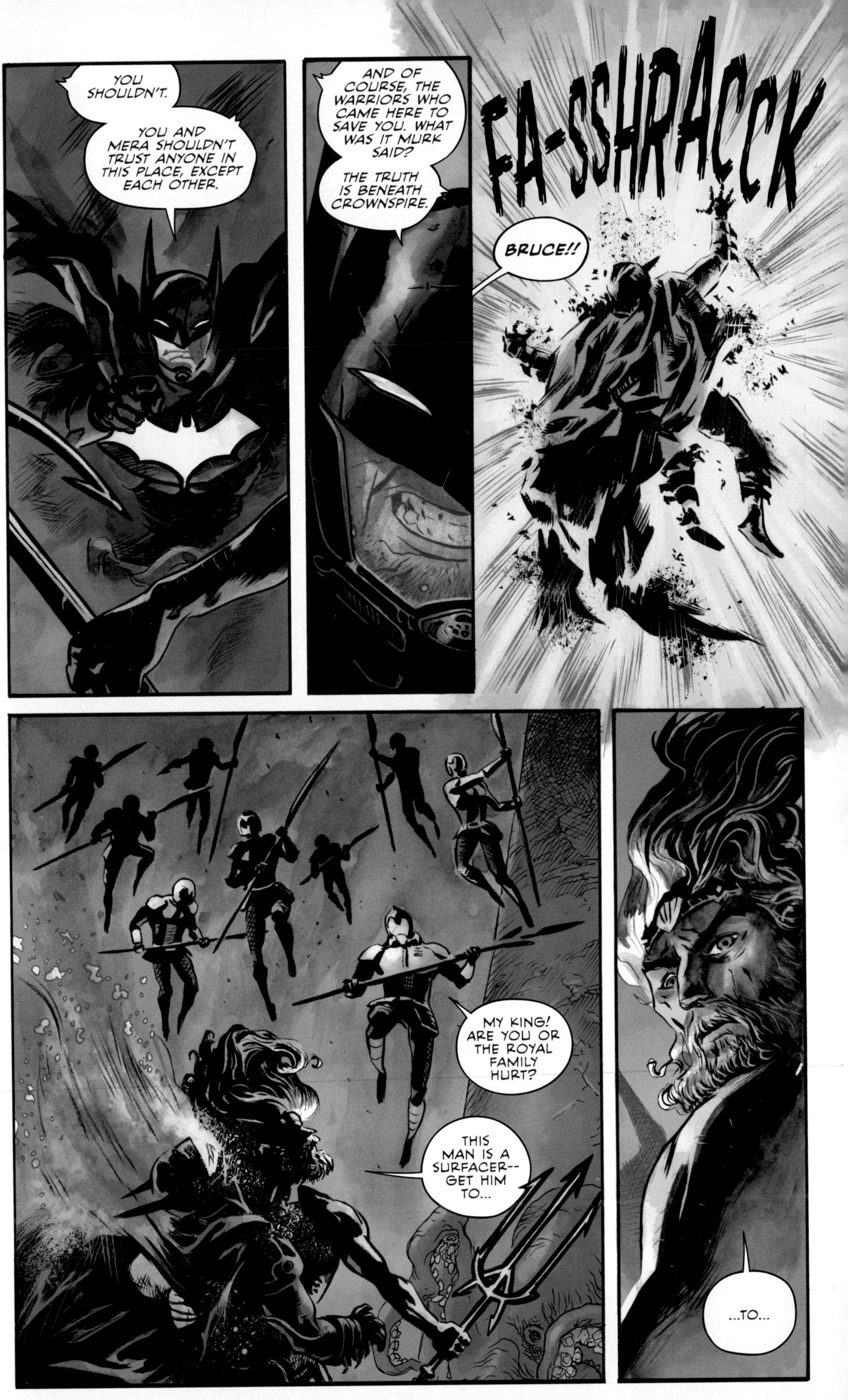
YOU SHOULDN'T.
YOU AND MERA SHOULDN'T TRUST ANYONE IN THIS PLACE, EXCEPT EACH OTHER.
AND OF COURSE, THE WARRIORS WHO CAME HERE TO SAVE YOU. WHAT WAS IT MURK SAID?
THE TRUTH IS BENEATH CROWNSPIRE.
FA-SSHRACCK
BRUCE!!
MY KING! ARE YOU OR THE ROYAL FAMILY HURT?
THIS MAN IS A SURFACER-- GET HIM TO...
...TO...

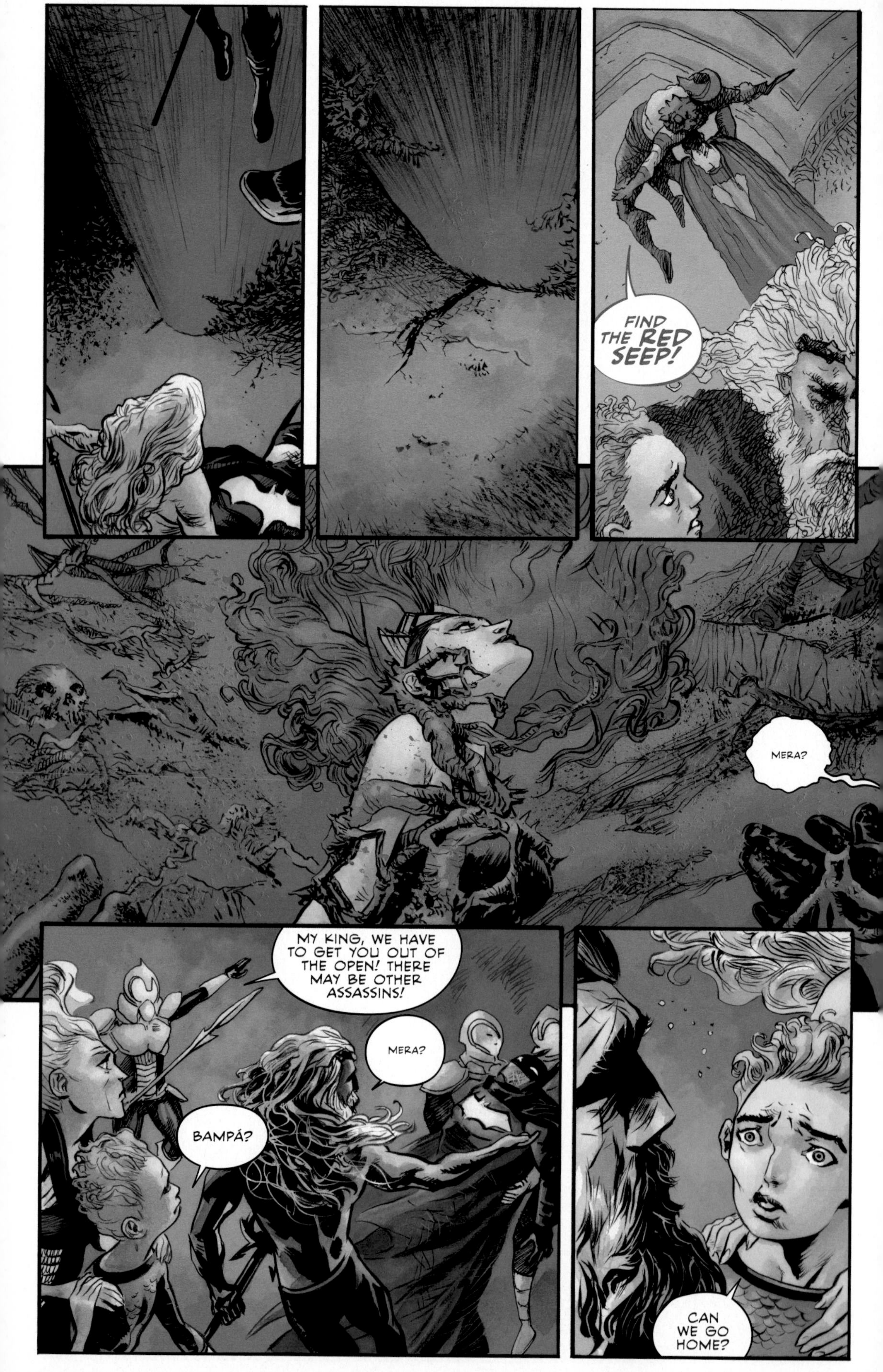
FIND THE RED SEEP!
MERA?
MY KING, WE HAVE TO GET YOU OUT OF THE OPEN! THERE MAY BE OTHER ASSASSINS!
MERA?
BAMPÁ?
CAN WE GO HOME?

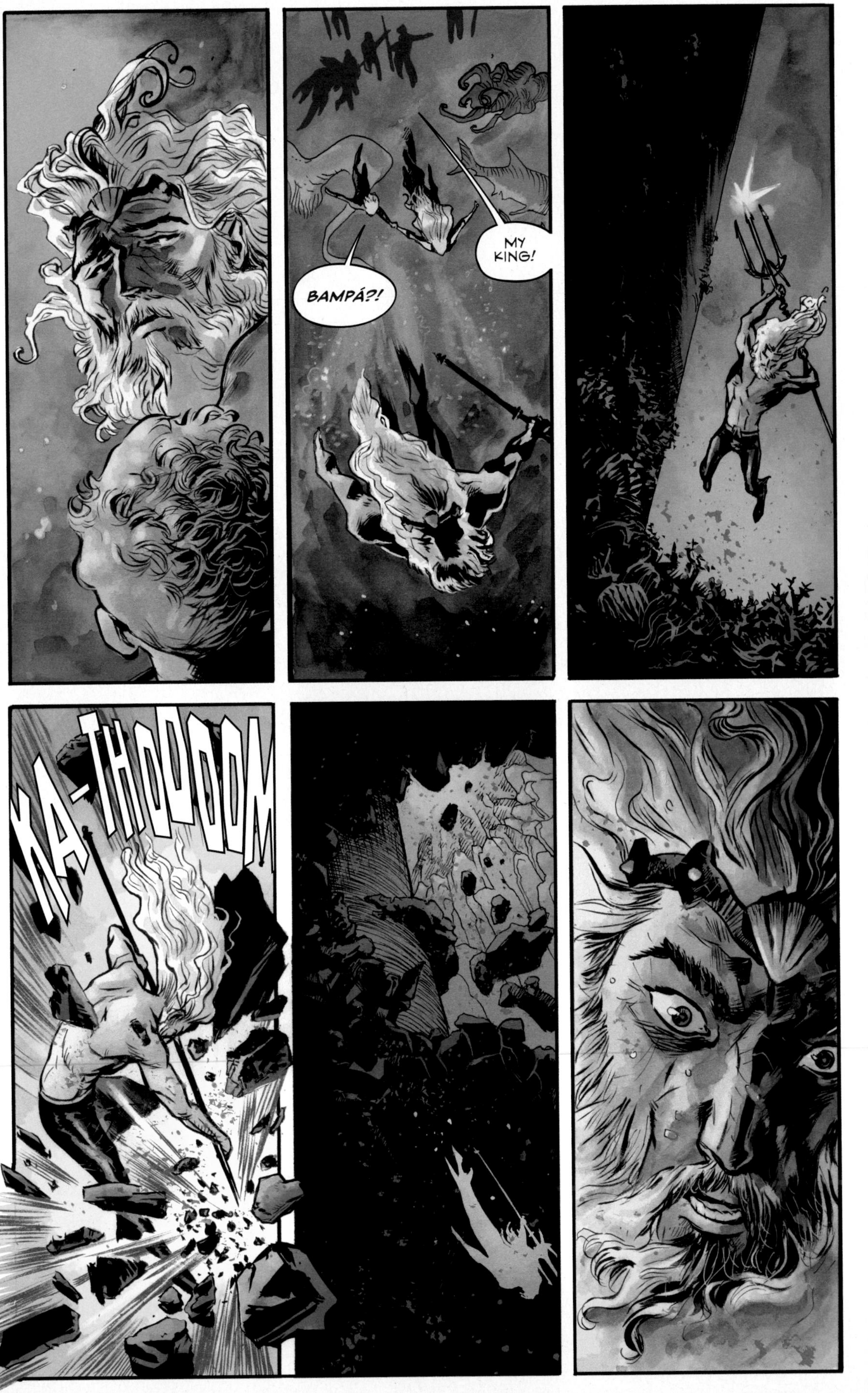
BAMPÁ?!
MY KING!
KA-THOOOOM

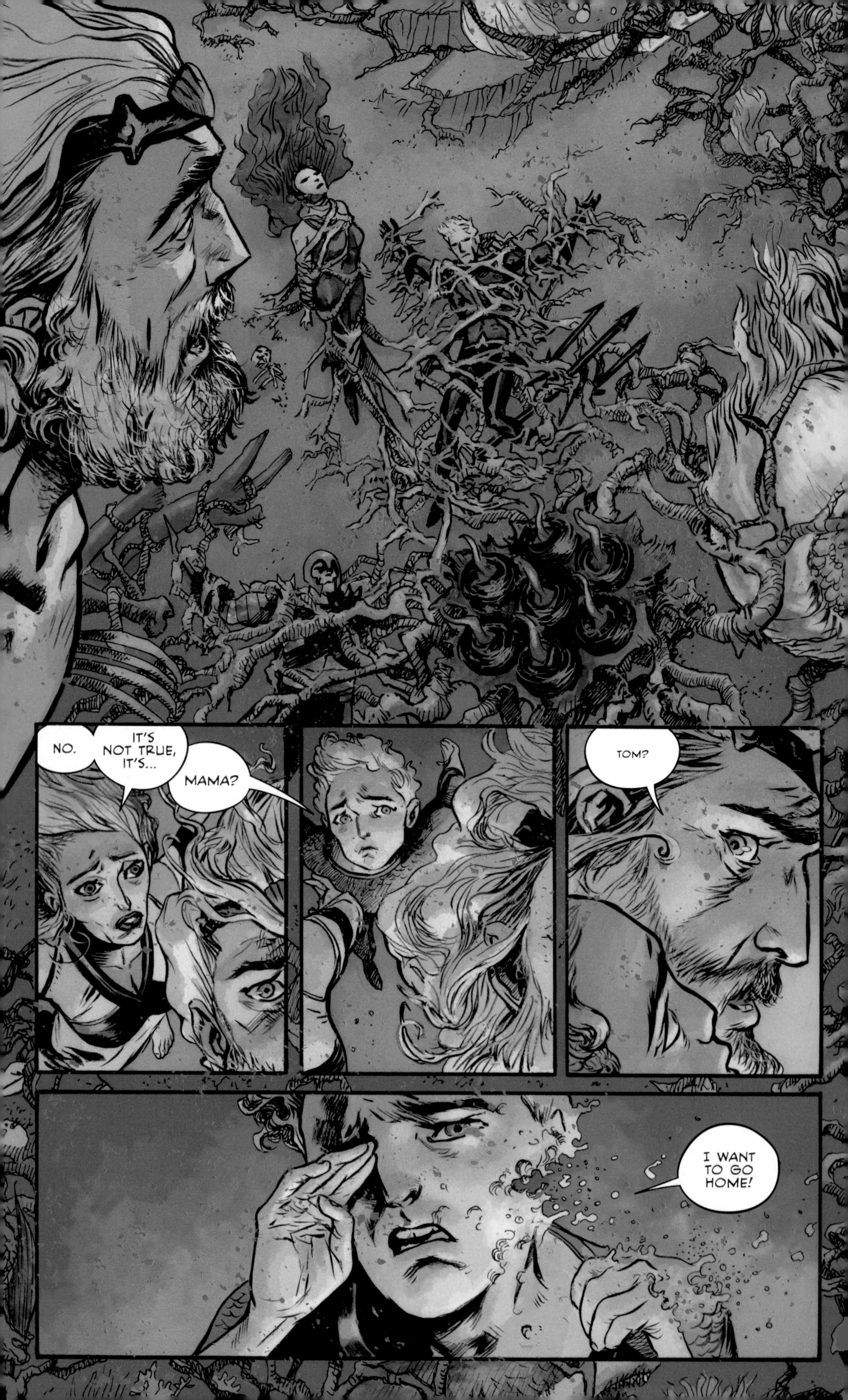
NO.
IT'S NOT TRUE, IT'S...
MAMA?
TOM?
I WANT TO GO HOME!

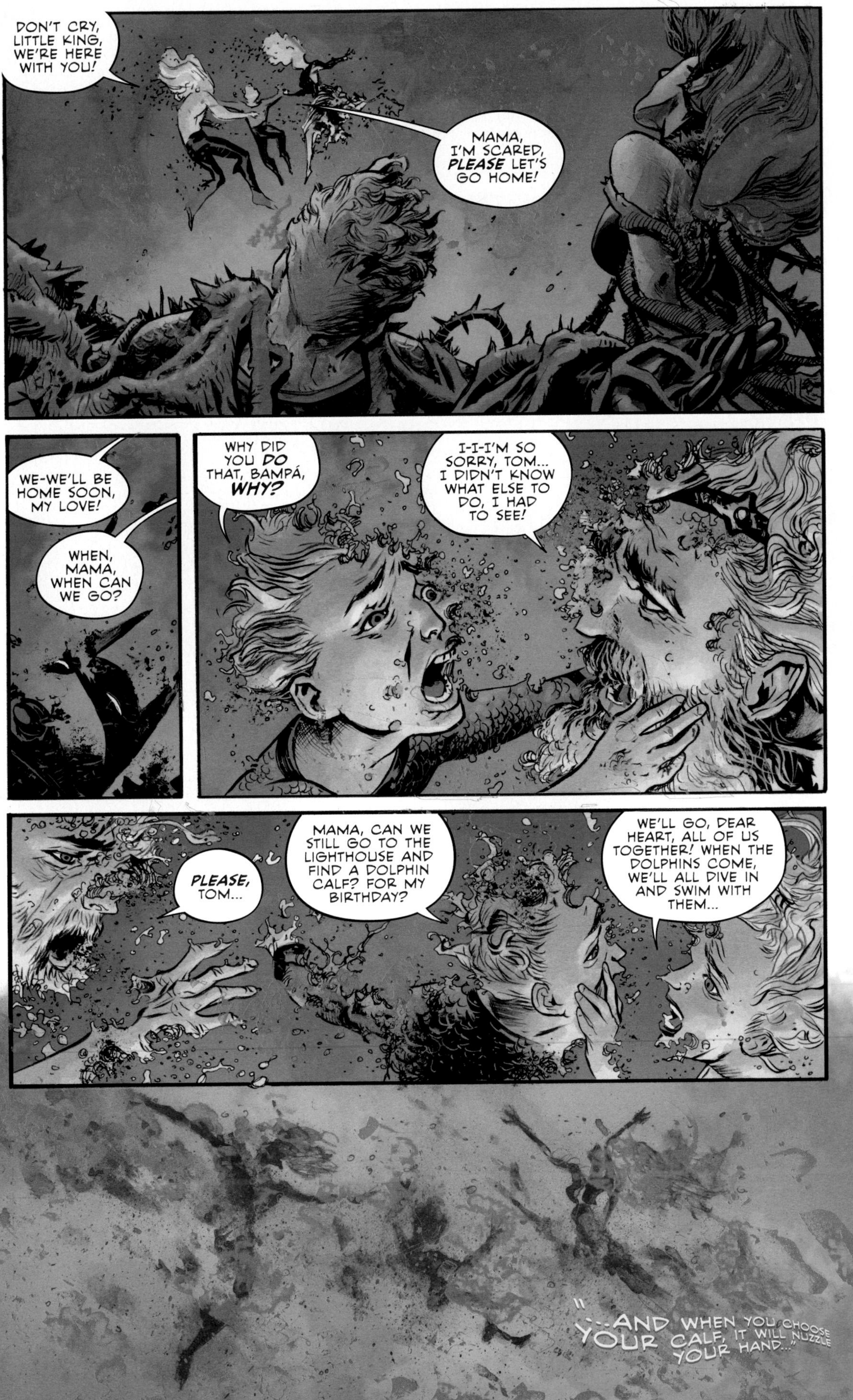
DON'T CRY, LITTLE KING, WE'RE HERE WITH YOU!
MAMA, I'M SCARED, PLEASE LET'S GO HOME!
WE-WE'LL BE HOME SOON, MY LOVE!
WHEN, MAMA, WHEN CAN WE GO?
WHY DID YOU DO THAT, BAMPÁ, WHY?
I-I-I'M SO SORRY, TOM... I DIDN'T KNOW WHAT ELSE TO DO, I HAD TO SEE!
PLEASE, TOM...
MAMA, CAN WE STILL GO TO THE LIGHTHOUSE AND FIND A DOLPHIN CALF? FOR MY BIRTHDAY?
WE'LL GO, DEAR HEART, ALL OF US TOGETHER! WHEN THE DOLPHINS COME, WE'LL ALL DIVE IN AND SWIM WITH THEM...
"...AND WHEN YOU CHOOSE YOUR CALF, IT WILL NUZZLE YOUR HAND..."

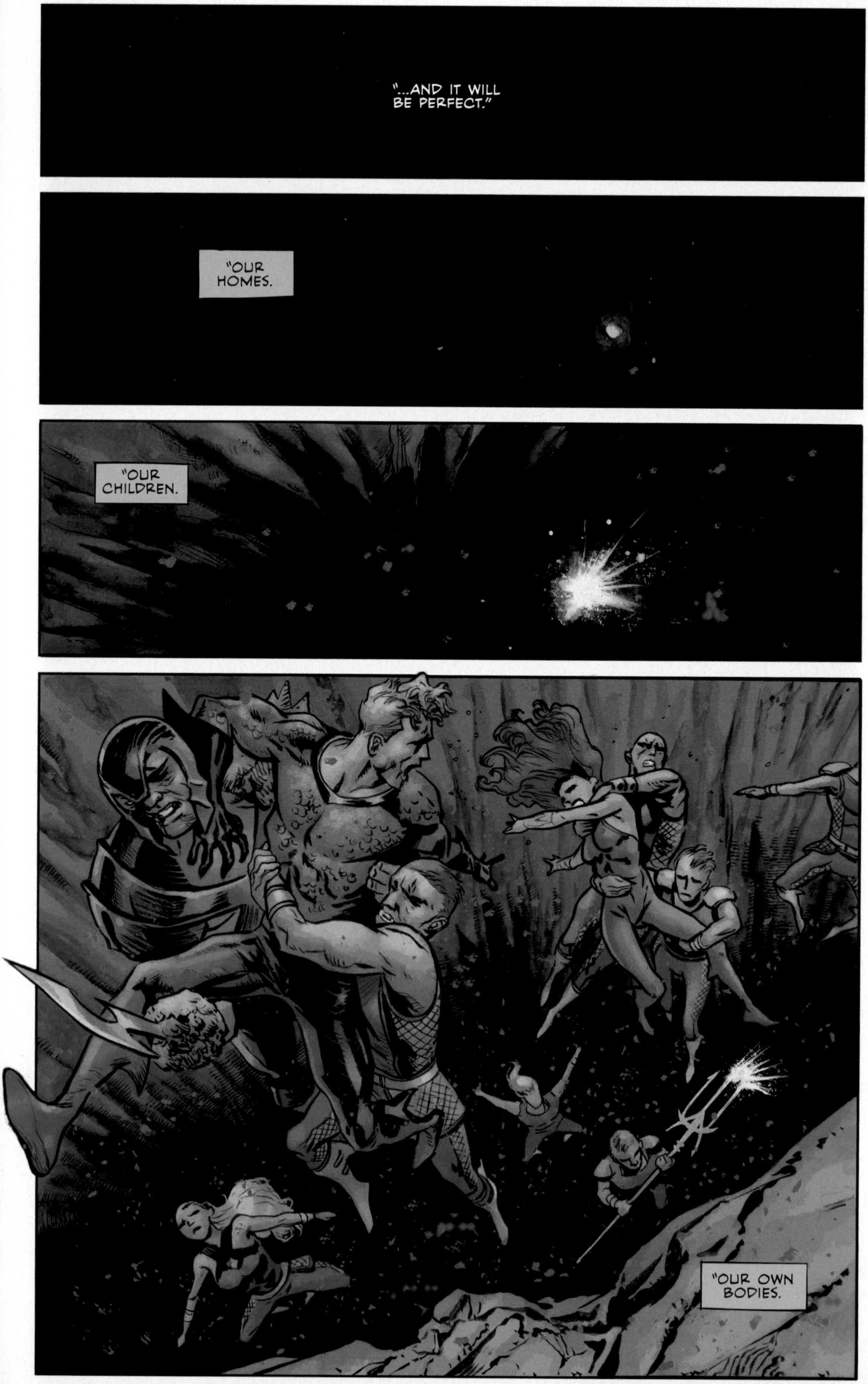
"...AND IT WILL BE PERFECT."
"OUR HOMES.
"OUR CHILDREN.
"OUR OWN BODIES.

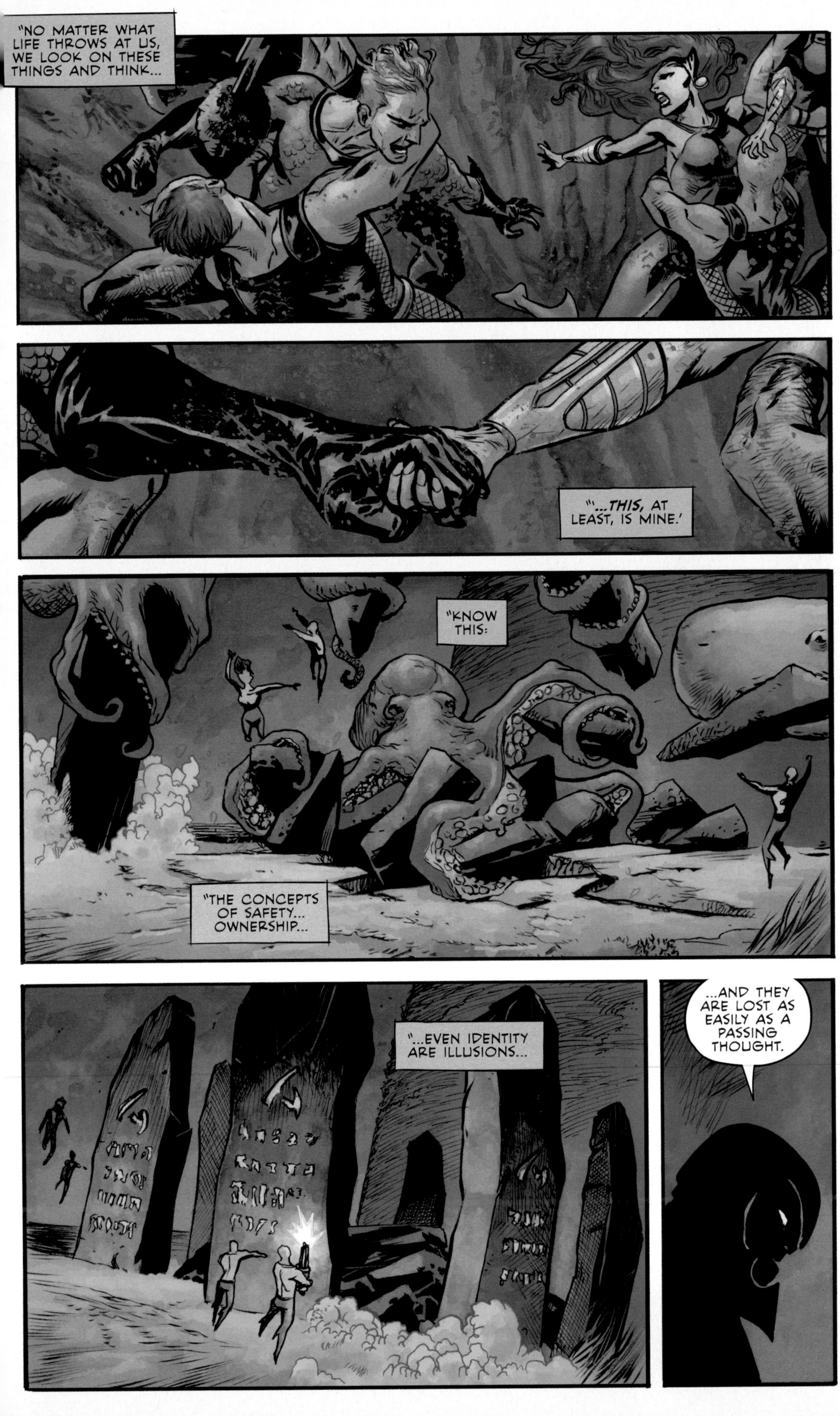
"NO MATTER WHAT LIFE THROWS AT US, WE LOOK ON THESE THINGS AND THINK...
"'...THIS, AT LEAST, IS MINE.'
"KNOW THIS:
"THE CONCEPTS OF SAFETY... OWNERSHIP...
"...EVEN IDENTITY ARE ILLUSIONS...
...AND THEY ARE LOST AS EASILY AS A PASSING THOUGHT.

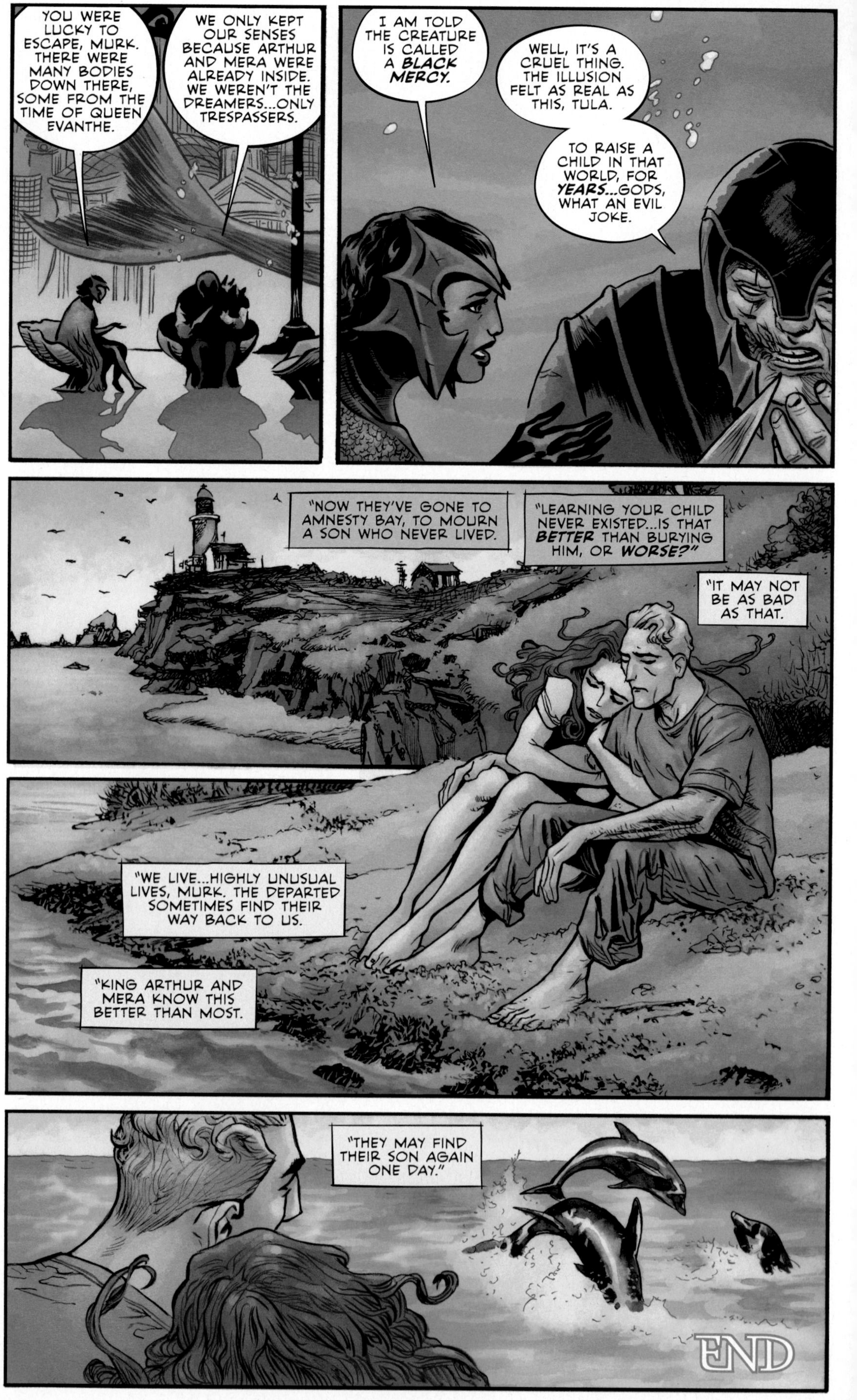
YOU WERE LUCKY TO ESCAPE, MURK. THERE WERE MANY BODIES DOWN THERE, SOME FROM THE TIME OF QUEEN EVANTHE.
WE ONLY KEPT OUR SENSES BECAUSE ARTHUR AND MERA WERE ALREADY INSIDE. WE WEREN'T THE DREAMERS...ONLY TRESPASSERS.
I AM TOLD THE CREATURE IS CALLED A BLACK MERCY.
WELL, IT'S A CRUEL THING. THE ILLUSION FELT AS REAL AS THIS, TULA.
TO RAISE A CHILD IN THAT WORLD, FOR YEARS...GODS, WHAT AN EVIL JOKE.
"NOW THEY'VE GONE TO AMNESTY BAY, TO MOURN A SON WHO NEVER LIVED.
"LEARNING YOUR CHILD NEVER EXISTED...IS THAT BETTER THAN BURYING HIM, OR WORSE?"
"IT MAY NOT BE AS BAD AS THAT.
"WE LIVE...HIGHLY UNUSUAL LIVES, MURK. THE DEPARTED SOMETIMES FIND THEIR WAY BACK TO US.
"KING ARTHUR AND MERA KNOW THIS BETTER THAN MOST.
"THEY MAY FIND THEIR SON AGAIN ONE DAY."
END

AQUAMAN

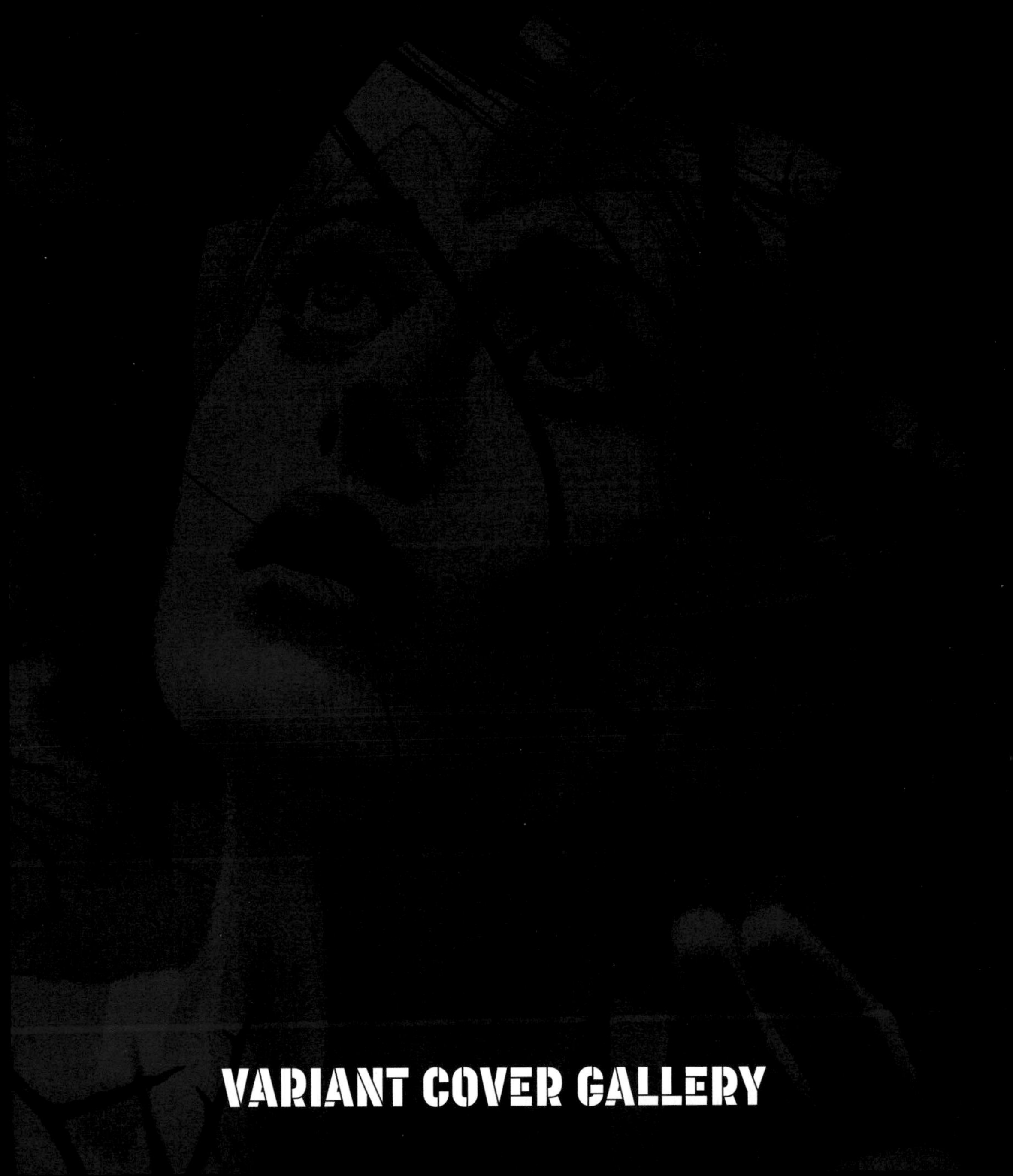

VARIANT COVER GALLERY

AQUAMAN #31 variant cover by JOSHUA MIDDLETON

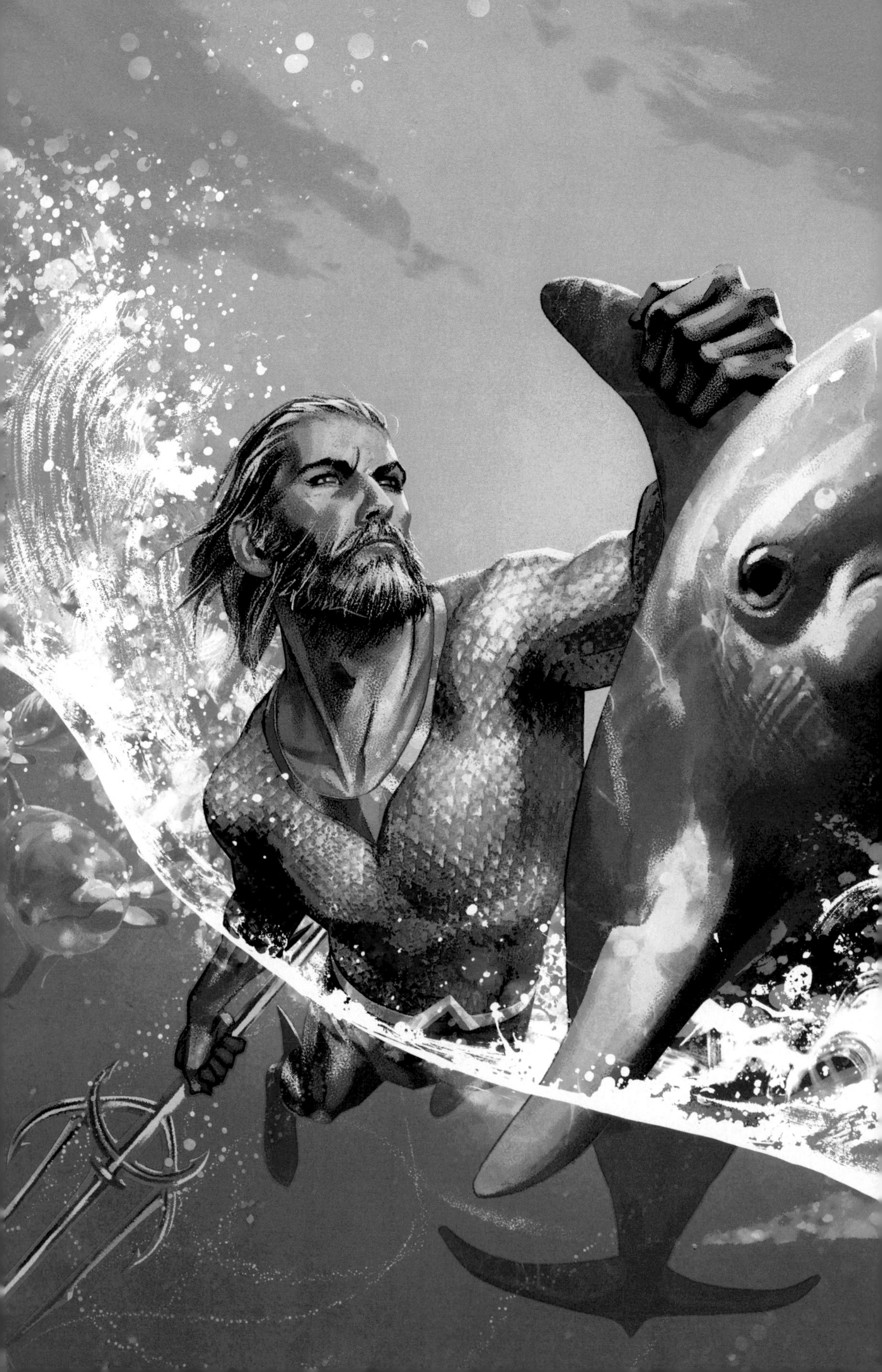

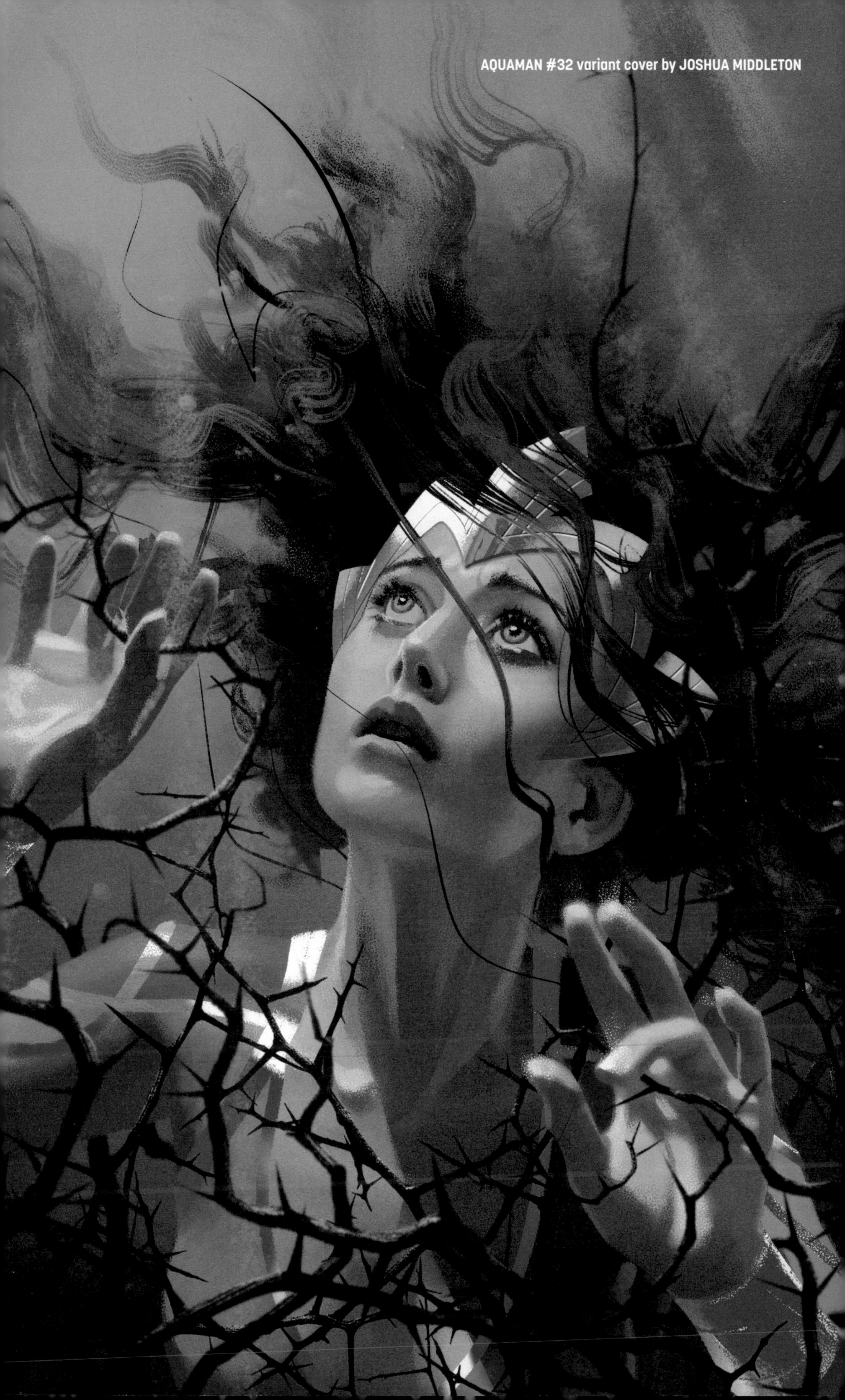

AQUAMAN #32 variant cover by JOSHUA MIDDLETON

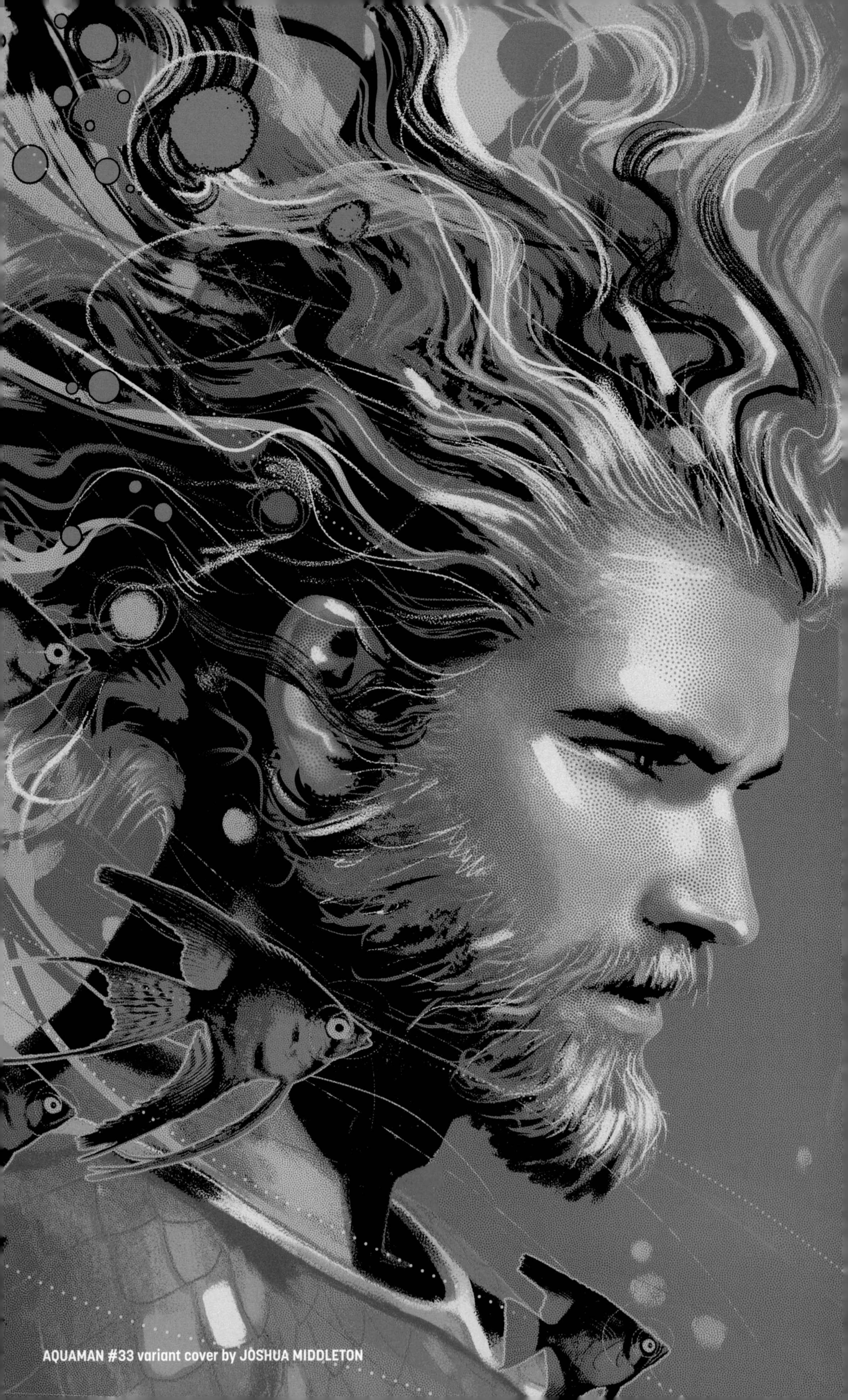

AQUAMAN #33 variant cover by JOSHUA MIDDLETON

AQUAMAN character sketches by MAX FIUMARA

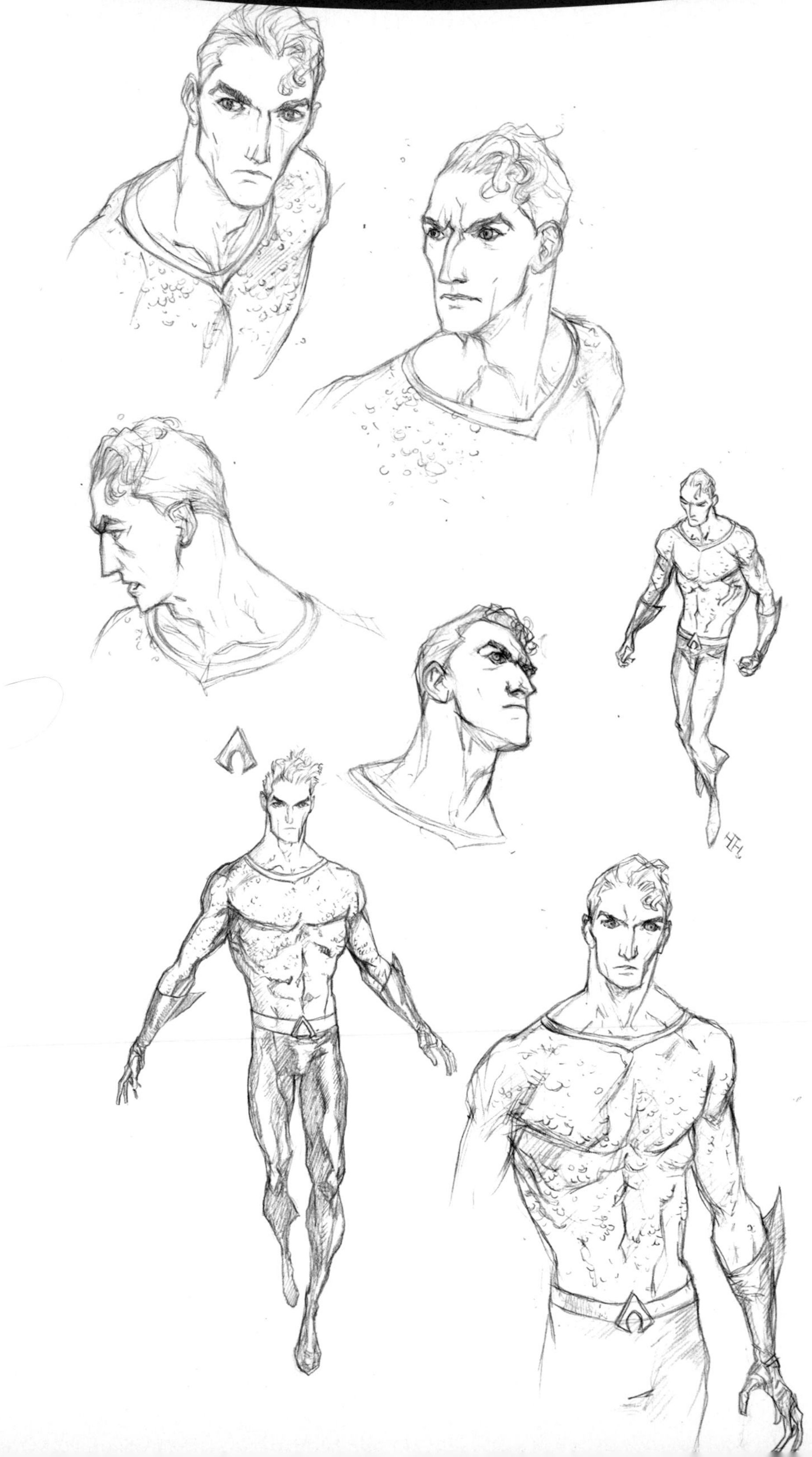

[redacted]

MERA character sketches by MAX FIUMARA

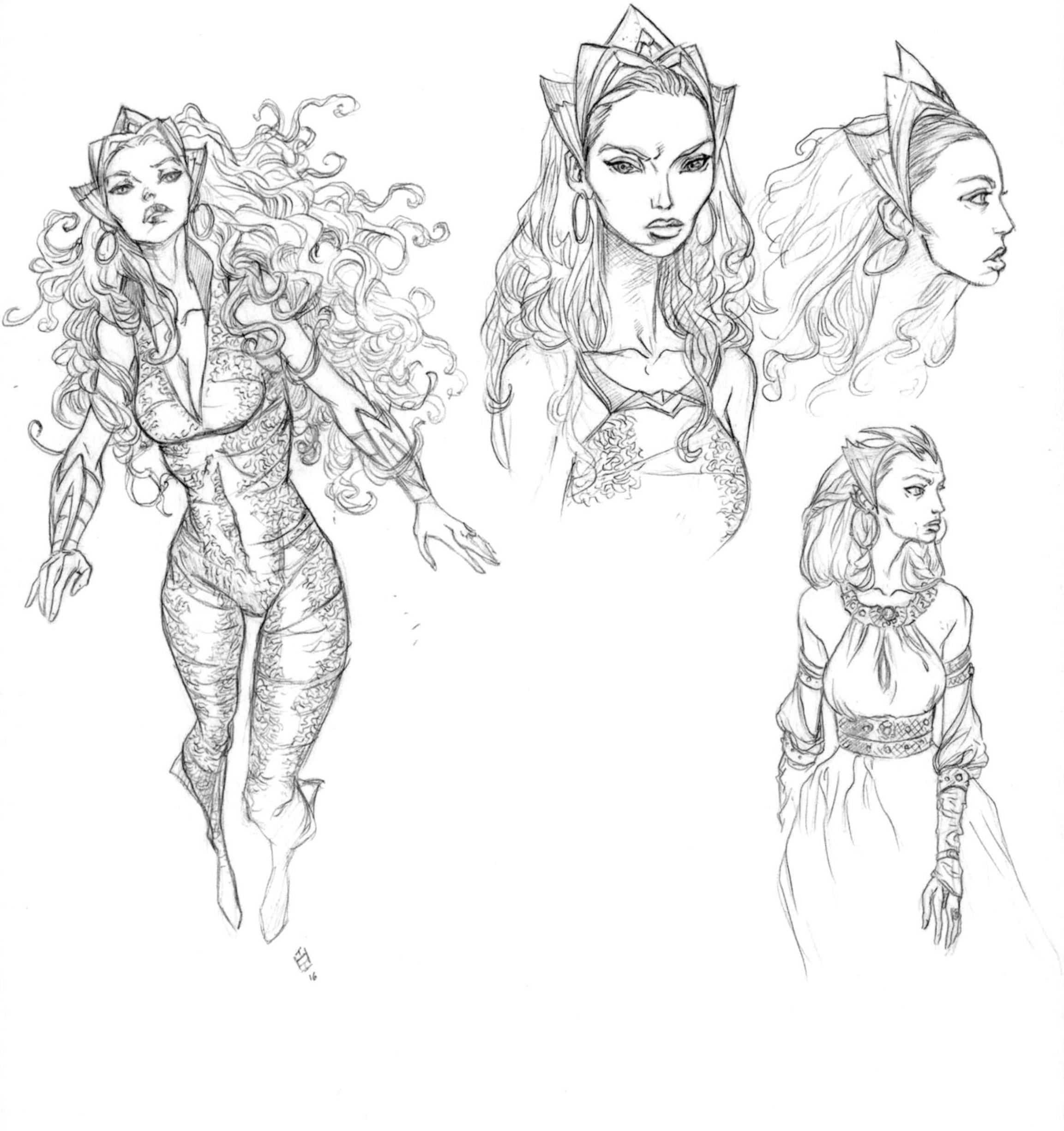

HAL JORDAN character sketches by MAX FIUMARA

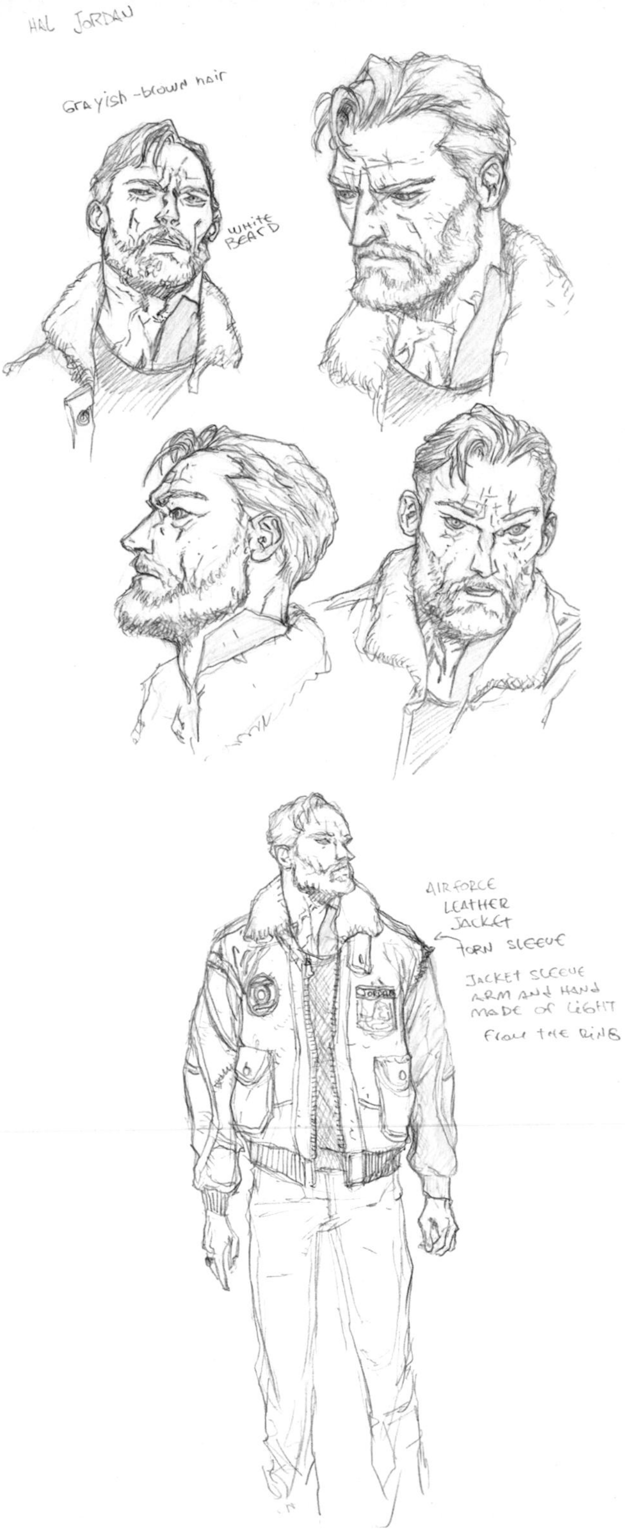
HAL JORDAN
Grayish-brown hair
WHITE BEARD
AIR FORCE
LEATHER
JACKET
TORN SLEEVE
JACKET SLEEVE
ARM AND HAND
MADE OF LIGHT
FROM THE RING

DIANA character sketches by MAX FIUMARA

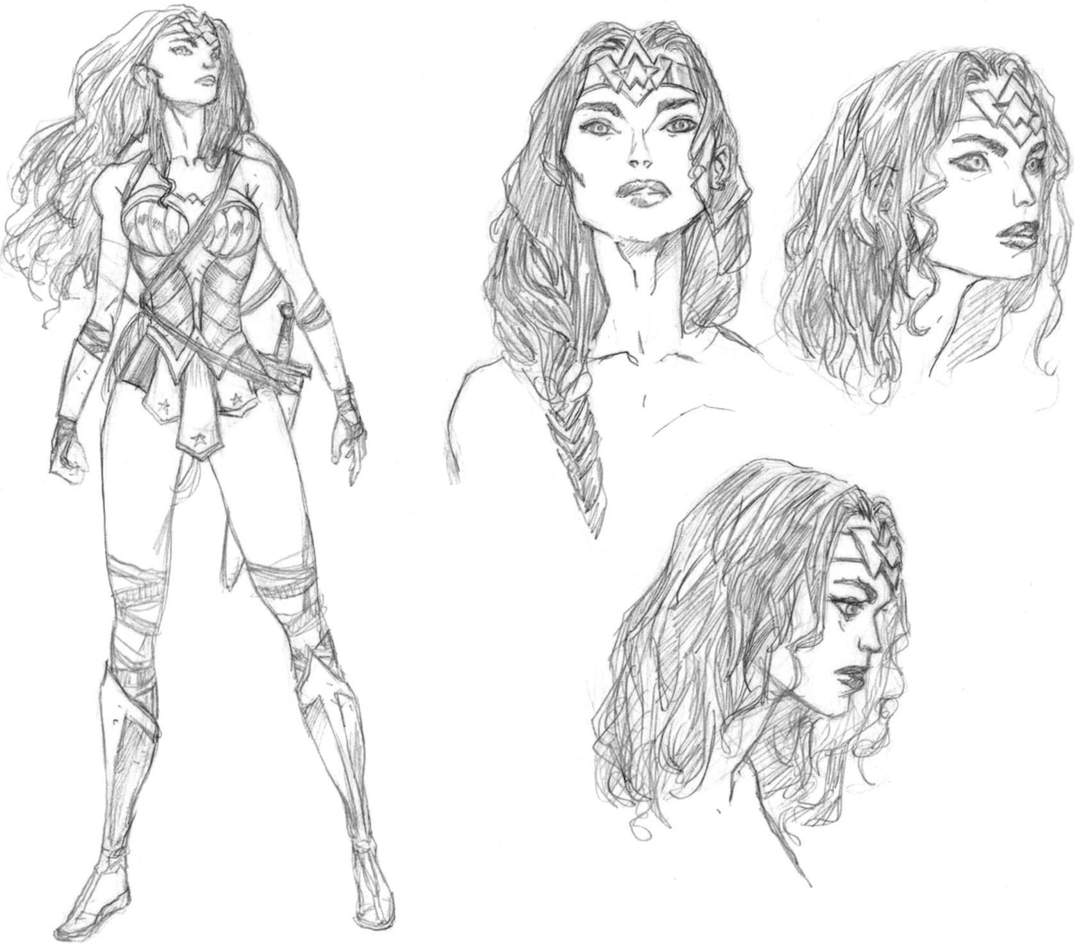

SUPERMAN character sketches by MAX FIUMARA

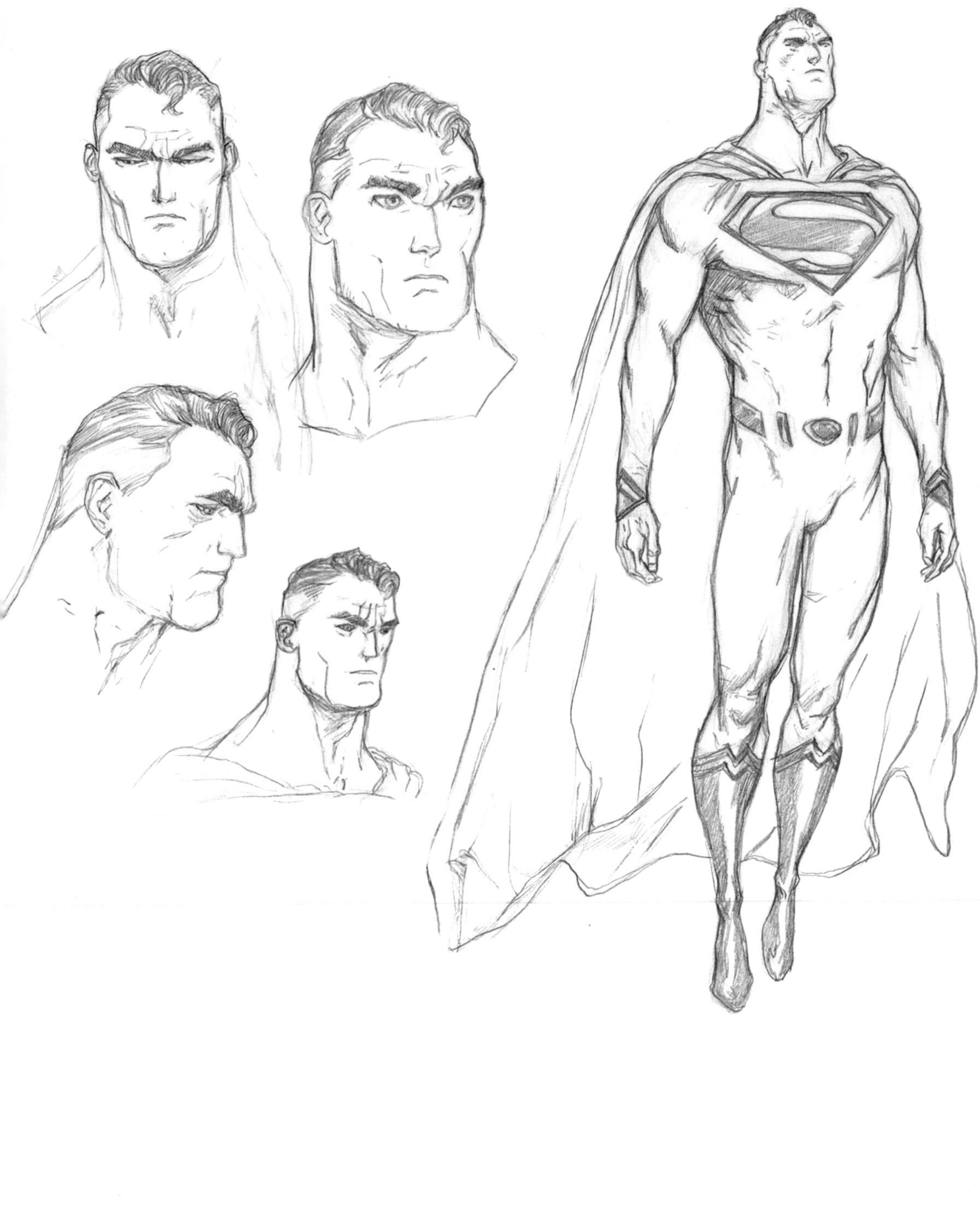

AQUAMAN, 20 YEARS LATER character sketches by MAX FIUMARA

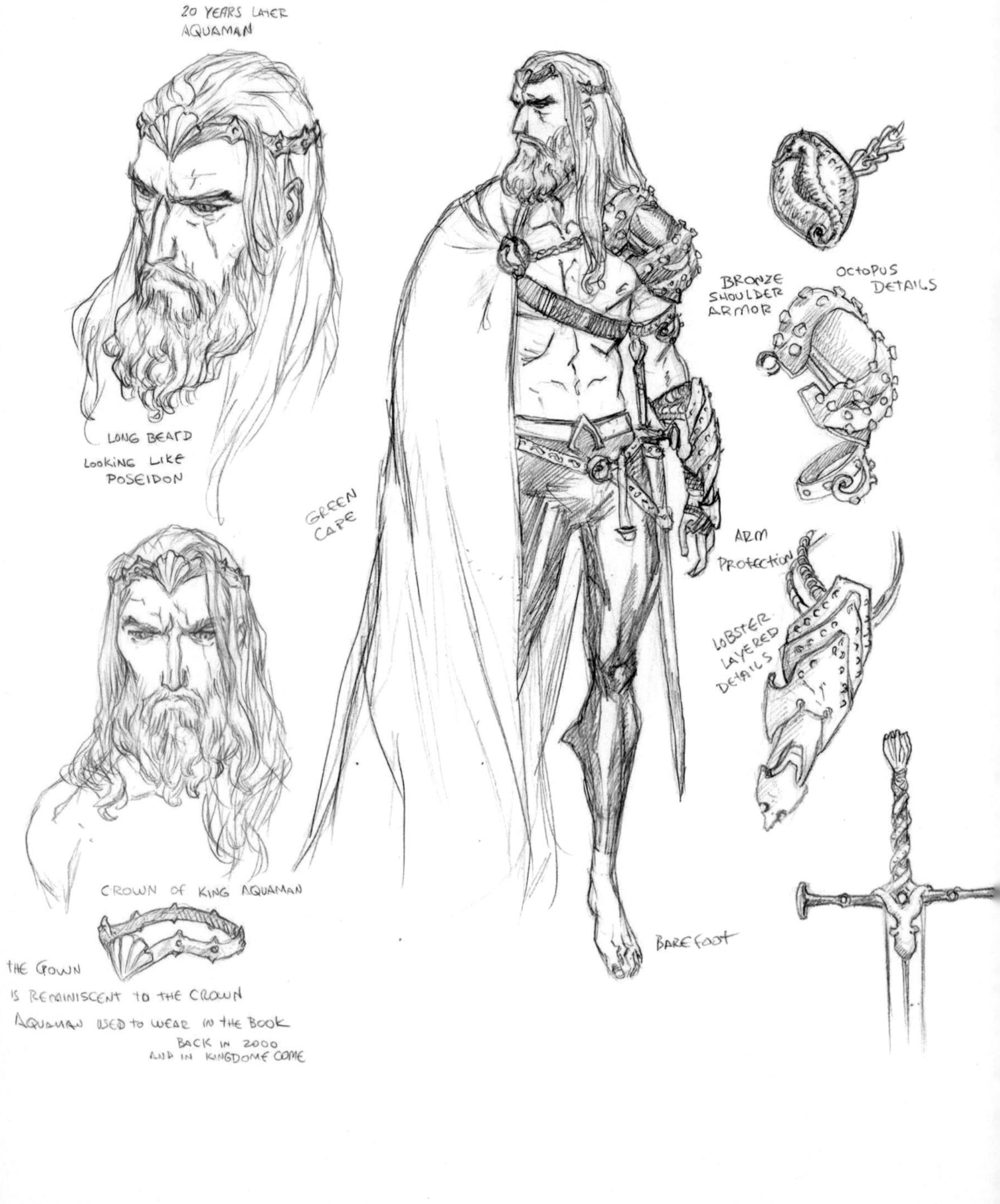
20 YEARS LATER
AQUAMAN
LONG BEARD
LOOKING LIKE
POSEIDON
GREEN
CAPE
BRONZE
SHOULDER
ARMOR
OCTOPUS
DETAILS
ARM
PROTECTION
LOBSTER
LAYERED
DETAILS
CROWN OF KING AQUAMAN
THE CROWN
IS REMINISCENT TO THE CROWN
AQUAMAN USED TO WEAR IN THE BOOK
BACK IN 2000
AND IN KINGDOME COME
BARE FOOT

CROWNSPIRE ANNUAL #1 cover sketches by MAX FIUMARA

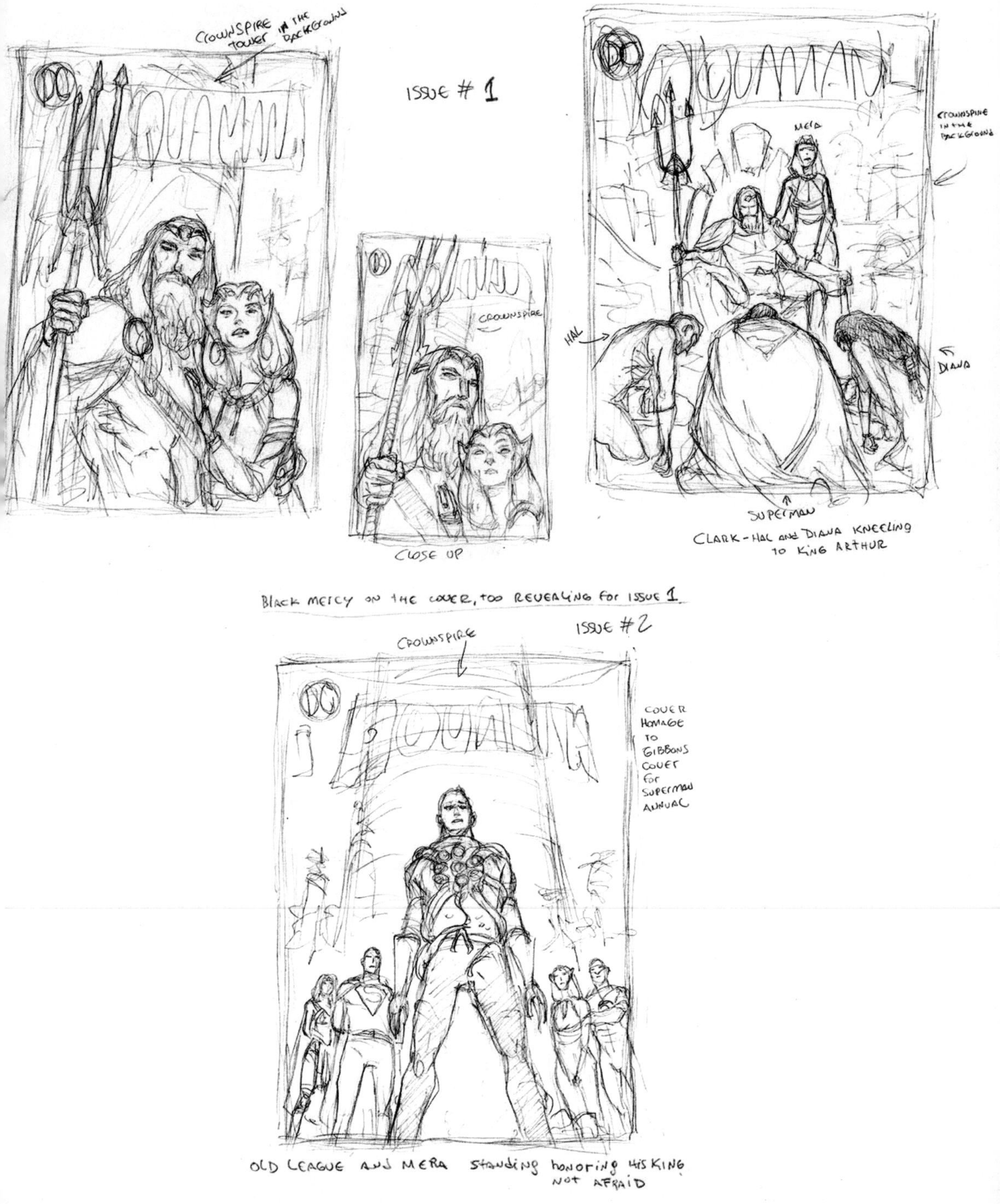
CROWNSPIRE TOWER IN THE BACKGROUND
ISSUE #1
CROWNSPIRE
CLOSE UP
MERA
CROWNSPIRE IN THE BACKGROUND
HAL
DIANA
SUPERMAN
CLARK-HAL AND DIANA KNEELING TO KING ARTHUR
BLACK MERCY ON THE COVER, TOO REVEALING FOR ISSUE 1.
ISSUE #2
CROWNSPIRE
COVER HOMAGE TO GIBBONS COVER FOR SUPERMAN ANNUAL
OLD LEAGUE AND MERA STANDING HONORING HIS KING NOT AFRAID

[redacted]

AQUAMAN concept sketches by RIC[redacted]DO FEDERICI

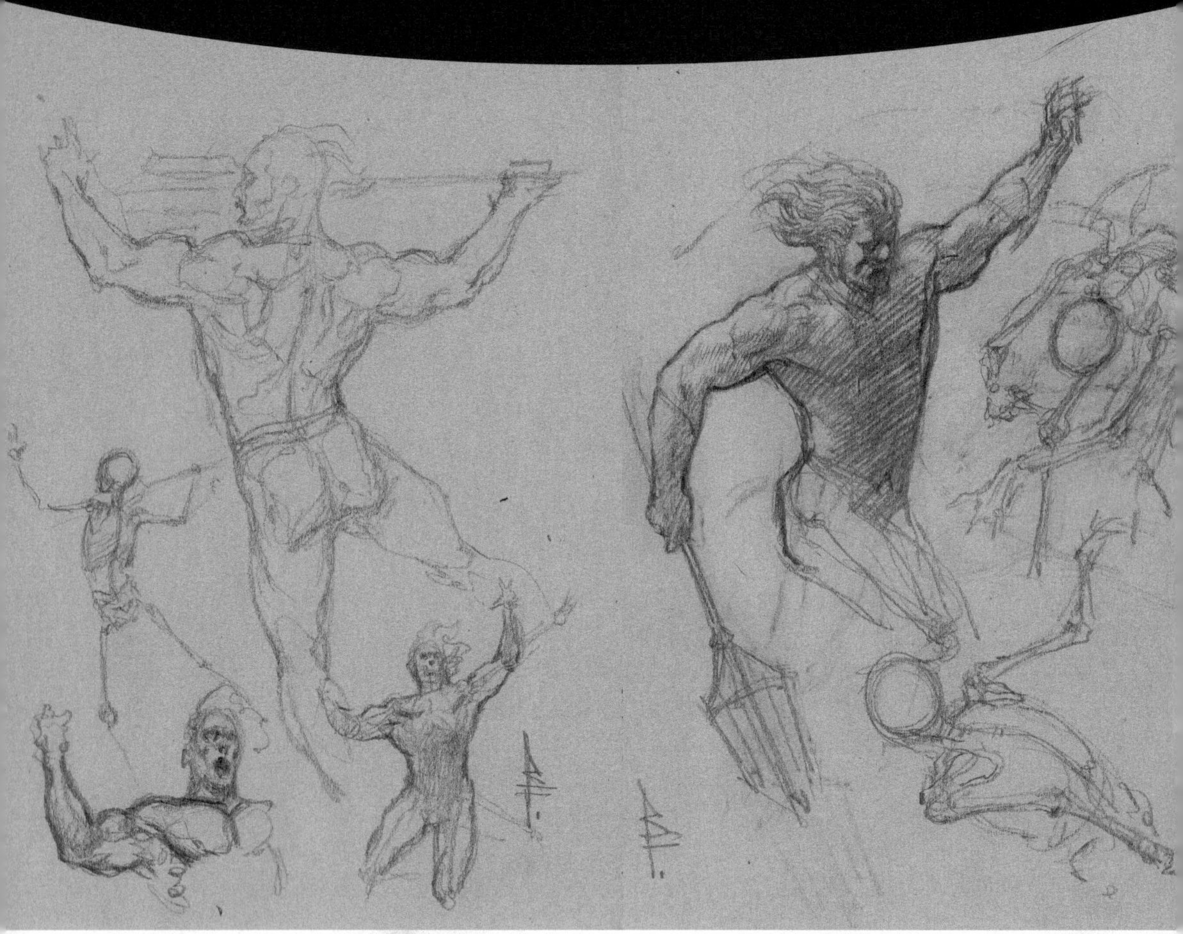

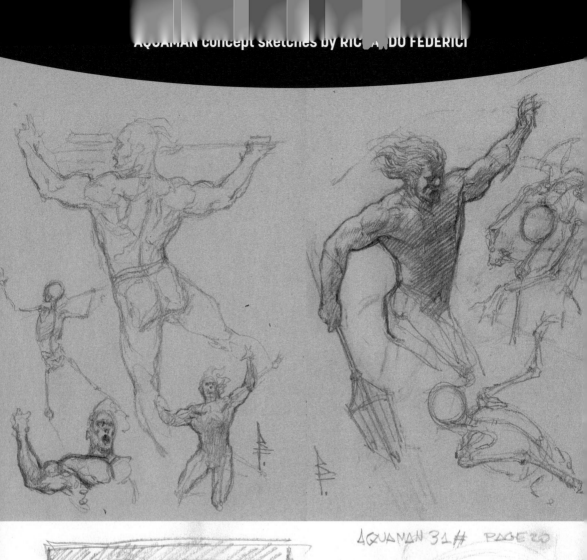

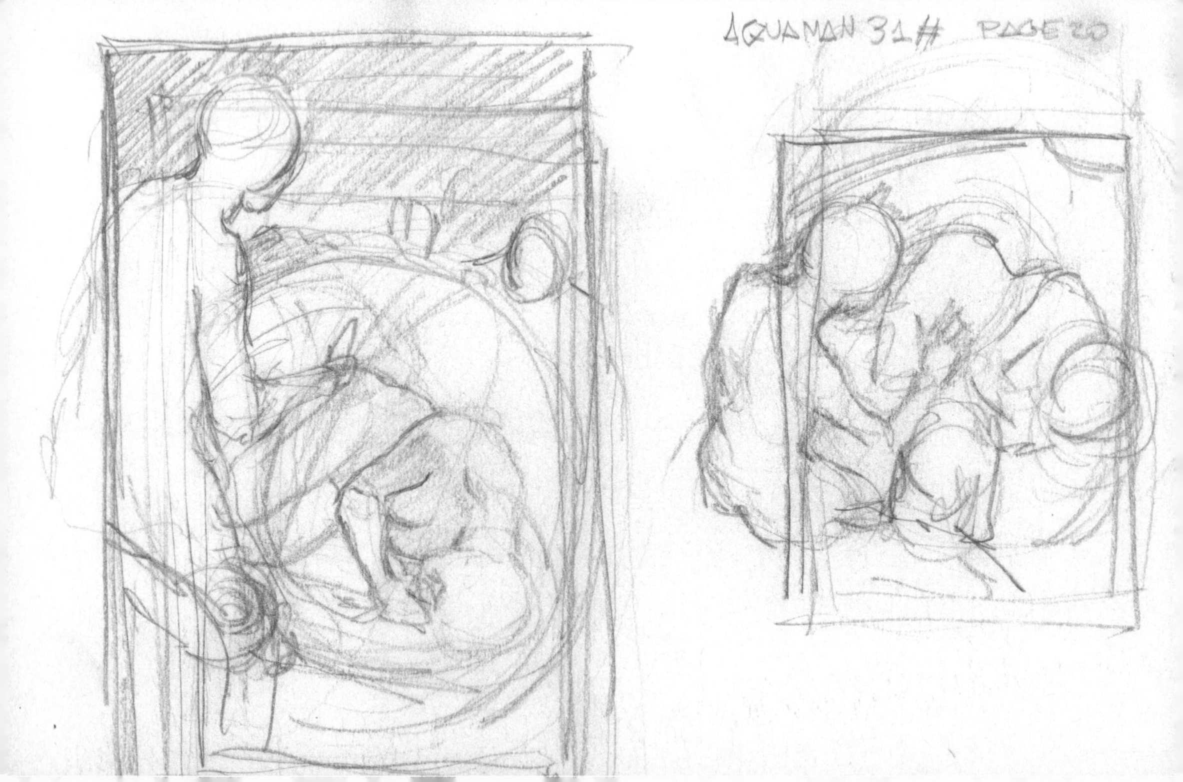
AQUAMAN 31# PAGE 20

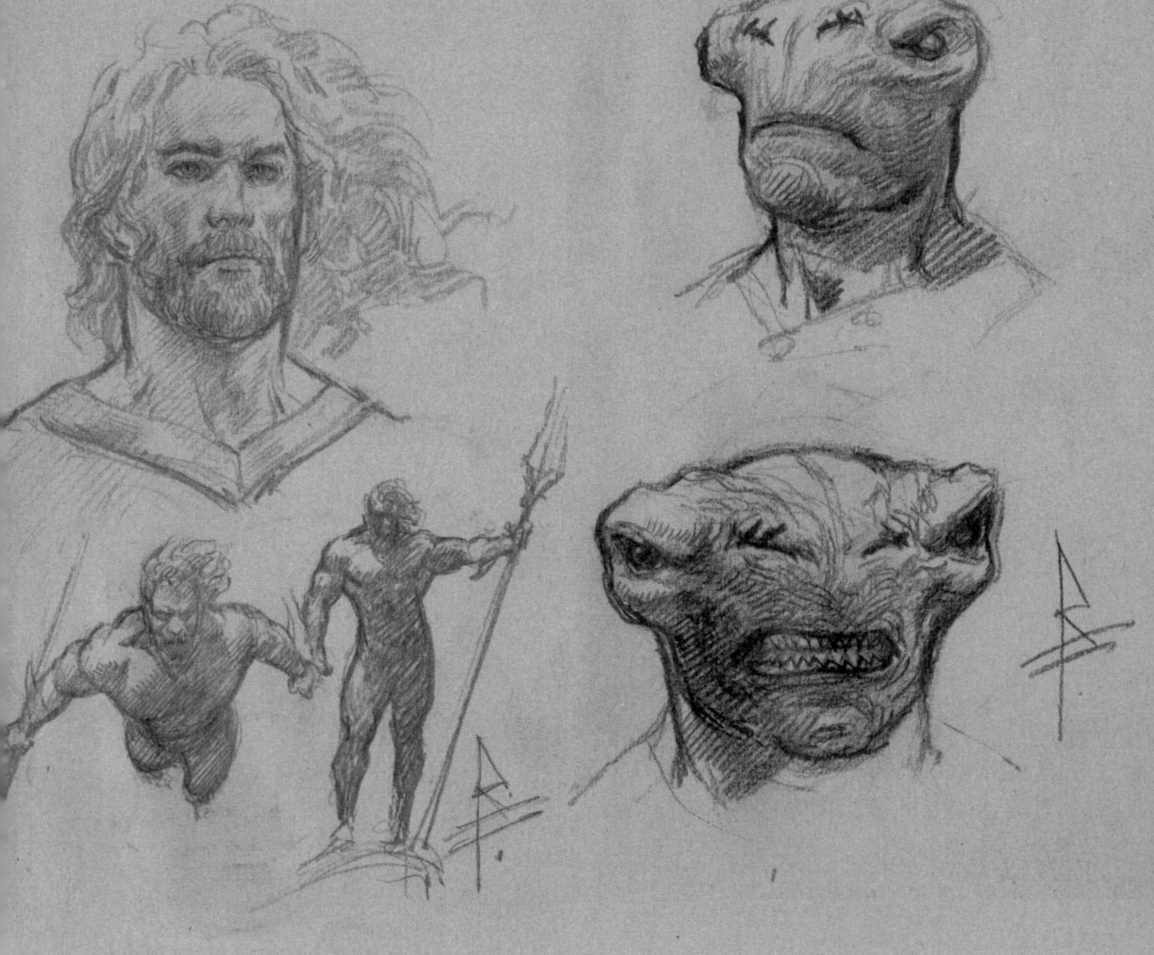

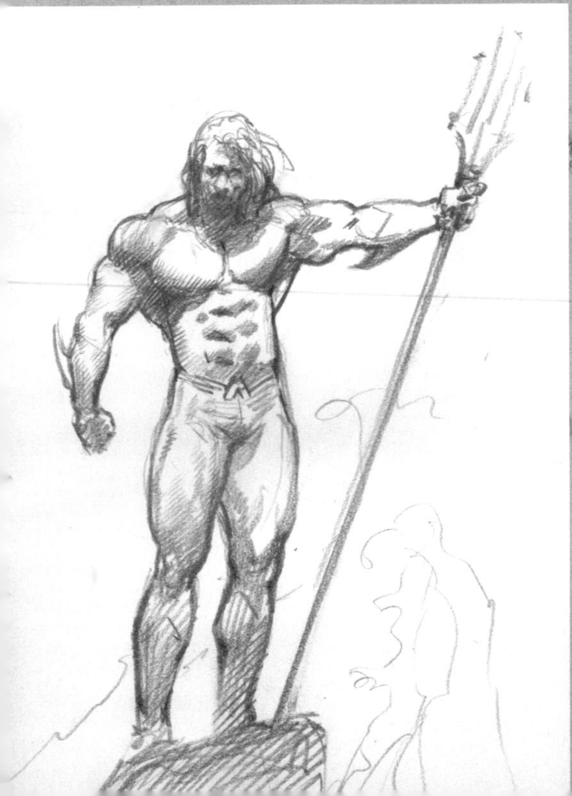

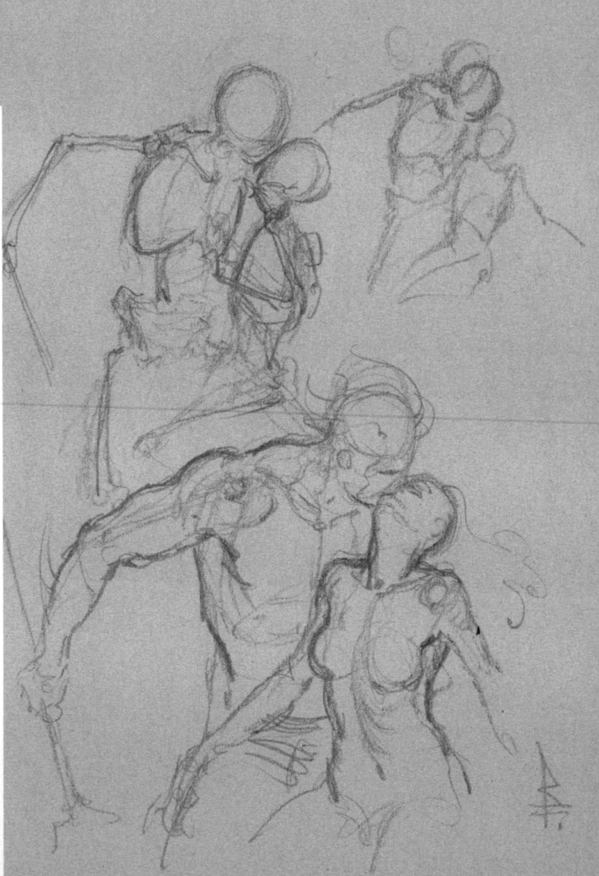

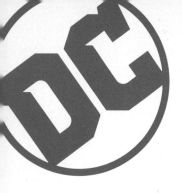

"All aboard for AQUAMAN!"
–NERDIST

"A solid primer on Aquaman's new status quo."
–COMIC BOOK RESOURCES

DC UNIVERSE REBIRTH
AQUAMAN
VOL.1 THE DROWNING
DAN ABNETT * PHILIPPE BRIONES * SCOT EATON * BRAD WALKER

AQUAMAN

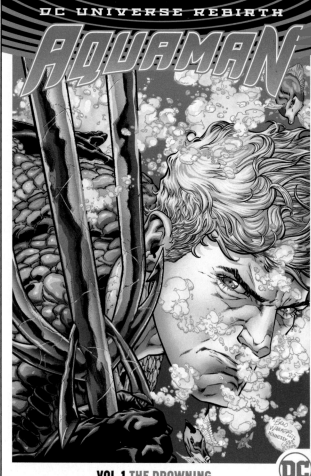

VOL. 1: THE DROWNING

DAN ABNETT with PHILIPPE BRIONES, SCOT EATON and BRAD WALKER

DC UNIVERSE REBIRTH
AQUAMAN
"I am all aboard for AQUAMAN..." NERDIST
VOL.2 BLACK MANTA RISING
DAN ABNETT • SCOT EATON • BRAD WALKER • PHILIPPE BRIONES

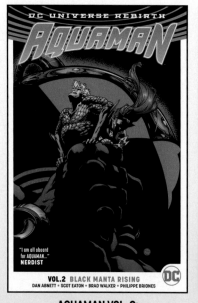

AQUAMAN VOL. 2: BLACK MANTA RISING

DC UNIVERSE REBIRTH
AQUAMAN
"I am all aboard for AQUAMAN..." NERDIST
VOL.3 CROWN OF ATLANTIS
DAN ABNETT • SCOT EATON • PHILIPPE BRIONES • BRAD WALKER

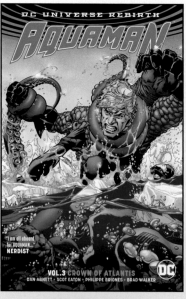

AQUAMAN VOL. 3: CROWN OF ATLANTIS

READ THE ENTIRE EPIC

AQUAMAN VOL.
UNDERWORL

AQUAMAN VOL.
THE CROWN COMES DOW

Get more DC graphic novels wherever comics and books are sold!

"AQUAMAN has been a rollicking good ride so far… The mythology Johns has been building up here keeps getting teased out at just the right rate, like giving a junkie their fix." **– MTV GEEK**

"With Reis on art and Johns using his full creative juices, AQUAMAN is constantly setting the bar higher and higher."
– CRAVE ONLINE

AQUAMAN
VOL. 1: THE TRENCH
GEOFF JOHNS
with IVAN REIS

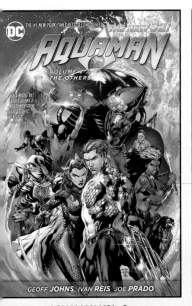

AQUAMAN VOL. 2:
THE OTHERS

AQUAMAN VOL. 3:
THRONE OF ATLANTIS

READ THE ENTIRE EPIC!

AQUAMAN VOL. 4:
DEATH OF A KING

AQUAMAN VOL. 5:
SEA OF STORMS

AQUAMAN VOL. 6:
MAELSTROM

AQUAMAN VOL. 7:
EXILED

AQUAMAN VOL. 8:
OUT OF DARKNESS

Get more DC graphic novels wherever comics and books are sold!

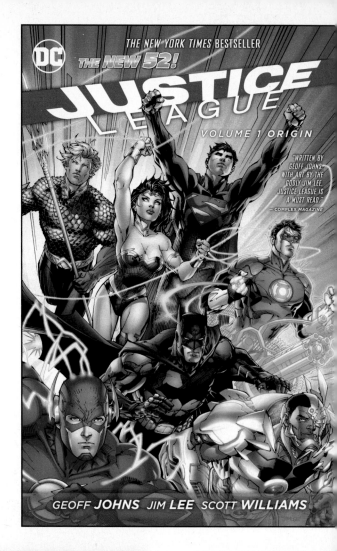

> "Welcoming to new fans looking to get into superhero comics for the first time and old fans who gave up on the funny-books long ago."
> **– SCRIPPS HOWARD NEWS SERVICE**

JUSTICE LEAGUE

VOL. 1: ORIGIN
GEOFF JOHNS and JIM LEE

**JUSTICE LEAGUE
VOL. 2: THE VILLAIN'S JOURNEY**

**JUSTICE LEAGUE
VOL. 3: THRONE OF ATLANTIS**

READ THE ENTIRE EPIC

JUSTICE LEAGUE VOL. 4
THE GR

JUSTICE LEAGUE VOL. 5
FOREVER HEROE

JUSTICE LEAGUE VOL.
INJUSTICE LEAGU

JUSTICE LEAGUE VOL.
DARKSEID WAR PART

JUSTICE LEAGUE VOL. 8
DARKSEID WAR PART